KEPT IN A SHOEBOX
The Popular Experience of Photography

Edited by
Brian Lewis
and
Colin Harding

Yorkshire Art Circus
Everyone has a story to tell. We find ways of helping them tell it.

NATIONAL MUSEUM
PHOTOGRAPHY • FILM • TELEVISION
PICTUREVILLE • BRADFORD

1992

Published jointly by Yorkshire Art Circus, School Lane, Castleford WF10 4QH and the National Museum of Photography, Film & Television, Pictureville, Bradford BD1 1NQ

Distributed in Yorkshire by Yorkshire Art Circus, School Lane, Glass Houghton, Castleford WF10 4QH and nationally by Turnaround, 27 Horsell Road, London N5 1XL

Editorial and Research Team:
Kerry-Anne Aitcheson, Pat Borthwick, Pam Davenport, Steve Davenport, Penny Fell, Olive Fowler, Tony Lumb, Char March, Margaret Pilkington, Wendy Robson, Reini Schühle and Steven Sneyd

Design and Technical Team:
Adele Broadley, Bob Cox, Jane Crumack and Janet Qureshi

Printed by:
Thornton and Pearson Ltd, Rosse Street, Thornton Road, Bradford BD8 9AS.

Typesetting by:
Mousehouse, Hornbeam Park, Harrogate HG2 8QT.

ISBN 0 947780 85 8

Classification: Photography/General Interest

Yorkshire Art Circus is supported by:
Yorkshire and Humberside Arts
West Yorkshire Grants
Wakefield MDC

The NMPFT is part of the National Museum of Science & Industry

FOREWORD

Yorkshire Art Circus is a unique book publisher, bringing to all members of its community the opportunity to write about their lives and experiences, and to put them in print. The National Museum of Photography, Film and Television is a unique museum, interpreting for everyone the media which form part of all our lives. With such complementary aims, it is almost inevitable - and entirely logical - that these two Yorkshire institutions should become partners in a unique project.

This book started with Yorkshire Art Circus interviewing visitors to the Kodak section of the Museum, 'The Story of Popular Photography'. Gradually, this circle of story-tellers spread to include friends, colleagues and strangers, all of whom shared their pictures and their experiences of photography.

Snapshots are intensely personal documents, with a power totally unrelated to their technical, compositional or artistic merits. Usually, they cannot be interpreted without access to the information which only exists in the memories of the photog-raphers and/or their subjects. That is why this is a collection, not only of photographs but of photographs with stories.

These stories touch on many aspects of the story of popular photography, and so we have included a number of historical 'fact boxes'. These demonstrate, among other things, that many of the things which excited the pioneers of photography continue to exert a fascination today.

Colin Ford, National Museum of Photography, Film & Television
Brian Lewis, Yorkshire Art Circus

INTRODUCTION

In a shoe box at home there is a postcard addressed to my grandmother, dated August, 1963. From a deckchair in Weston-Super-Mare my mother writes: 'Dad gone for a walk on his own to see the camera shops (no interest to us). Thanks for sending the camera, it arrived safely. We have bought a colour film so hope it turns out OK. We should have some good ones.' We did indeed get 'some good ones'. We still have them, kept in the same shoe box as my mother's postcard, together with hundreds of other snaps. Snaps of family and friends, pets and possessions, holidays and weddings. A record of the complex relationships and social rituals that make up our lives.

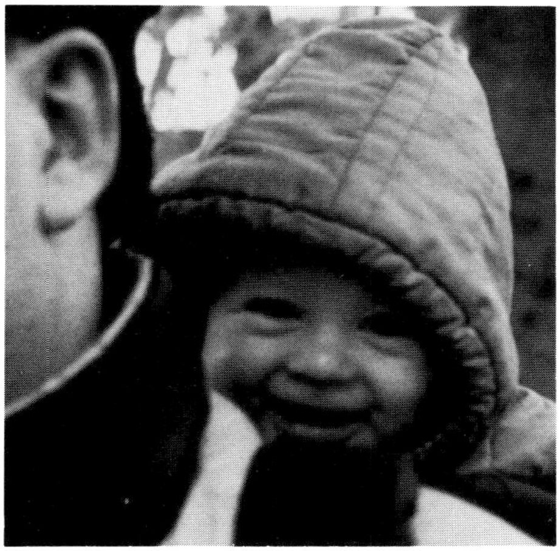

There is, of course, nothing unusual about having such a collection. Most families have a similar hoard - hidden away in wardrobes,cupboards and drawers, in albums, boxes or old handbags. Accumulated over several generations, they are a treasured part of the domestic clutter with which we surround ourselves. Familiar, comfortable and often predictable images, they conform to a visual language which we can all understand. Each collection shares a common pattern and yet each is unique. Family snaps are an essentially private medium. We invest them with all the weightof our personal experience. The images, no matter how technically poor they might be, are enriched by the many layers of meaning that we bring to them. We become emotionally involved when we view them. Remove this level of understanding and involvement and you diminish the photograph. Family photographs can of course be viewed objectively, from 'outside', as it were, but then we move into a fundamentally different realm - that of social history, sociology, or the history of photography.

After about 1900, with the introduction of cheap, easy-to-use cameras combined with a developing and printing service, photography became accessible to everyone. For nearly a century, snapshots have been very much a part of most peoples lives. From the outset it was clear that this new form of self-expression was to be no respecter of class barriers. Taking snapshots quickly became one of the most democratic of pastimes. Indeed, it is hard to think of another leisure activity that appeals to such a broad range of social and income groups. By the 1930s it was estimated that over half of the households in this country already owned a camera. Today, three-quarters of the entire adult population own one. In 1989 the British spent 1.3 billion on photographic equipment, film and developing and printing services.

Since the turn of the century there have been enormous technical advances in the equipment and materials available to the snapshot photographer. The last forty years in particular have been a period of rapid development in photographic technology. It is now easier than ever to produce a sharp, correctly exposed photograph. Colour is now the norm and built-in electronic flash has brought the snapshot indoors. Whether indoors or out, however, the things that people choose to photograph and the way in which they photograph them have changed very little.The subjects that our parents and grandparents recorded in their family albums are essentially the same as those which make up the vast majority of snapshots today. The birth of a child is still the greatest incentive there is for buying a camera.

Colin Harding, National Museum of Photography, Film & Television

We would like to thank the following people for sharing their stories and photographs:

Adrian Abbot, Andrew Ailes, Angela Ailes, Jane Allsopp, Duncan Ambler, Rosemarie Anich-Erickson, Jenny Arniel, Simon Asker, Dennis Atkinson, Hassan Badat, Kerri Baker, Julie Barber, Margaret Barrie, Diane Barron, Brian Beedle, Deb Beetlestone, G N Birch, Pauline Blake, Judy Blue, Marie Bolton, Chris Bourne, Matt Bourne, Janet Bowstead, Stephen Boyd, Deborah Brackish, Anne Bridges, Lisa Broad, Joan Brookes, Ted Brookes, Mr & Mrs Brown, Tom Burns, Eula Cameron, Jerry Caplan, Peter Carroll, I Carven, Margaret Chambers, John Charlton, Mohinder Singh Chatrik, Chris Childs, Grace Clark, Phil Clark, Mr and Mrs N Clarke, Ian Clayton, David Clegg, Gill Cliff, D Andrew Coldwell, Maureen Colquhoun, Jess Crowther, Terry Cryer, Brian Curran, Steve Darnley, Glen Davis, Freda Dennis, Joyce Dillon, Christine Dixon, Andrew and Evelyn Dobson, Reginald and Sylvia Dolton, Jerry Doe, Andrea Dorsman, Sylvia Dyson, Brian Dudley-Barrett, Tracey Duggan, Nick Eastwood, Margaret Edwards, Maureen Ellis, J Ellis-Beech, Nisha Elsherbini, Kath Exley, Ian Fell, Stephen Flett, David Franks, Frances Froggett, Sue Furness, Diane Gibson, Carole Golby, Mabel Goldthorpe, Susan Gott, Sarah Graham, Sandra Goldberg, Paul Goodman, W D Graham, Elizabeth Grattan, Celia Greatorex, Duncan Green, Victoria Greet, Andrew and Wendy Grimshaw, Celia Greatrex, Lynsey Haigh, Patti Hall, David Hammond, Jenny Hampshire, Nick Hampshire, Edna Hardacre, Barbara Hardcastle, Joyce Harding, Doug Harding, Reginald Hargreaves, C and H Harrison, Kay Hartley, Jane Hartwell, G Hawkin, Jude Heinitz, Pete Hellings, Joyce Hepshaw, Janet Hepworth, Alf Hirst, Greg Hobson, Chris Hodgson, E Hodgson, Leanne Hooley, Anne Hughes, Bernadette Illingworth, Georgina Jackman, Donald and Mary Jenkinson, Ken and Pat Johnson, Sandra Kay, Alan Kaye, Rajia Khanam, Christine King, Geoff King, Mary King, Wim Kranendonk, Michelle Lane, Richard Langron, David Law, Darren Leaf, Grace Lee, Samantha Leonard, Sara Lin, Fiona Lloyd, Liz Lloyd, David McAndrew, Stephen McClarence, Dennis McConnel, Jane McDowell, Clare McHugh, Liz and Alan McIlroy, Fiona MacIntyre, Garry McIntyre, Nikki McIver, Rachel McQuillan, Linda Malkin, Janet Marsh, Jean Marshall, Beryl Massey, Liz Matthews, Clare Maynall, Brian Millard, Alison Miller, Gill Miller, Sally Mitchison, Bill Mycock, J Neesam, Paula Nicholl, David Norfolk, L Nunn, Frank O'Brien, Mandy Oades, Viv Oakes, David Odey, Joanne Ottewell, Louise Owen, Steve Owen, Father Paul, Emma Park, J Parr, Phil Paver, Jean Pearson, Kevin Pearson, Malcolm Picken, Alan Pilkington, Abigail Poole, Peter E Presford, Janet Qureshi, Sue Raynor, Michael Reddy, Andrea Reed, Kevin Reynolds, Brian Richardson, Jane Ridgeway, Richard Van Riel, Walter Roberts, Alice Robinson, Rony Robinson, Pete Robinson, John Robinson, Joyce Rogers, Mario Rodgers, Ken Rowley, Melanie Rudd, Tony Rudge, Ros Rushworth, Gill Sandford, Elizabeth Sandie, John Sargeant, Kathryn Scott, Richard Scott, Brenda Sharpe, Kiersty Sinclair, Bernal Siswick, D Skidmore, Barry Smith, Mandy Southwick, Janet Spears, June and John Speller, Kath Stewart, Cheron Stevenson, Bob Stoker, Kath Stott, Simon Sykes, Sung Meng Tang, Alice Taylor, Roger Taylor, Sarah Taylor, R Telford, Viv Thom, Denise Thompson, Melanie Thompson, Viv Thorne, Gaynor Thorpe, Joan Thornton, Kandice Threapleton, Susan Tilford, Catherine Tinson, Shirley Tomkinson, M Uttley, Katrina Verity, Kate Waldram, Gary Walker, Ruth Walker, Andy Wallace, Helen Walther, Tony Ward, M Watson, Tim Whawell, Stewart Wheeler, Pauline Wigglesworth, Rachel Wilds, Stephen Winstanley, Ben Wood, Caroline Wood, Kim Whotake, Ellis Williams, Elsie Williams, Steve Williams, Edna Wilson, Kathleen Wood, Mary Wood, Gerry Woodgate, Alice Wyatt, Rachel Yates, Fuyi Zhang

CHAPTER ONE

YOU PRESS THE BUTTON, WE DO THE REST

Kodak advertising slogan 1888

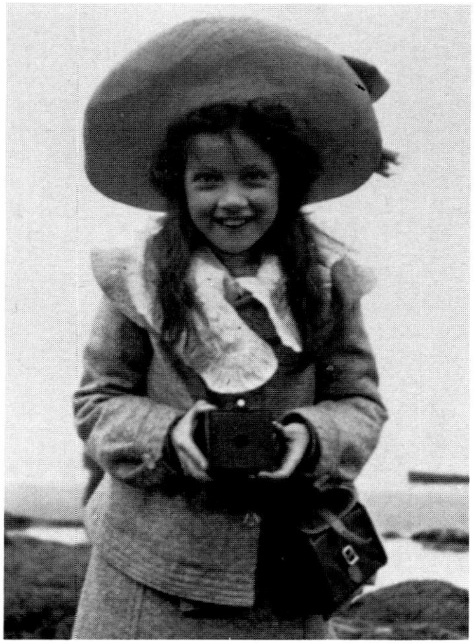

THE KODAK, 1888.

Popular photography can properly be said to have started with the introduction of this camera. It was invented by George Eastman, who also devised the name 'Kodak' - short, distinctive and easily pronounced in all languages. After the last exposure, the entire camera was returned to the factory where the film was processed, a set of prints made and a new film loaded before it was returned to its owner. For the first time everyone, regardless of their knowledge or skill, could enjoy the pleasures of photography.

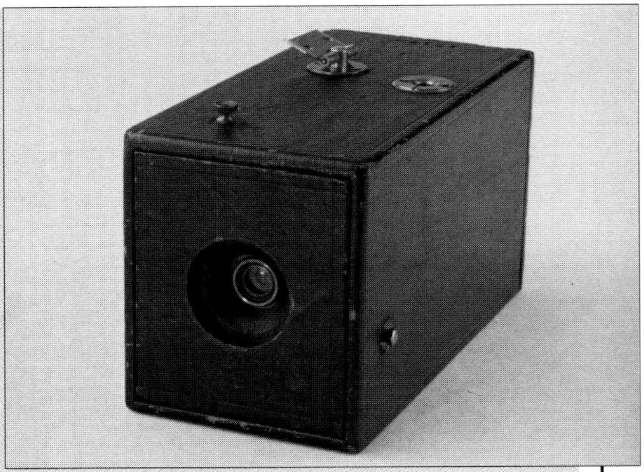

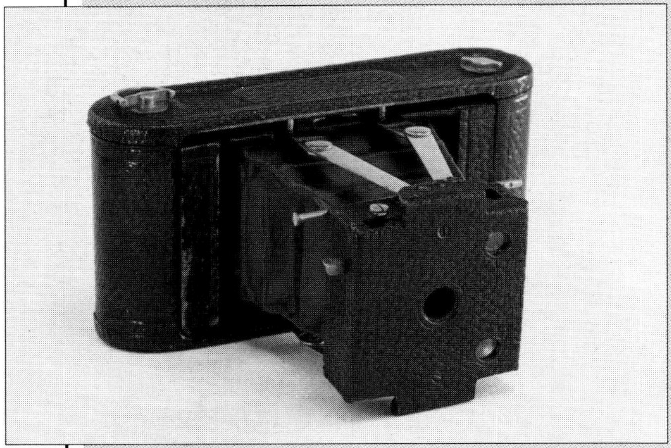

THE FOLDING POCKET KODAK, 1897.

A milestone in camera design, this pioneered a whole generation of popular folding rollfilm cameras. A standard design for many years, Kodak alone made over two hundred different models of folding camera. The last, the Kodak 66, was made in 1960.

When closed, the Folding Pocket Kodak was less than two inches thick and could slip easily into a coat pocket - hence the name.

THE BROWNIE, 1900

Originally designed to appeal to children, the humble 'Box Brownie' provided an introduction to photography for millions of people. Although cheap and simple to use, Brownies were not toys. They were capable of producing perfectly good photographs. Following on from the success of the original model a whole range of Brownies were made. By the time the last one appeared in 1980, nearly one hundred different models of Brownie camera had been produced.

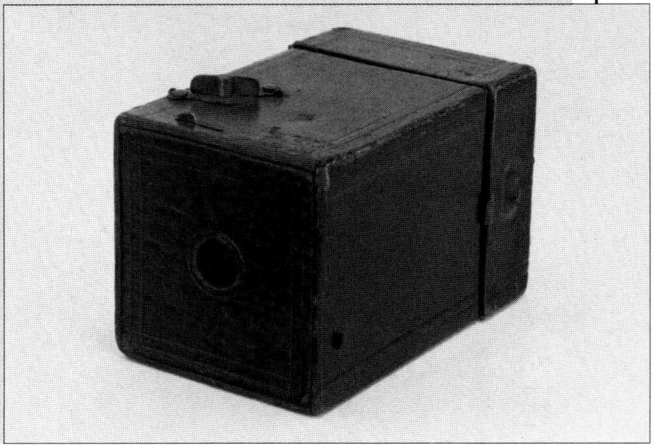

THE LEICA, 1925

Designed by Oskar Barnack, this was the first successful precision 35mm camera. A landmark in camera history and a classic of industrial design, it set 35mm photography on the road to the pre-eminent position which it enjoys today. The success of the Leica owed much to the precision of its manufacture and the quality of its lenses. Improvements in film emulsions meant that quality enlargements were possible from the small (24mmx36mm) negatives that the Leica produced.

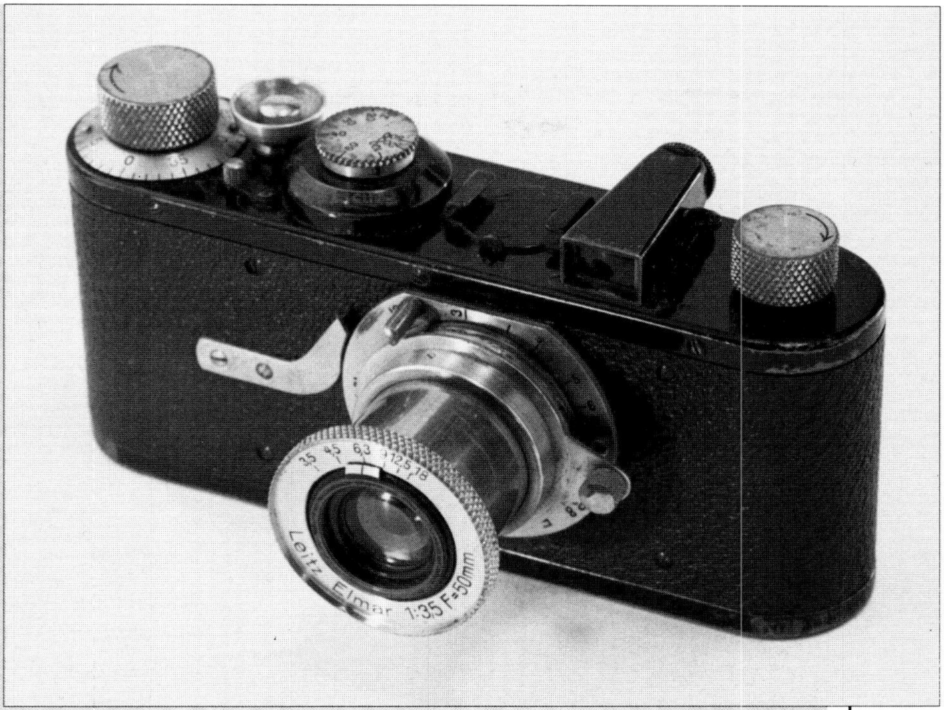

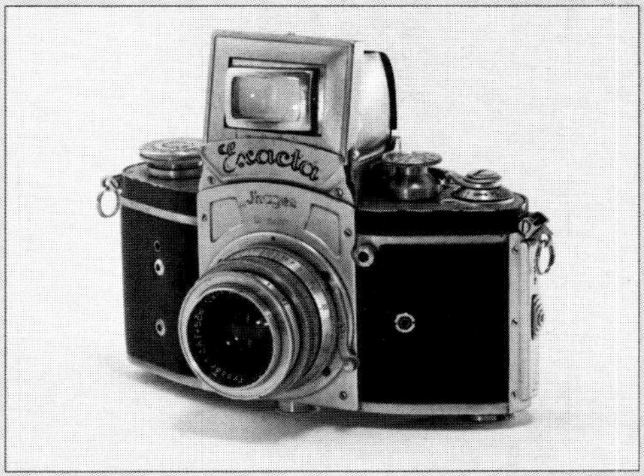

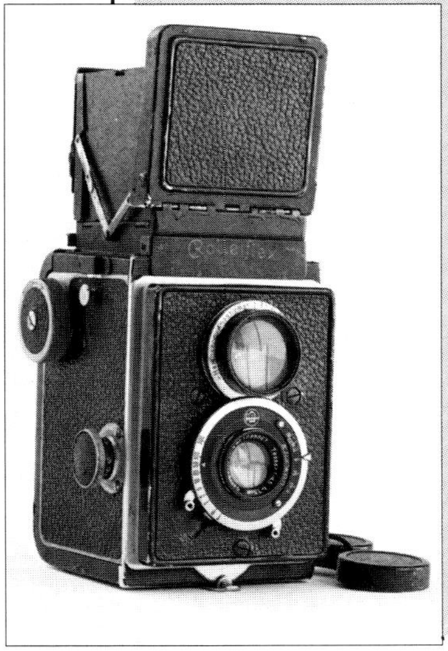

THE ROLLEIFLEX, 1928

The Rolleiflex, made by the German firm of Franke and Heidecke, was the first modern twin-lens reflex camera. The design was to remain popular for several decades, but has in recent years given way in popularity to the single-lens reflex. Similar cameras are still used by many professional photographers.

THE KINE EXACTA,1936

Made by the Dresden firm of Ihagee, this was the first commercially successful single lens reflex camera for 35mm film. Apart from the viewfinder, it is very similar in appearance to modern 35mm SLRs, of which it is the direct ancestor.

THE POLAROID LAND CAMERA, 95, 1948

Invented by Edwin Land, this was the first 'instant print' camera. It produced a sepia-coloured print in about one minute.

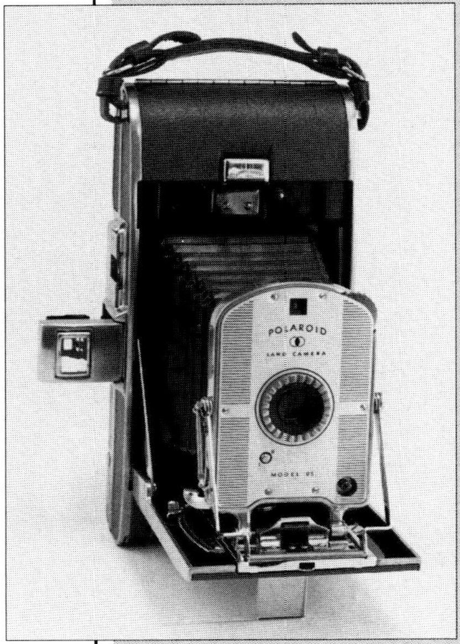

Other models of Polaroid Land camera were produced to follow on from the success of the original. In November, 1956, the one millionth Polaroid camera was sold. The Type 95 was the prototype for Polaroid's range of instant cameras and was manufactured, with slight variations, until 1961.

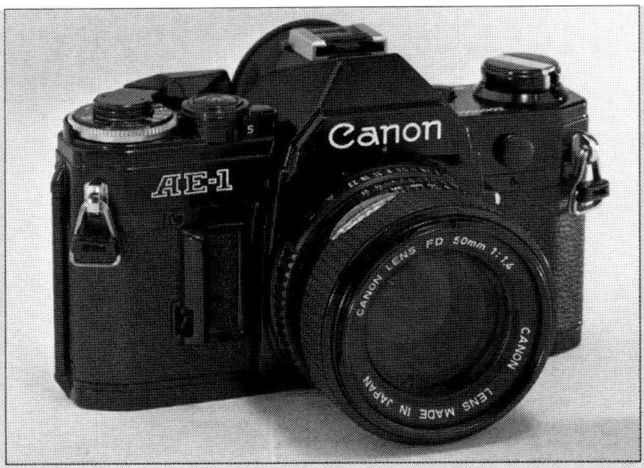

THE CANON AE-1, 1976

The AE stands for Automatic Electronic. This camera was the first to use a micro-processor, similar to those used in computers. A CPU, or Central Processing Unit, acts like a 'brain' to control all the camera functions. Over five million Canon AE-1s were sold, making it the most popular 35mm SLR ever produced.

THE KODAK INSTAMATIC, 1963

Many snapshooters found it difficult to load their cameras using roll film. Instamatic cameras overcame this problem by adopting a system of cartridge loading. Film was contained in a plastic 'Kodapak' cartridge which could simply be dropped into the back of the camera and which would fit only one, the correct, way. An immediate success, over seventy million Kodak Instamatics were eventually sold. In 1972 Kodak introduced their range of Pocket Instamatics.Based on the same principle, these took a smaller size film cartridge.

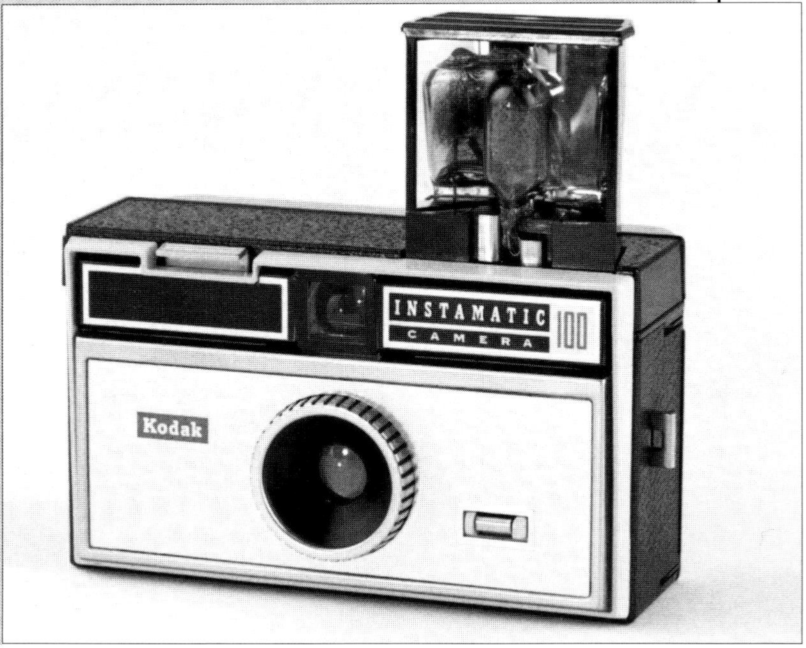

THE KONICA C35 AF, 1977

The forerunner of today's point-and-shoot compacts, the Konica C35 AF was the very first camera to incorporate automatic focusing. This was based around an integrated electronic circuit designed by the Honeywell Corporation of America. The camera also featured automatic electronic flash and exposure control. All the photographer has to do is centre the subject in the viewfinder and press the shutter release button.

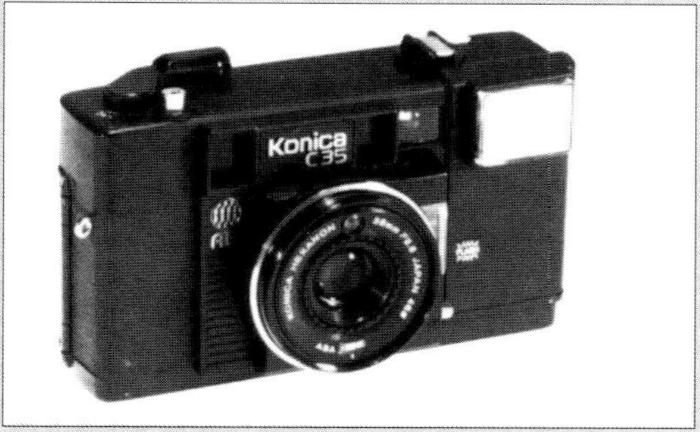

THE KODAK DISC CAMERA, 1982

In these cameras the traditional roll of film was replaced by a disc. Although technologically very advanced, disc cameras were not a commercial success. The quality of their photographs could not compete with those from 35mm cameras with a negative of over ten times the size. The last disc cameras were made in 1988.

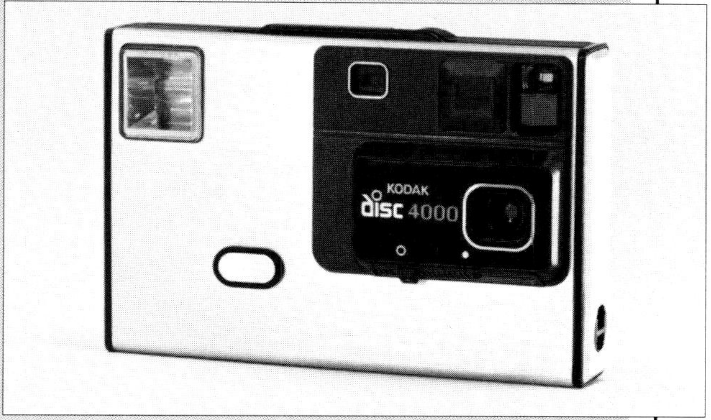

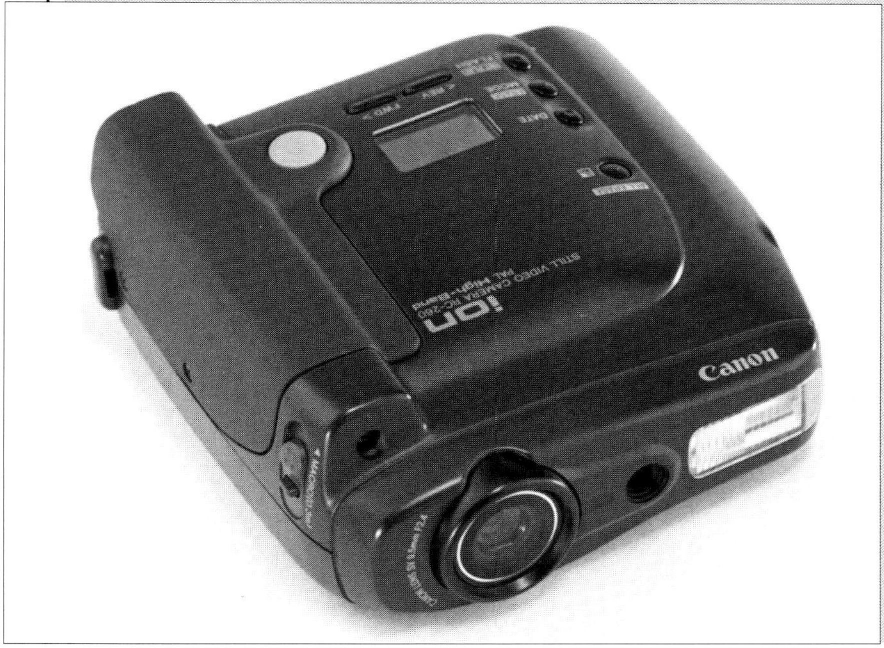

THE CANON ION, 1992

This is the first 'still video' camera to be designed for the amateur market. Instead of film, the Ion uses a computer floppy disc. Up to fifty photographs can be recorded on each disc. These can then be played back for viewing on an ordinary domestic television set.

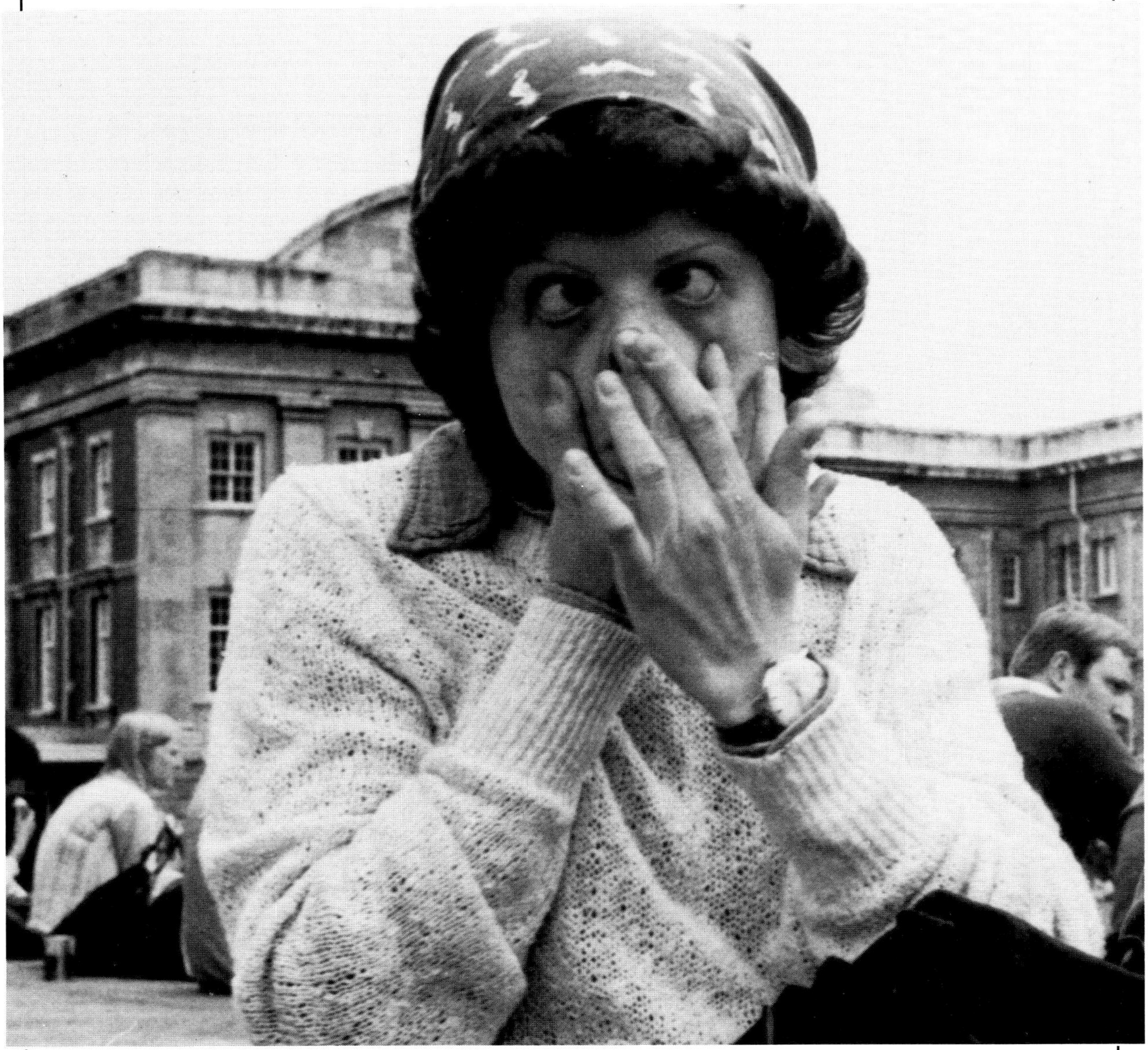

I said to my wife,
'But surely they had a camera'.
'Oh, no', she said, 'She's not bonny and he's not bonny,
the kids aren't bonny either,
so why should they?'

CHAPTER TWO

SHE'LL ALWAYS BE YOUR LITTLE GIRL BECAUSE YOU TOOK A PICTURE

Kodak advertisement 1955

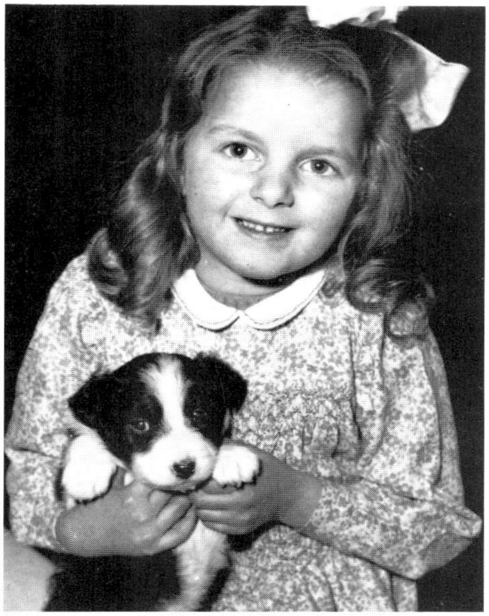

❧ My grandmother had a wooden box inlaid with mother of pearl. In this she kept all the family photographs. One, dated 1887, showed my great grandmother, who was a teacher, and her illiterate farmer husband sitting together. She looked very prim and he was holding a sickle.

When I was young I used to love that box because it carried our family history. All of the old photographs were there: pictures of my parents, who were cousins, as young people, then my father going off to war, followed by my mother going off to war and me as a girl. Then they stopped. It was as if, just before she died, my grandmother had tired of taking photographs.

That's when the collection came to my mother. Mum carried it on and enlarged it because she was thinking of creating a family album; pictures and text.

Recently my husband bought a camera and we are adding our bits and pieces but beyond that there are those which my daughter is taking. She is seven and a year ago we bought her a Mothercare camera. It had a red casing but after a time this broke away and when my husband peeled it off we found a small black camera inside. She likes this because she says it looks more grown up. She is following on the tradition of taking family photographs.

❧ I think old family photographs are great pleasure givers. When we were kids, my sister and I loved to ask Mam to get out the old, imitation pigskin handbag and let us look at the old photos. Mam would explain to us where they were all taken and who was on them. Some aunties and uncles were unrecognisable as youngsters but we would laugh a bit and then shake our heads slightly when we came to people who had gone.

When our children were born and Mam and Dad got older we would still get the bag out and reminisce. Inevitably the time comes when parents are no longer there, so it is you who has to explain to your children who is on the photos.

All too often after the funeral these sepia treasures are thrown away as the house is cleared. I didn't let that happen. I still have the old handbag full of insurance policies, birth and marriage certificates and old bills, but I have now sorted the old photos and put them into modern plastic pockets. They are stored in ring binders and are catalogued.

Some evenings, when my wife and daughter and I are at a loose end, we get out the albums and reminisce. The plastic envelopes, though, aren't the same as getting the old handbag out.

❧ I've seen collections of family photographs kept in a whole variety of conditions. One afternoon I saw two collections. One friend kept his in beautiful uniform albums of plastic wallets. The other was kept in a child's scrapbook.

"Why are some pages covered in white blobs?" I asked.

"Oh, that's the paste and water. When we split up he wrote asking for his pictures back. I tore them out one night, crying all the time, and never rearranged the pages. I've kept some of him but I made sure that he didn't get any of me."

❧ This picture of my new son was taken eight minutes after his birth at 10.13pm on Friday 29 August. The camera was a Rollei Miniature. I was shooting on Boots 100 ASA at 1.250th second. Flash provided the lighting at F8.

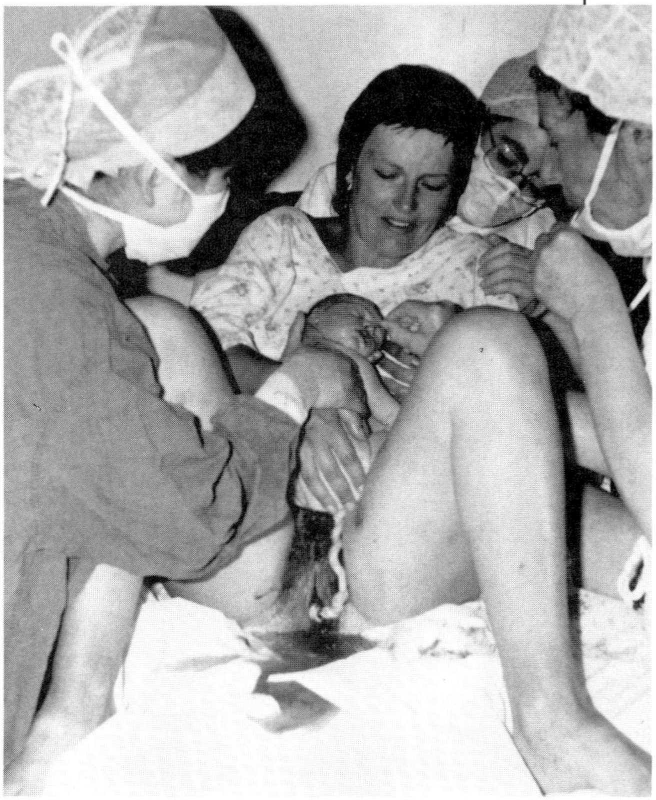

❧ At our maternity hospital it is automatic to take a picture of all the premature babies. I was very glad of that when they took Jacob up into the special care unit. I could go up, but it was comforting to have a small photograph of him by my bed. It made him seem more real.

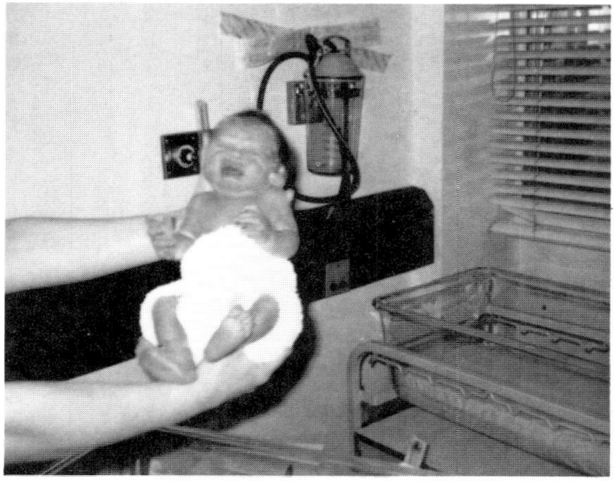

❧ In those days it was the vogue for babies of a few weeks old to be photographed naked lying on a sheepskin or fluffy rug. Mercifully by the time I was born this fashion had passed, but there remains in the family album a picture of my eldest brother looking suitably angelic, kicking happily at about four months old.

I remember being about five (he would be thirteen then) and enjoying the ritual of the heavy album; learning the names of relatives I hadn't yet met. I always thought Peter looked beautiful and was very proud of being his little sister.

At ten, sharing the album with my best friend Jenny, we noticed for the first time scratchmarks across Peter's groin. It was time for the magnifying glass and sure enough Peter didn't have what boys are supposed to have. We giggled an awful lot but were confused too. Of course, I didn't dare ask Mother. At fifteen, revisiting the album, I wasn't sure whether Mother had had the photographer remove Peter's penis from the negative because it was indecent to be so exposed or because of its extraordinary size. So much for a Catholic upbringing.

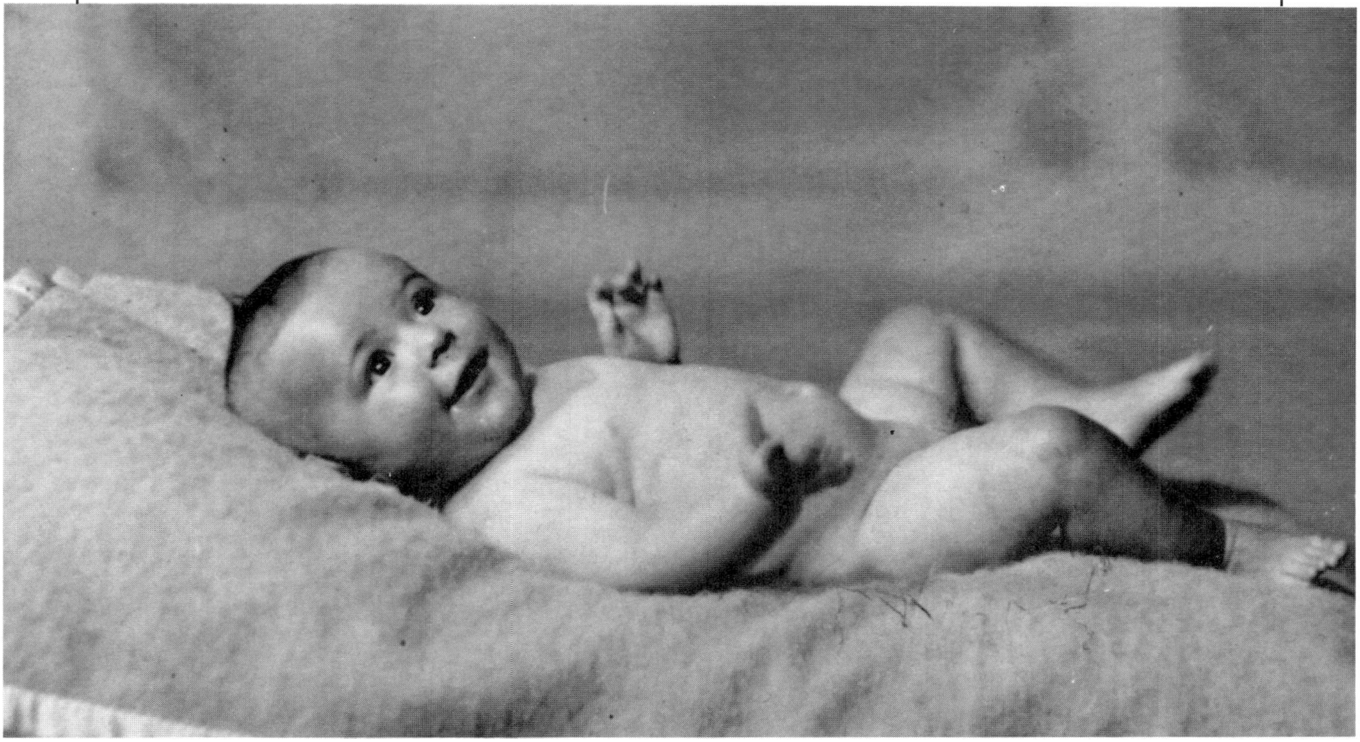

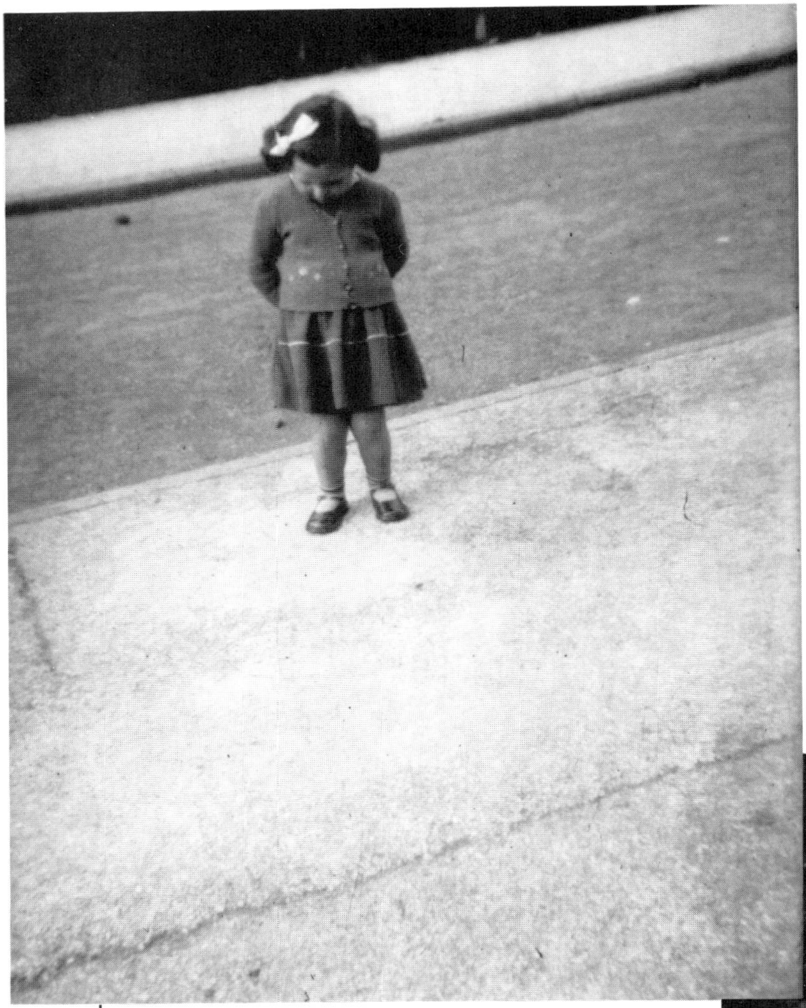

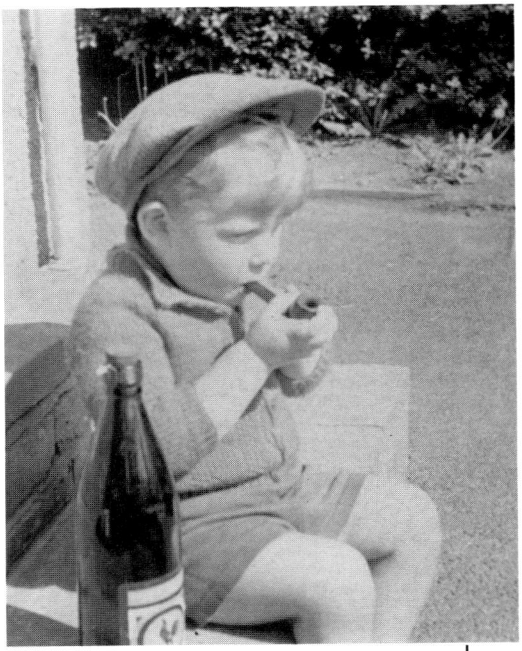

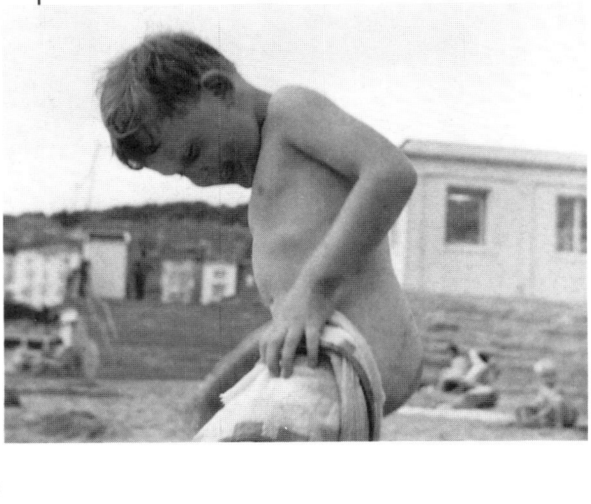

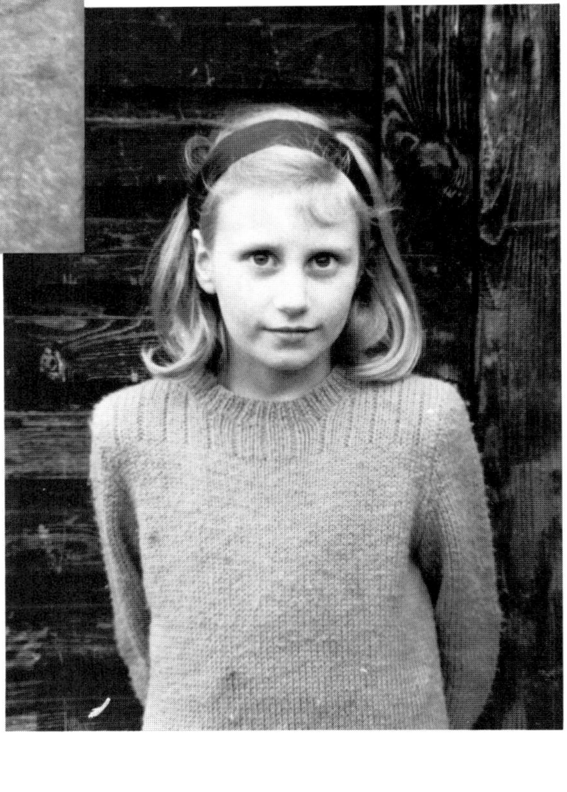

❧ I've got an old sepia photograph I really love. It shows an old man holding a baby. Their grouchy faces are almost identical. The grumpy little baby was a cousin of my Dad. Whilst the picture makes me laugh, I can never forget that when the baby grew into a child he was run over and killed.

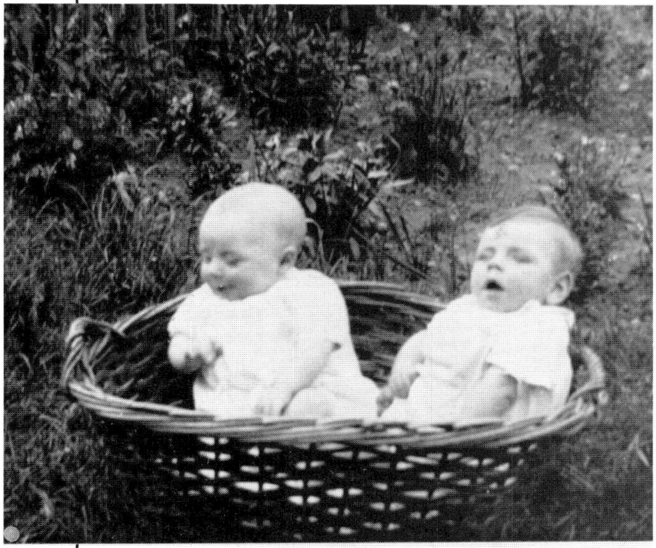

❧ My mother's sister, my Auntie Mill, had Barry two months before I was born. The only photograph which survives from that time is of the two of us in a wicker basket. He has masses of hair and there's me, completely bald. For some reason I was embarrassed by this when I was a child, though I don't see why I should have been. I suspect Barry was to blame. He was always better than me at everything. He could read first, he could ride a bike, he could grow hair. The funny thing is that in later life he went bald and I didn't.

❧ My stepdad took up photography when I was six. I remember he always made me and my sister sit posing for him every night for months on end. We used to dread coming home from school, as the last thing we wanted to do was pose for photos, but he used to get very angry and threaten us with loss of our pocket money if we didn't pose.

❧ When I was a very small child we used to spend our summer holidays in Weston-super-Mare. Once, when we were walking along the prom, my father picked me up and put me inside a litter bin. I was only about three years old and the top of the bin came up to my shoulders so I couldn't climb out. He then walked away saying that he was going to leave me there. When I started to cry he took out his camera and photographed me. I still can't figure out why he thought it was alright to cause me such distress just so that he could take a funny snap.

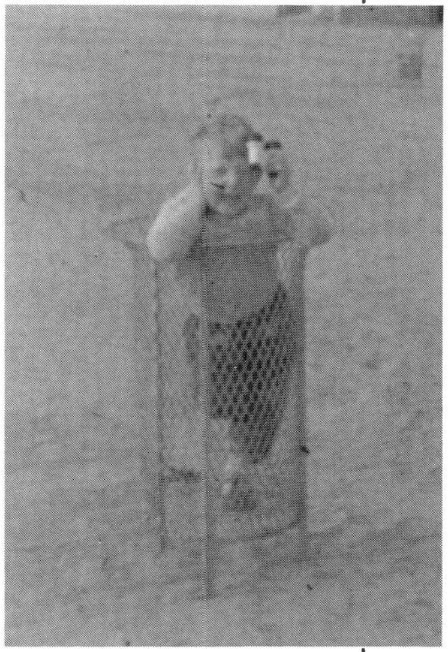

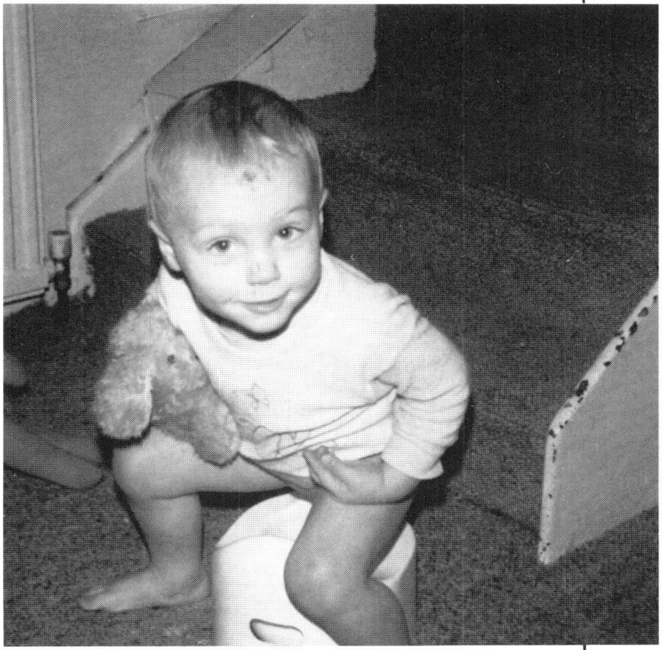

❧ My daughter is only six. Already she wants to get rid of certain photographs which embarrass her. We have one of her sat on her potty. She hates it.

❧ Grace, my daughter, is five and usually has no interest in boys other than in avoiding them. She has a big brother, you see. During the school holidays I found her gazing misty-eyed at her school photo. She explained it made her go all funny when she looked at Gavin from her class.

❧ When I was a schoolboy we would have a school photograph taken every couple of years. The camera was set on a tripod and at a steady rate scanned the lines of five hundred or so boys. We used to say that if you were quick enough you could have your picture taken at one end and, by running along the back, also manage to be taken at the other end of the photograph.

I wish that schools would take that sort of picture now, they're more interesting than the individual photographs you get these days. You know the sort of thing, a big picture for you and one each for the grandparents. These come with the bill and the ransom note; pay up or have three children who think they'll lose face. They're expensive and are in no way as interesting as the picture my mother kept rolled up in the bedroom wardrobe.

CIRKUT CAMERA.
The camera used by the school phtographer in this story was a 'Cirkut' camera made by the Eastman Kodak Co. Introduced in 1904, this was one of the best-known and most widely-used of panoramic cameras.

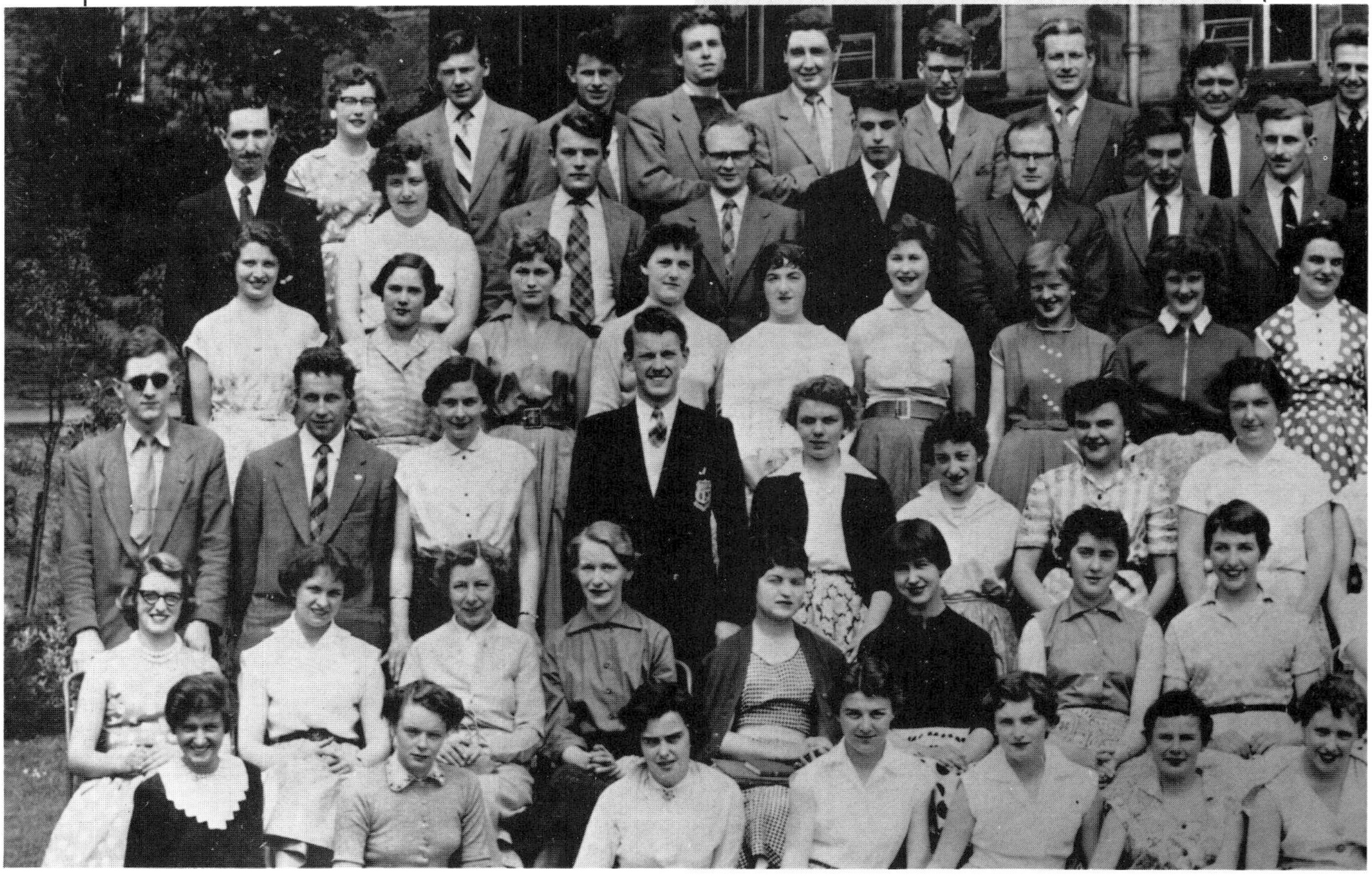

Cirkut cameras worked by traversing the subject to be photographed. A clockwork motor inside the camera rotated a gear wheel on the camera base which engaged with a rack around the top of the tripod. As the gear wheel turned, so the camera swivelled. The camera turned slowly. Someone standing at one end of the group could run to the other end and so appear twice.

The last Cirkut cameras were made in 1941 but some are still being used for group photographs. In 1953 a Cirkut camera was used to take a panoramic photograph of the Coronation procession,the photographer taking position on the roof of Buckingham Palace.

❧ I think photos have a huge amount of power. I know they do over me anyway. I got thrown out when I told my parents I was a lesbian. I was literally given ten minutes to pack and get out.

It really preys on my mind that they have all the family photographs. Loads of them with me on, me growing up, me on holiday, at different family events, me in my new Brownie uniform - yuk!! All sorts of bits of me and my past that they still have full access to and, through them, power over me. I'll never see any of them again.

I haven't seen or spoken to my parents now for seven years - don't even know where they live now. It just feels really sad and cruel that now I can't even see what I looked like at twelve years old, can't know which friends were at my seventh birthday party, or what the village looked like when we went on holiday and I broke my arm.

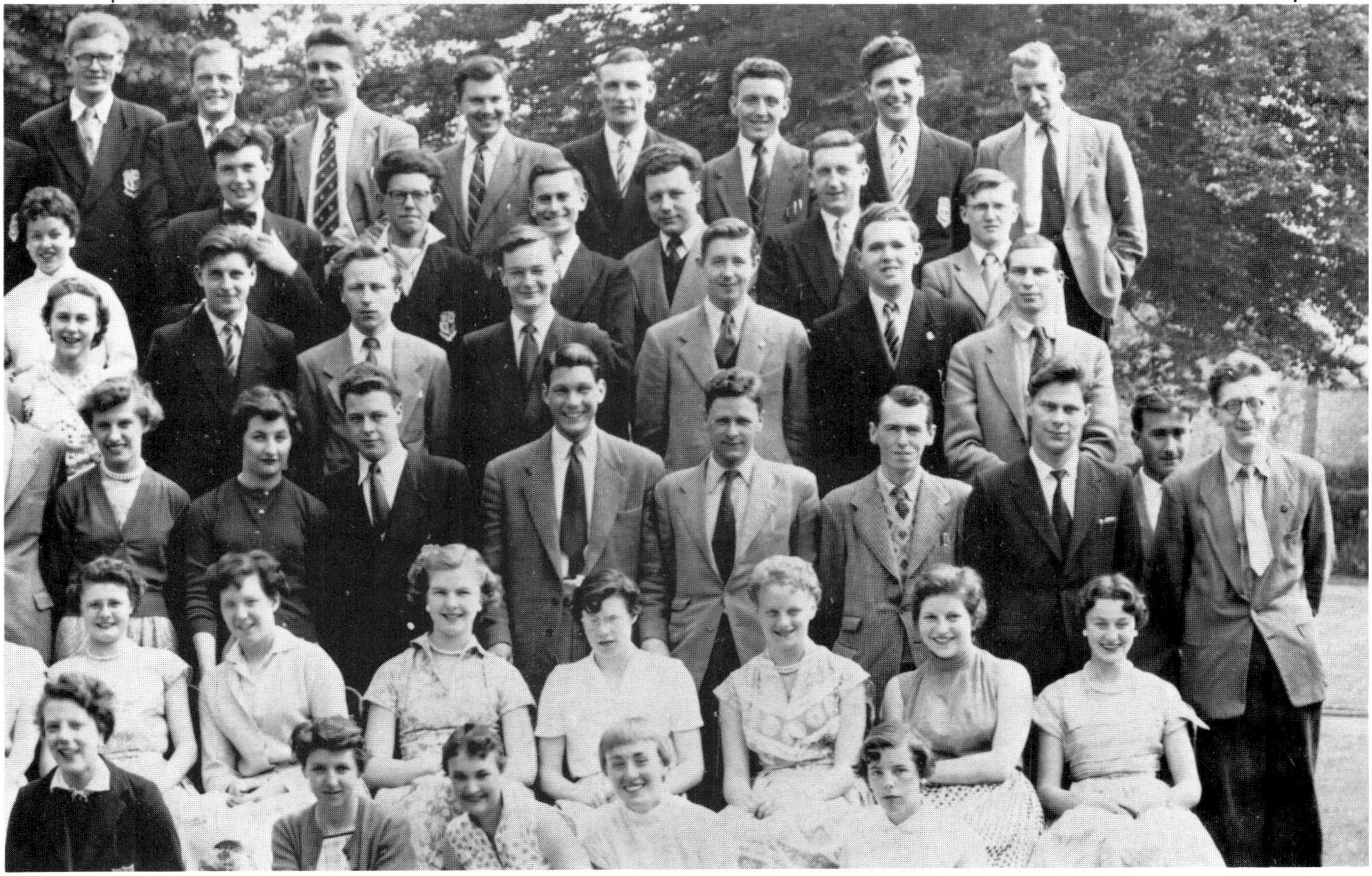

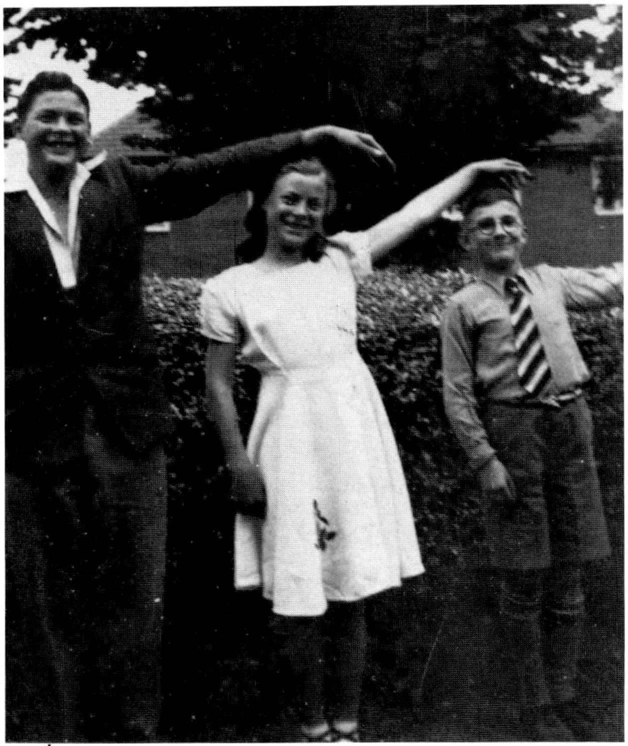

❧ My mother, who seems to delight in scoring points at my expense, couldn't phone me fast enough to let me know about my cousin's knighthood. She also reminded me, once again, about him being the youngest Air Vice Marshal in the RAF. Her phone call was laughable - I hadn't seen my cousin or his sister for over forty years.

My mother, in her usual way of wanting the world to pose for her, had lined us all up for a photograph. Each had one arm outstretched - like a set of Ovaltinies: my cousin, his sister in the middle, and myself at the end.

It's interesting to think how prophetic that photo turned out. Despite there being only a few years between our ages, he reached the pinnacle of social class and career structure whereas, in my mother's estimation, I'm still the bottom of the pile.

❧ Everything on the day trip was fine; nice weather, plenty to eat, everyone was happy. We even remembered to bring the camera. Perhaps we were having too much of a good time because the cheeky little boy running in the photograph locked the keys in the car. We had another two hours of enforced paradise before a very, very nice man was able to open the car for us.

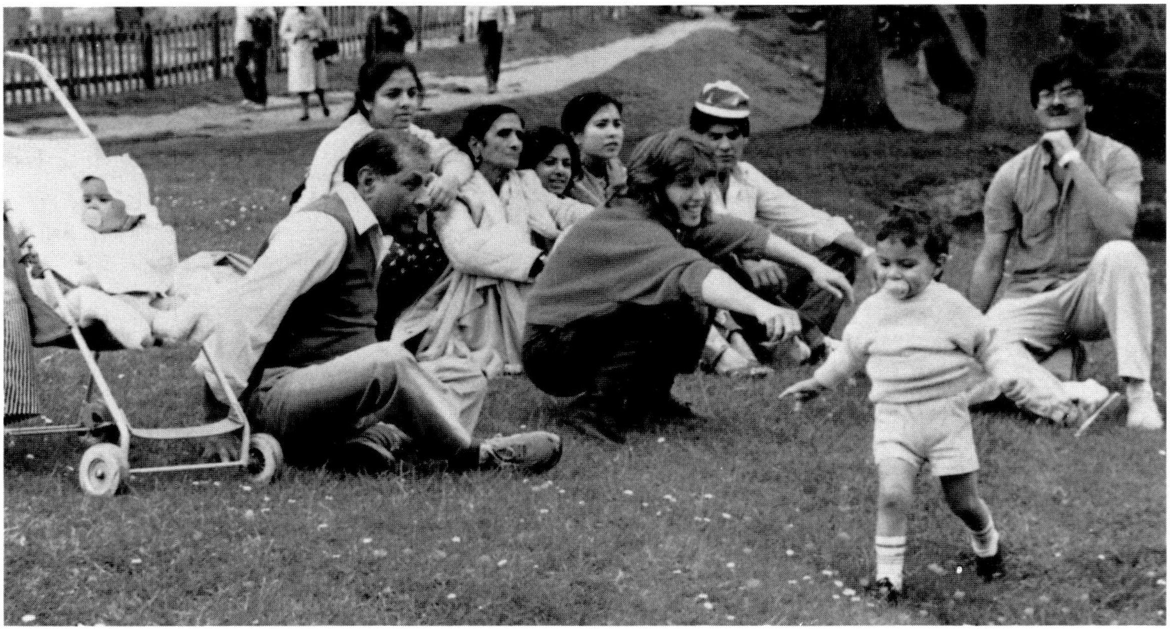

❧ I take photographs as a memory trigger, so there are plenty of the family in all sorts of situations. My husband likes to take landscapes and buildings, beautifully composed, but without the intrusion of people. When I look through our photos there are hardly any of me. I think about how sad I felt when my mother died and there were very few photos of her because she disliked being snapped. I wonder if my children would feel the same if anything happened to me, but I don't think it sounds right to say to my husband, "Take some photos of me in case I die."

❧ When I graduated from university my parents attended the ceremony which was held at the Albert Hall. In the basement of the building a number of photographers had set up small temporary studios to take official portraits. My mother asked me repeatedly with growing concern and, eventually, anger to have a proper photograph taken to mark the occasion. I stubbornly refused to cooperate.

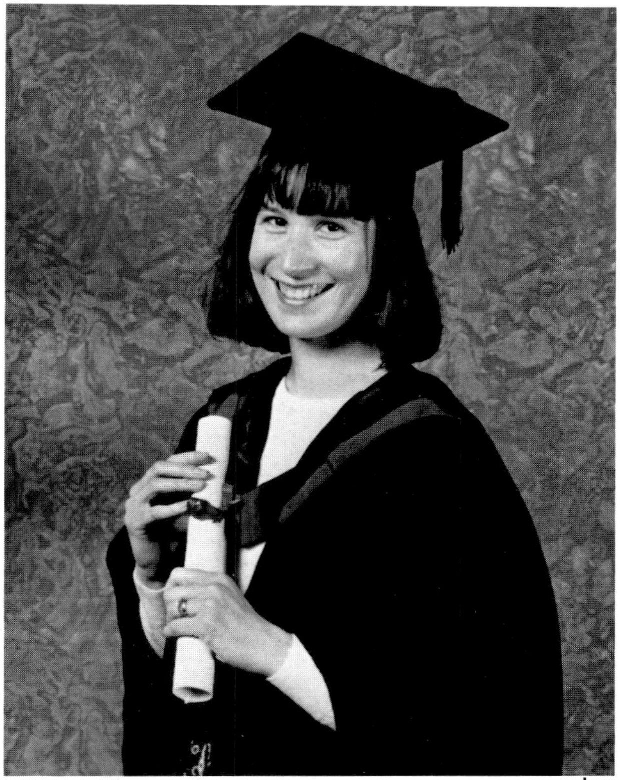

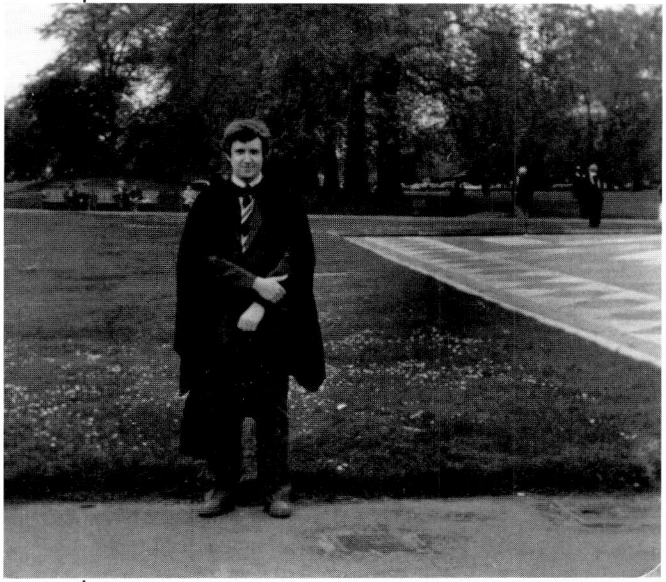

It all meant very little to me and I felt that simply by agreeing to attend in the first place I had done more than enough. Eventually I conceded to having a snap taken in Hyde Park with my gown on!

That snapshot now has pride of place on top of their telly. It is blurred and I am standing too far away from the camera, but it is the only photograph that my parents have of my graduation day.

I don't think my mother will ever forgive me for refusing to be photographed. Looking back, I can see that I was wrong. It was little enough to ask of me in return for all that they had done and it would have meant so much. Every time I see that photograph I am ashamed at how selfish and inconsiderate I was on that day.

❧ My aunt got married just after the First World War. She had a little girl but, sadly, soon afterwards became ill - TB I think - and died, leaving a three-year-old daughter. My uncle remarried and more or less decided to start his life again. He never referred to his first wife and did not keep any photographs of her. Since he lived at the other end of the country, our contacts became fewer and fewer until finally they stopped altogether. Fifty years later my mother died and while sifting through her treasures I discovered my father's very old battered wallet. It contained a studio portrait of his sister, aged about eighteen, her wedding photograph and a snapshot of her cuddling her small daughter in the grounds of a hospital. I almost destroyed them but something prompted me to write and ask my cousin if she would like them. She replied saying all photographs of her mother had been lost or destroyed when her father remarried and all her life she'd longed to know what her mother looked like, but had given up hope.

Later, at an emotional meeting, I was able to give her the precious photographs and see the look on her face when, at the age of fifty-five, she saw what her mother looked like for the first time in her life.

Who would have guessed that photographs hidden away for half a century could give such happiness and re-unite a family?

❧ We never were a family for holding hands or kisses, not even goodnight ones. Yet here I am at about five years old perched on my dad's shoulders at Skegness. The picture makes it look like me and my dad were really close. Perhaps we could have been but, come to think of it, I can't ever remember having time on my own with him. It's still the same, my mother always has to be there. Nothing's changed.

❧ This was taken at Butlin's, Skegness, in 1946; the time I went with Uncle John, Auntie Freda and my cousin Pamela. I can't remember much about the holiday except, "Wakey, Wakey!" and keeping fit to music in a field. Some things were free but I think that we had to pay for these bikes. The plan was to have one for the grown ups and one for us but Pamela wouldn't sit with me so I pedalled alone. Take a look at our clothes. I am dressed in a very smart tailored dusty pink coat and Uncle John has tie, pullover and coat on. This at the height of summer. In his lapel he has a Butlin's badge. I still have it. The other one, the old sailor and the slogan "Skegness Is So Bracing", has gone astray.

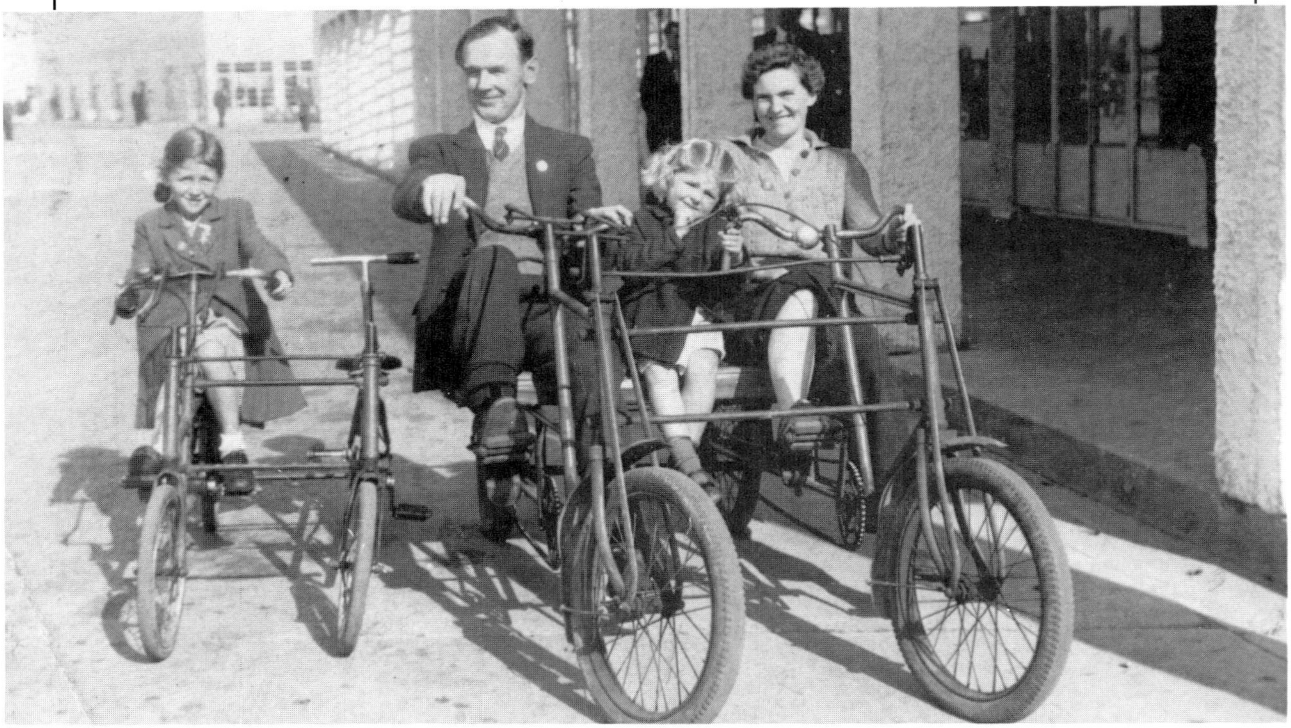

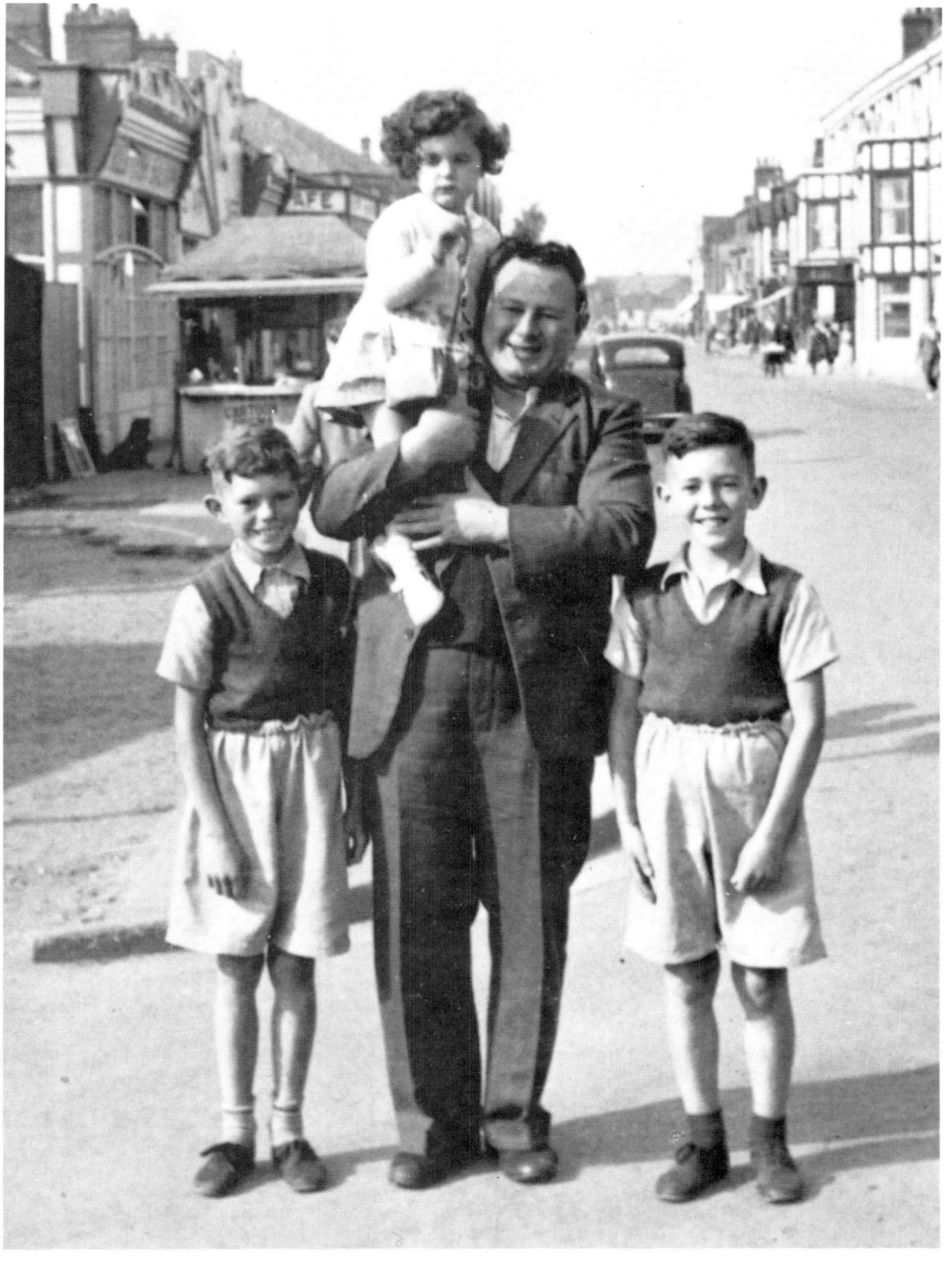

❧ We went on holiday almost every year when I was young. It's very interesting to me that my mother always managed to collect holiday photos of her three children even though we never had a camera. We always came home with a key ring viewfinder, one for each child. The viewfinder was a small plastic container with a tiny round lens which magnified the picture. They were pretty inexpensive.

❧ My mother cut her first husband off all the family photos. Years ago this was. I remember it was weird flicking through the albums with neatly cut-out blanks. Last Christmas my half-brother was clearing out some stuff for her and found a picture of his dad. He'd never seen a photo of his own dad before You can't imagine, it can you? I couldn't even imagine it and I'd lived with it all. He was really shocked - shaken - but dead chuffed too. Anyway, he went running downstairs and showed Mum and she just couldn't cope at all. All those years on and one photo just sent her into a total panic.

❧ In a way I'm lucky to at least have this. This torn-in-half picture of my daughter as a baby is the only one I have of her at that age. He burned all the rest when we left him. I suppose it was his way of coping, by denying her existence. In fact he's said so since. I never could quite repair the damage to her. Her two halves always left a ragged gap somewhere around where her heart should be. Sellotape's no good for that sort of job.

❧ I have some photos of my sixteenth birthday party. My mum and dad went out as usual to the local Saturday night dance. Their last words were "No boys allowed!" Of course the boys were straight in when they left. The party went well and we managed to get rid of them before my parents' return.

What caught me out was Mum opening the envelope when the photos came back from the chemist and seeing the house full of boys. The camera never lies.

❧ Most of Dad's photos were taken on Wednesdays and Saturdays - his days off. Wednesdays always felt special because Mum and Dad would pick us up from school and, if it was a pleasant day, we would go for a run into Derbyshire before heading home. Mum was always self-conscious if cameras were around. I don't know why - she was so beautiful and elegant.

Of course, we were always happy to perform for the camera whether it be doing a Scottish jig in the middle of a country road or smiling angelically as we marched along in the school May Procession.

The irony is that the man who captured our childhood and provided all these happy memories is present on so few cine films and photos. He was too busy holding the camera.

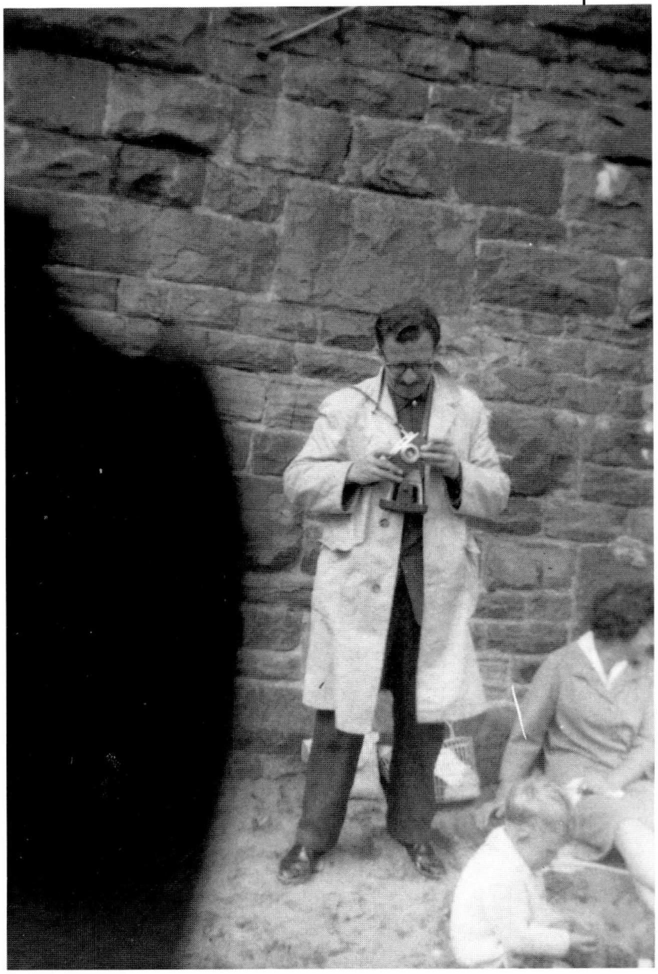

WOMEN SNAPSHOOTERS.

During the nineteenth century, photography was almost exclusively a male pursuit. The introduction of hand-held snapshot cameras in the 1890s encouraged many people to take up photography. Many of these enthusiastic amateurs were women.

'Modern Society' magazine observed in 1895 ; 'Young women have adopted this fad with such enthusiasm that they ruthlessly "snap-shot" anyone that comes within reach of their lens, and in any attitude, no matter how ridiculous and silly'.

By the 1920s women actually formed the majority of snapshooters. Indeed, the female market was so important that in 1928 Kodak Ltd introduced a range of cameras aimed solely at women. Named 'Vanity' Kodaks, they were sold in a variety of colours; Bluebird (blue), Cockatoo (green), Jenny Wren (brown), Redbreast (red) and Sea-Gull (grey). The idea was that cameras should be a fashion accessory, matching or complementing the colours of one's outfit. There was even an 'ensemble' available - a case containing a 'vanity' camera together with a matching lipstick holder, mirror and powder compact. From the earliest days, camera advertisements showed women behind the lens. As well as encouraging women to take up photography this was undoubtedly a device intended primarily to show how simple it was to take a snap. In 1910 the most famous of these characters appeared - the Kodak Girl. In her distinctive striped dress, the Kodak Girl was a familiar figure right up until the 1950s.

❧ My father would never allow my mother anywhere near the camera. Sometimes he would want a Man-with-Son or Man-with-Daughter pose and so would set the shot up completely - with my mum in his place. He'd actually mark on the ground where she had to stand. Then she'd be ordered over to the camera spot and given a set of barked

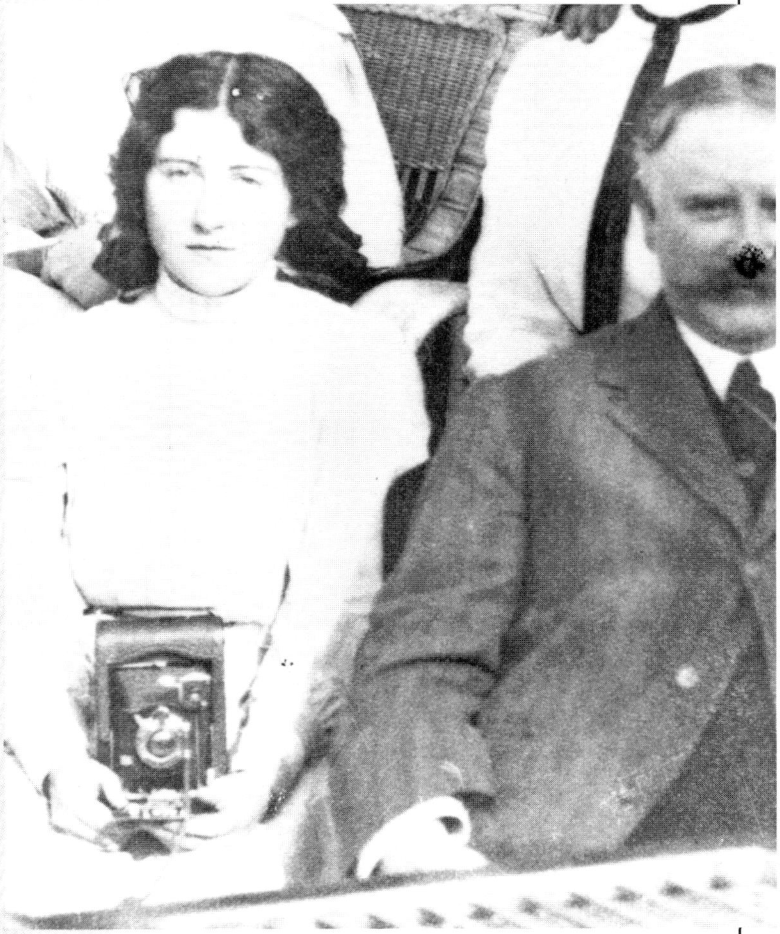

commands on where to put her fingers and what to press. He'd never try and explain to her how it worked so she could do it for herself. This done he'd run back to be in the photo - all smiles. Really natural, eh?

If he'd want two shots he wouldn't even let her wind it on but would run back and do it himself. The photos would usually come out with loads of camera shake - and with my Dad's head partly cut off. I'm pretty sure that was deliberate!

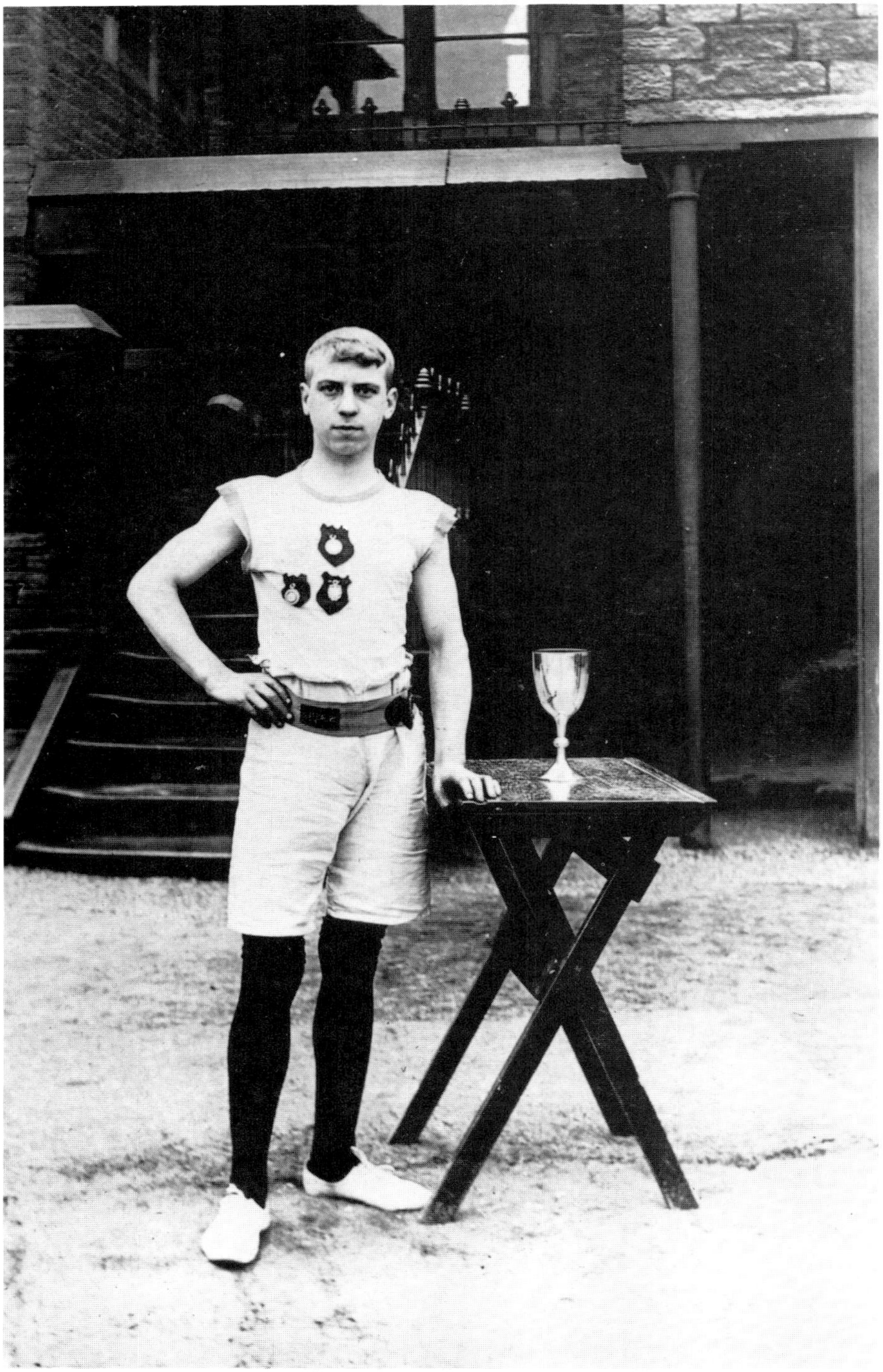

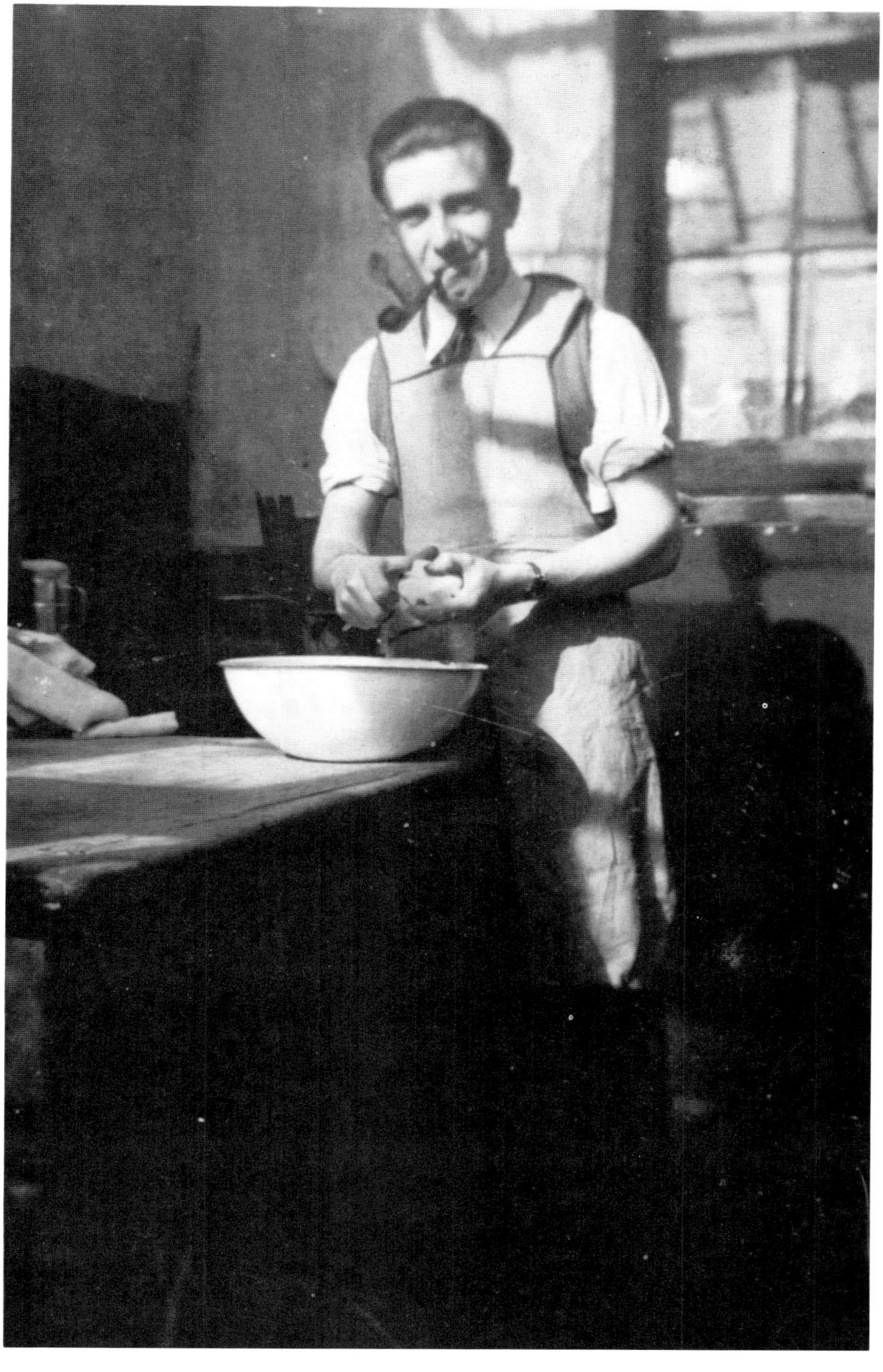

❧ In my youth teenagers hadn't been invented. I worked in a factory in Burnley then. The majority of workers were women so engagements and weddings were a constant talking point. I soon learnt that there was nothing they liked better than a good set of wedding photographs. They were always impressed by a posh do so I decided to let them see one in which I was a groomsman.

He had too, he was the brother-in-law of the bride and considerably older than any of us. The photographer is the little girl on the right. He was a photographer with the local paper. There were always a lot of posh wedding photographs hanging around their office. This was one he improved. I'm on the left with the Erroll Flynn pencilled-on moustache. The bride is the girl he was going with at the time.

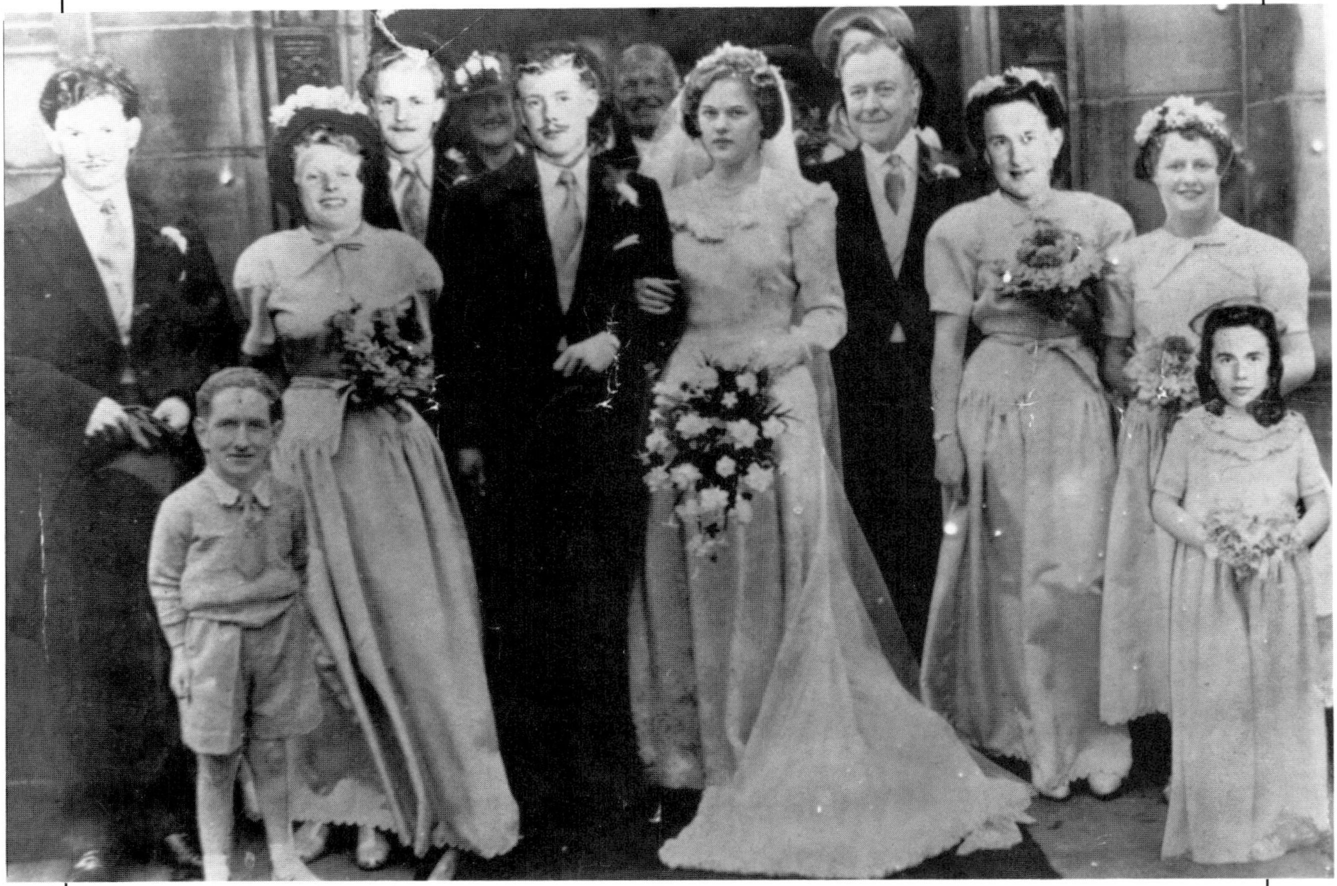

In fact, such was their enthusiasm that it seemed to cloud their critical faculties.

A few people caught on immediately. Those who didn't recognise the spoof were uneasy but didn't like to hurt my feelings. I always kept my face straight. I would let the embarrassment build up until eventually someone would ask, "Who's that little lad?".

"Oh, him," I would reply, "that's young Alan. He's got an old head on his shoulders, he has."

❧ I used to take a lot of photographs for this small brewery chain, publicity photographs of their restaurants and so on. Believe me, the quickest way to find out who is there with someone else's wife is to see who leaves suddenly as soon as they spot you setting up the camera!

❧ I have never fully understood why our ancestors dressed in their finery should choose to have the wedding photograph taken in the yard with what seems to be the lavatory door directly behind them!

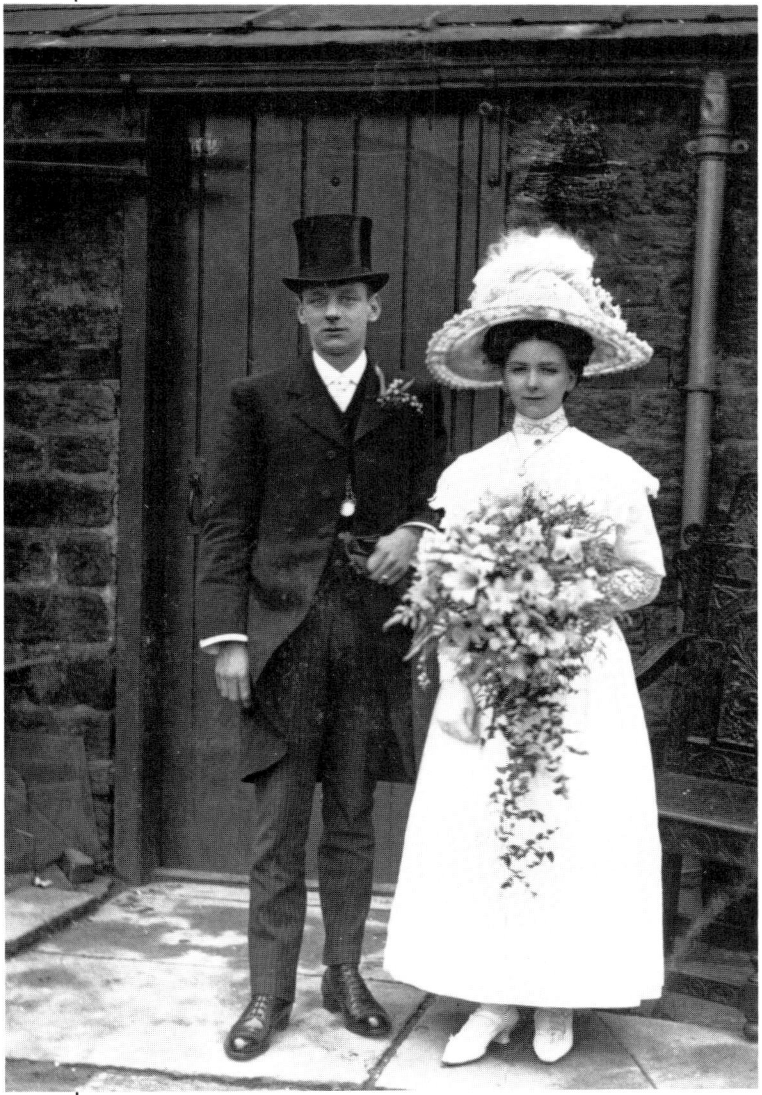

❧ Ernest and I got married in 1936. We couldn't afford a proper photographer at the wedding so a friend took the photographs with his camera. Unfortunately he tore the film taking it out of the camera, so we decided to have our picture taken at Robert's on Eldon Street. He was the photographer in Barnsley at the time and happened to be a friend of ours.

I remember Ernest had put even more Brylcream on than usual, his hair was really curly and he hated it. You were in danger of being called a pansy if you went round with curly hair then. My dress was white brocade and later I had it made into a dance dress. It finally ended up as a lovely pair of camiknickers. Ernest thought that they were very fetching.

❧ For some couples, having a good photographic record of their wedding is very important. When my husband and I got married we just took my Box Brownie camera to the Registry Office and got four of the guests to take it in turns to shoot a picture. It was a foggy November day so all the record we have of our wedding is captured in four misty photographs. It was second time round for him, so he'd been through all the business of hiring a photographer and even had a Super 8 movie of his first wedding. My commitment to our partnership would have been just as great with or without a marriage certificate, so neither of us set great store by wedding photographs.

The best wedding photo we could have had would have been of the looks on my workmates' faces when I turned up the next day with a plate of buns and announced that I'd got married on my day off.

❧ Around about 1940 I used to help my father develop and print wedding photographs he had taken. Once I remember, I was helping and as the photograph began to show on the paper it looked as though the bridesmaids had nothing on from the waist down.

This was something to do with the nylon dresses and the way nylon became transparent in certain lighting conditions. In fact, my father wrote to the manufacturers to tell them about it. I think shortly after that nylon began to be treated to stop this happening. I wish I knew what happened to those photographs.

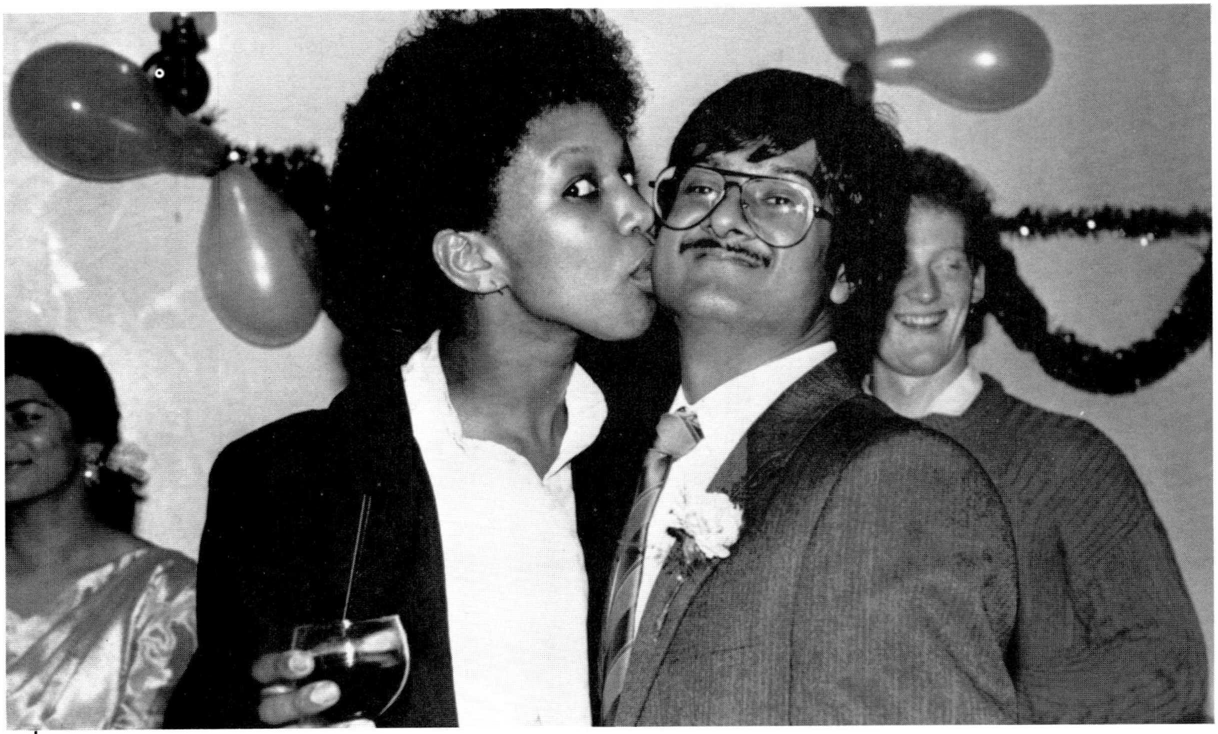

❧ For the wedding reception my mother arranged for a professional photographer to take pictures of the guests. When the results came back we were bitterly disappointed. It was lucky that my best friend volunteered to take some informal snaps of the party. This picture showing my new husband being happily molested by a college friend makes me laugh. Perhaps I like it even more because my mother-in-law can't bear to look at it.

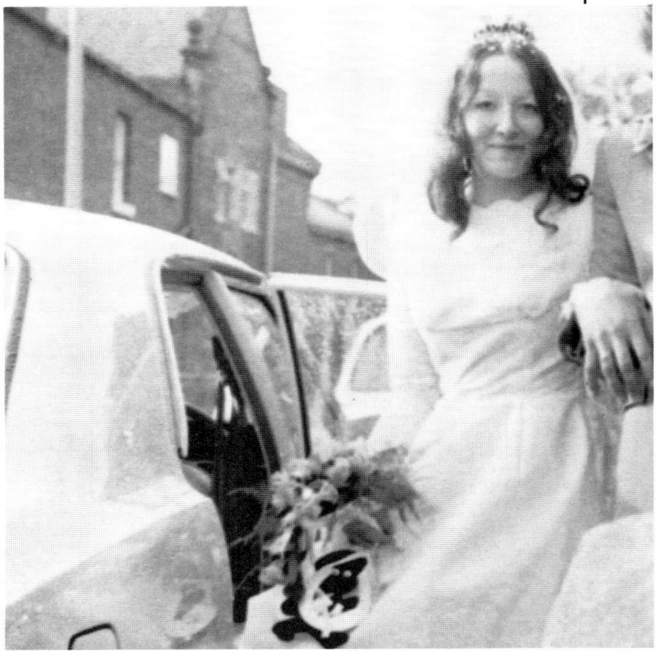

❧ Although I remain friendly with my ex-wife, her mother can't stand the sight of me. Alison was in stitches and had to go out of the room when she saw what her mother had done to our wedding photos. She had systematically gone through all the photographs and cut me out of the pictures. In some cases this has left just a photograph of my wife. In others I have been removed from the group and the picture has been sellotaped back together, leaving an image of my wife with the group while a mysterious hand dangles round her shoulder or waist.

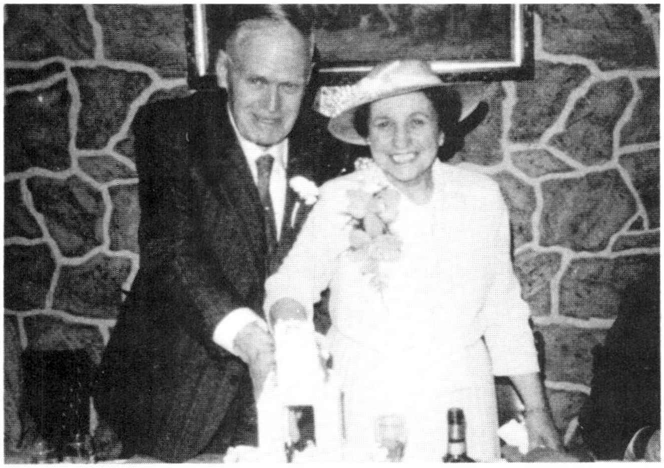

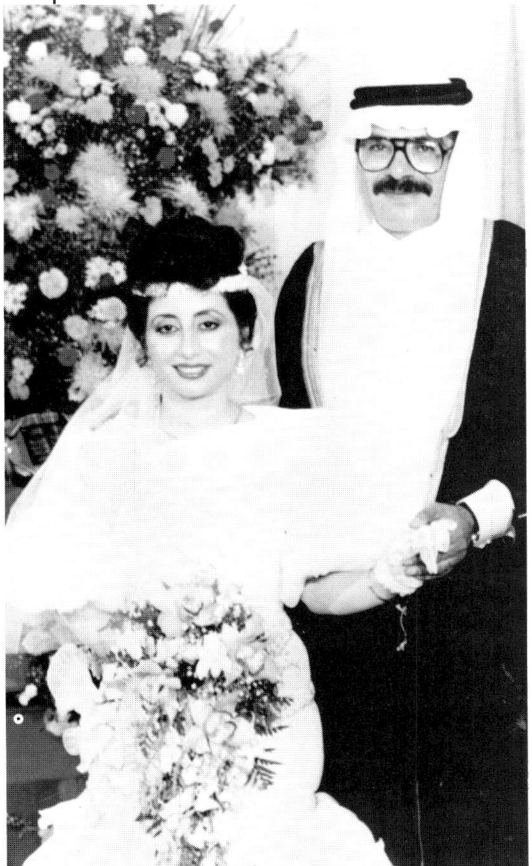

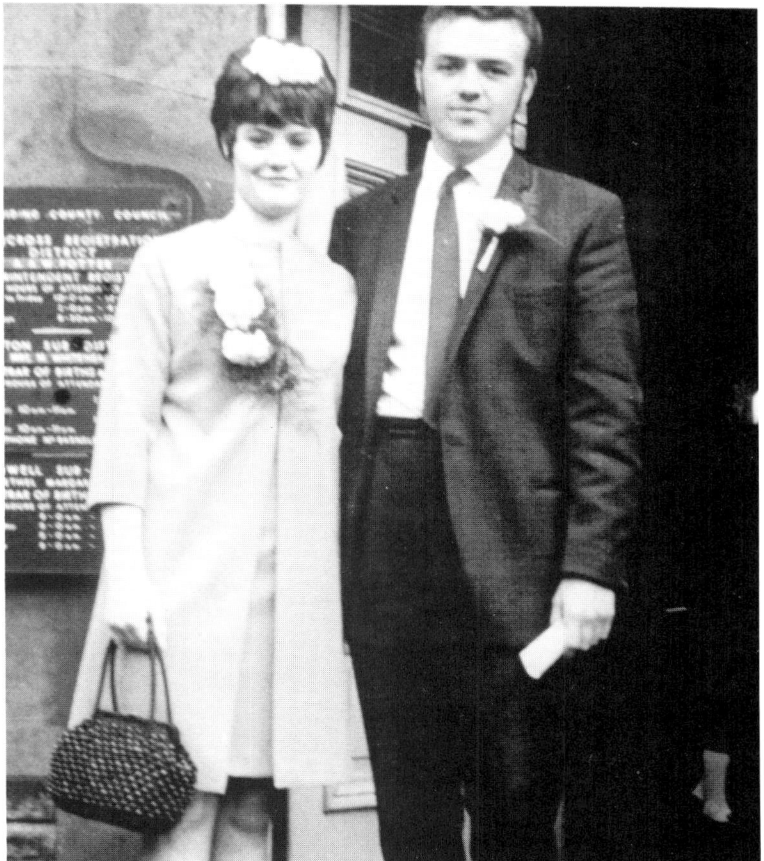

❧ I wonder how many of us would realise just how the years have changed us if we didn't have photographs?

I remember an incident at a friend's Silver Wedding. The celebrating wife was tall, slim and without a grey hair. Half way through the party she disappeared to re-emerge, to calls of approval, in her wedding dress, veil, shoes, the lot. She proved that she could still fit into the A-line white satin.

Three kids later, she still looked amazingly like herself of a quarter of a century ago. Her husband though had thinned a bit on top, thickened a bit round the middle and generally acquired a prosperous air on that Silver Wedding night. But Simon their eldest son, at twenty-four, bore an eerie resemblance to his father as the bridegroom.

So Simon posed with his mother for a second set of spot-the-difference wedding pictures. Everyone, including the father, joked about it but it seemed quite poignant too.

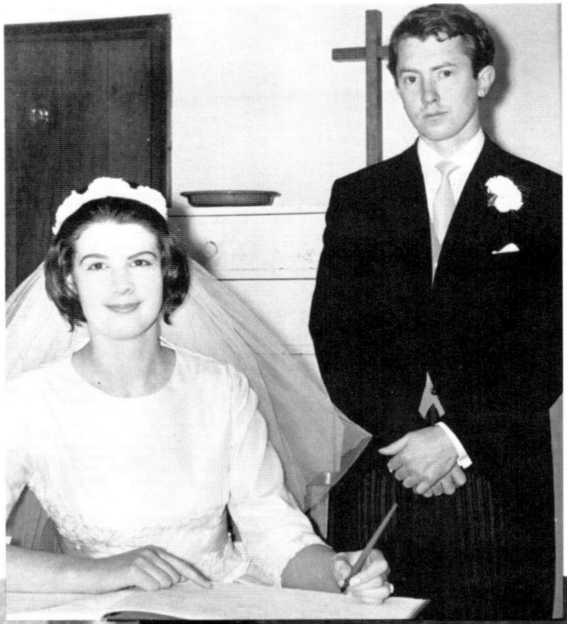

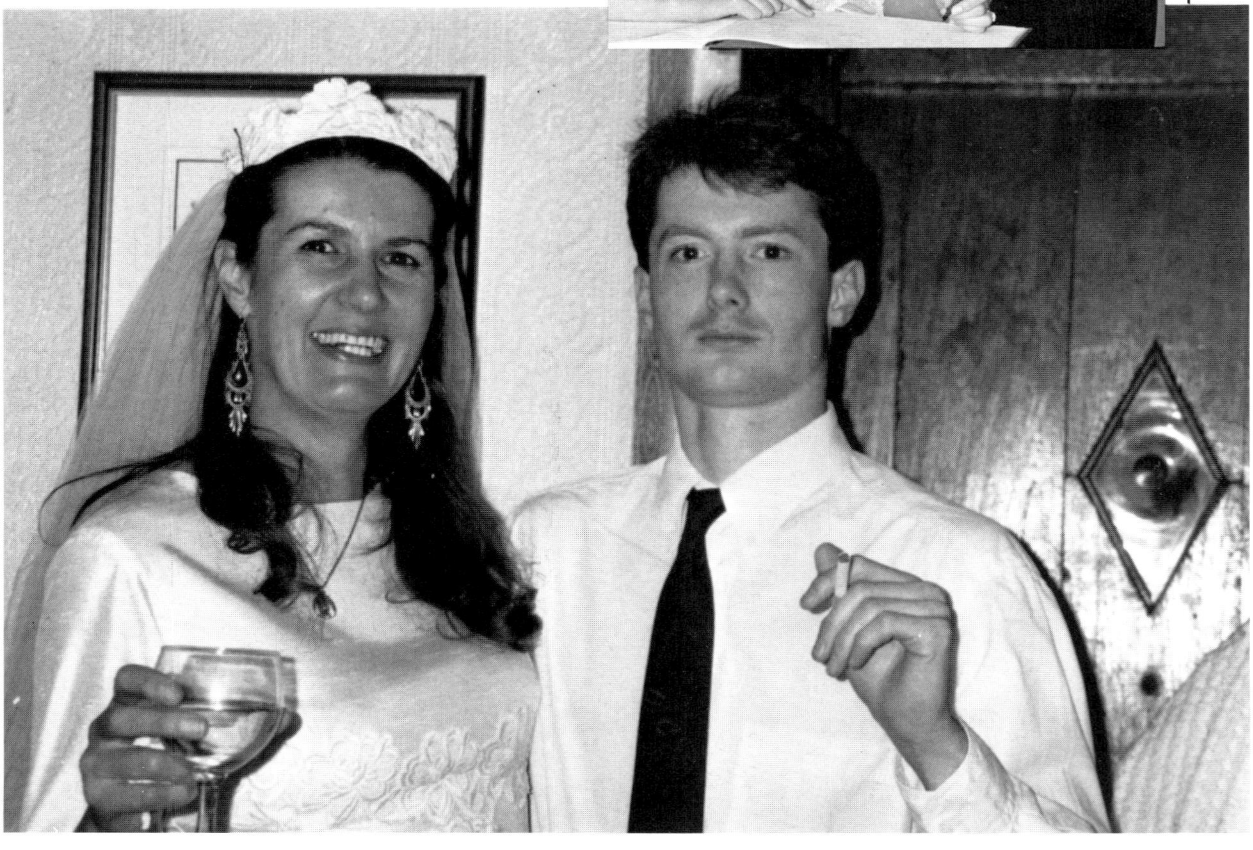

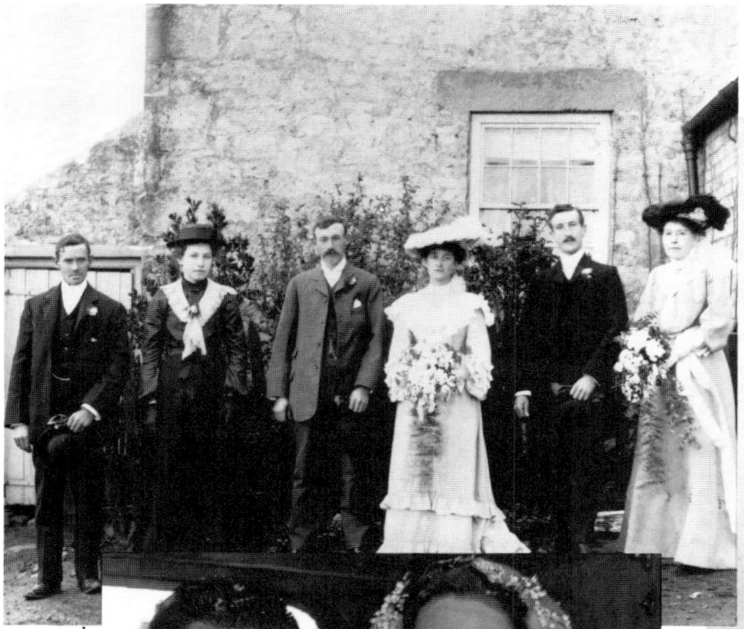

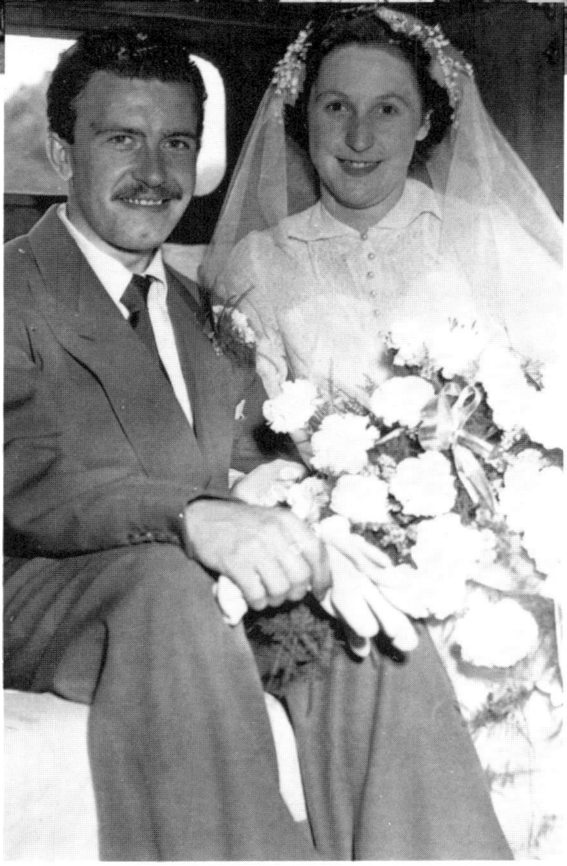

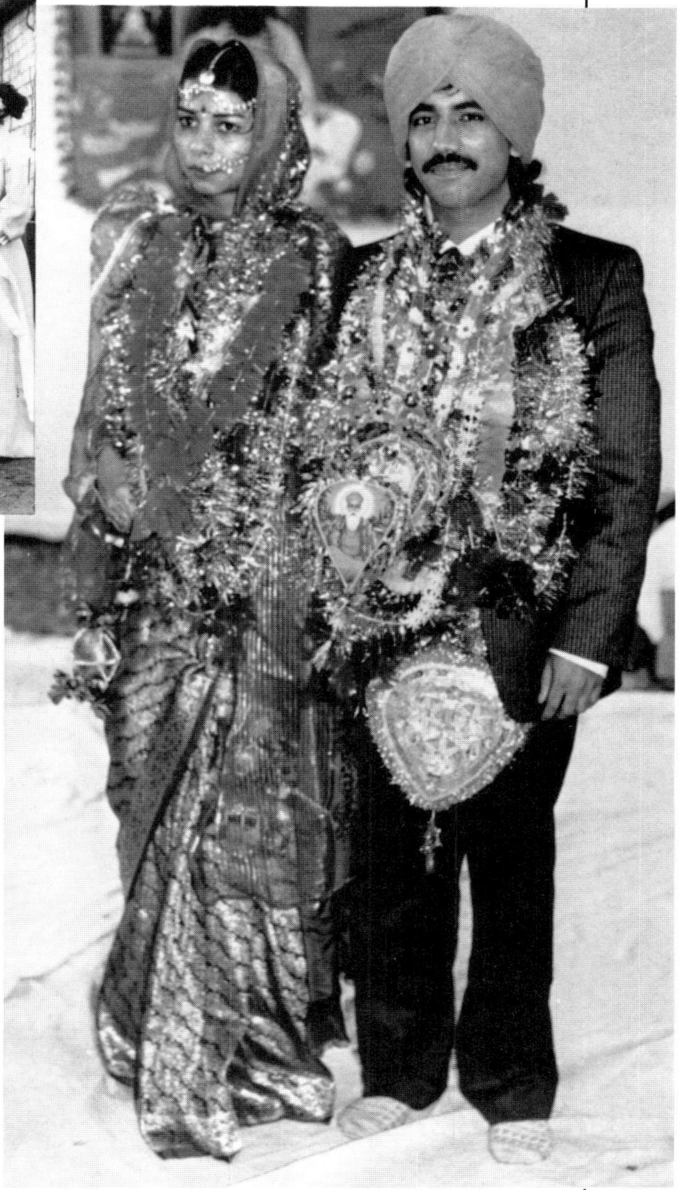

❧ I'd had enough of being a single parent, stuck on my own evening after evening, so I decided to put a personal ad in the Evening Post. I was amazed by the response. There are a lot of lonely blokes out there. Sifting through that pile of letters was a really good evening in itself.

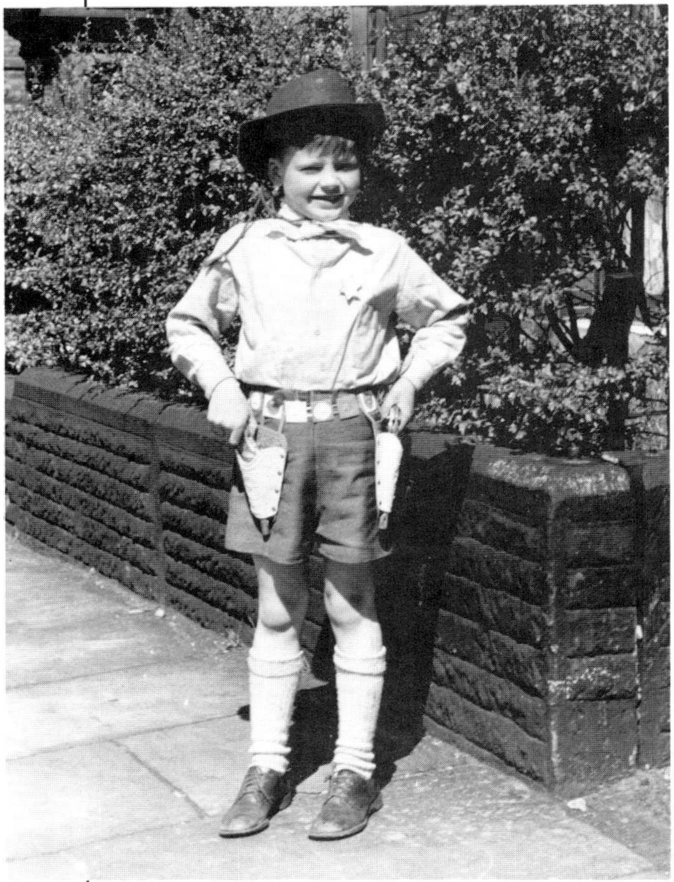

In the advert I'd requested that prospective suitors enclose a photograph. You should have seen some of them. One of them apologised for not having any recent photos and sent one of himself in a cowboy outfit when he was nine. Another, who sounded very nice in his letter, looked a real lounge lizard. The best looking of the bunch was almost illiterate whilst another looked as if he was a bit too fond of his T-reg Escort.

In the end I plumped for the bloke wearing his cowboy suit. He didn't look any different twenty years on.

We didn't last. He still behaved as if he was nine.

❧ When I was living in Brighton I had a relationship with a man who lived in London. I sent him a photograph of myself taken on the beach looking all seductive. We were only together for a couple of months, and afterwards I wished I hadn't sent that picture. I felt embarrassed and vulnerable.

❧ We had just got back from the pub after chucking out time. We'd all had a skinful and had walked two miles through the pouring rain. What's more, there were no street lights and we literally couldn't see our hands in front of our faces. To make sure we didn't lose our way we all held hands and stretched across the road. The blokes at each end felt their way along the walls that lined the road.

What we didn't realise was that at one point the road forked. At the fork there was a concrete post. I was in the middle of the human chain. The result can be seen in the photograph. At the time, I was too drunk to feel any pain, but the next day I suffered.

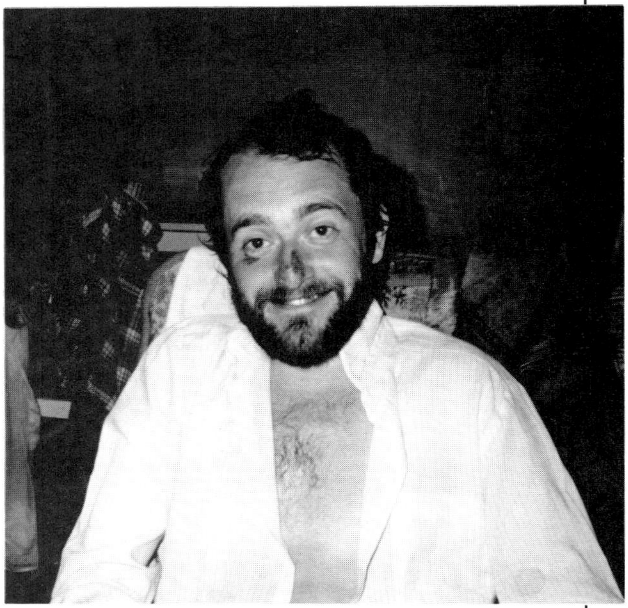

❧ I don't take many photos because I can't get the camera in my handbag. Mind you, I've got ten albums filled with different blokes I've met on foreign holidays over the past ten years!

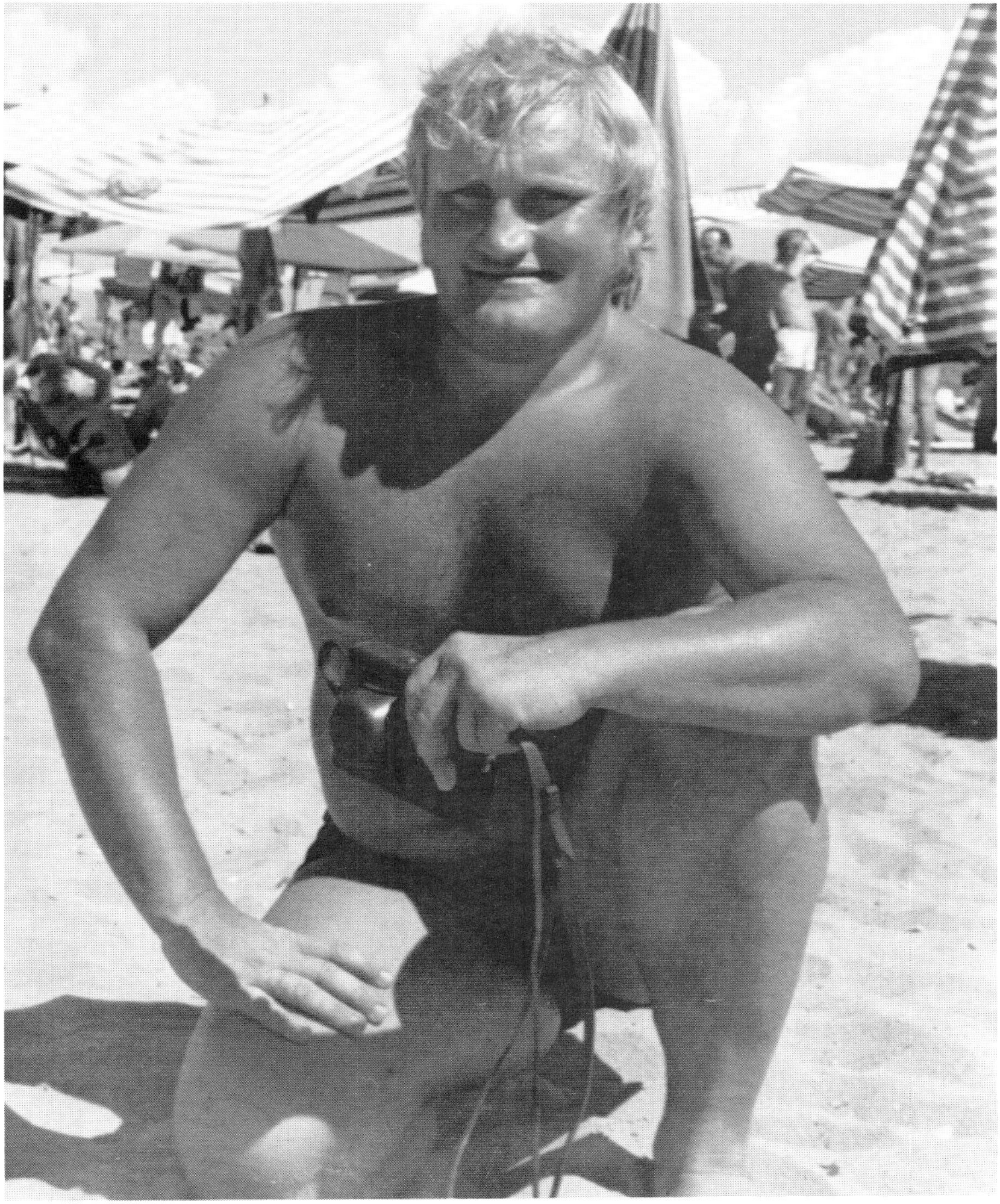

❧ My editor, an individual singularly devoid of that commodity always rare amongst his kind, a sense of humour, once enquired, "How come, whatever the job, flood, famine, pestilence or bloody plague, you always photograph some dozy bugger with an inane grin on his face?"

He had a point. Although, I invariably photograph a different dozy bugger each time. Not, as he seemed to be implying, the same one. However, even he would have been impressed by one example of the powerful need to smile when a camera is pointed at you.

Golden Weddings are a regular, if somewhat mundane, part of local newspaper life. Having said that, one such celebration in Castleford will remain forever etched in my mind. The usual routine on such occasions is for Father to grumble about having to wear a tie and Mother to insist on including all ninety-seven cards, the cake and half an allotment of flowers. This particular day, having negotiated these expected hurdles, I positioned the couple and had raised my camera, when Mother dashed to the sideboard and began rummaging through an assortment of bric-a-brac. "Mi teeth. I can't remember where I put mi teeth".

Father, mother and daughter then embarked on a thorough but fruitless search. The old lady was adamant that she would not face the camera toothless; I was ready for off, the old boy had gone back to his paper, then, with a flash of inspiration the daughter solved the problem. "Here, Mother. Put mine in, this lad can't wait all day."

The gleaming dentures were quickly pushed into place, or at least as near into place as they would go. I got my picture; what a picture, it still haunts me. The smile was grand if somewhat overstated, like a Steinway in the snug bar.

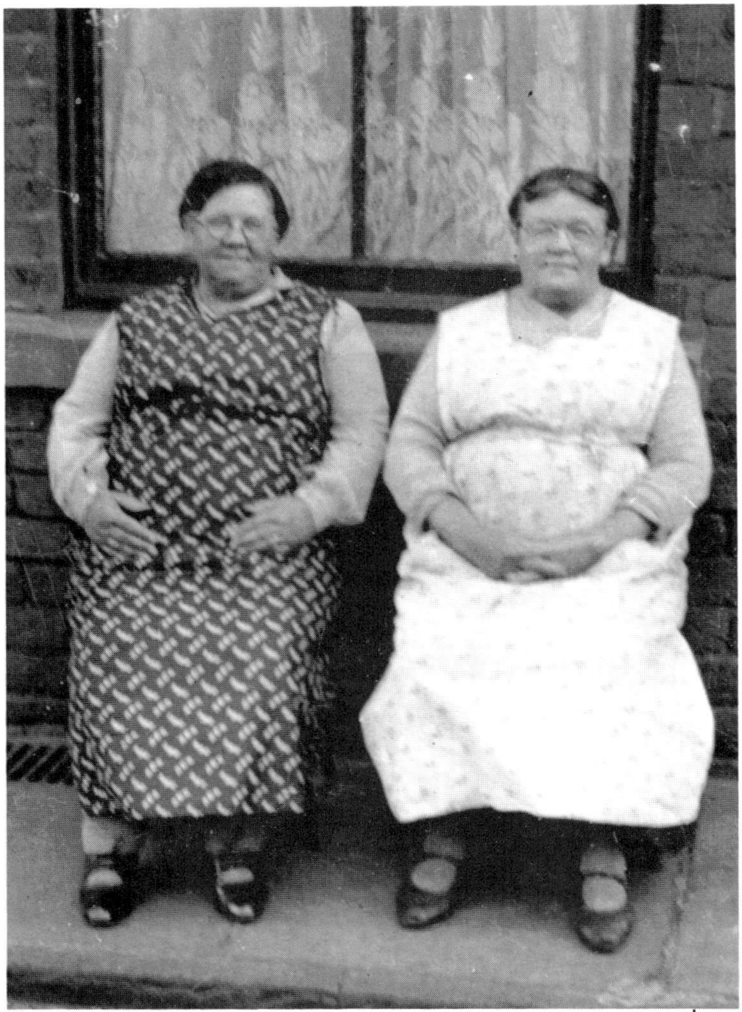

❧ When my husband's great grandmother came to visit us we thought it would be lovely to have a photograph of our young son with her. It was taken in our sitting room. When developed great great grandma was showing her bloomers. The photograph is now displayed in our family album with the corner cut off to maintain the old lady's dignity.

❧ I've been taking photos for many years now and develop and print my own. I wanted a formal portrait of my ageing parents but, before I had chance to take one, my father became ill with a suspected hernia. Then it turned out he had cancer.

I didn't want to take a photograph of him looking frail and weak, not at all the person I remembered as my father. His eyes looked large and sunken into his face. How I wish I had taken the photo when I first thought about it. This has taught me to get on with things rather than think about them for too long.

❧ I was never all that keen on photography, just the odd holiday snap here and there. My line was movies and later videos. My husband, on the other hand, is a very keen photographer. He has taken some really splendid shots. I own an automatic which does it all.

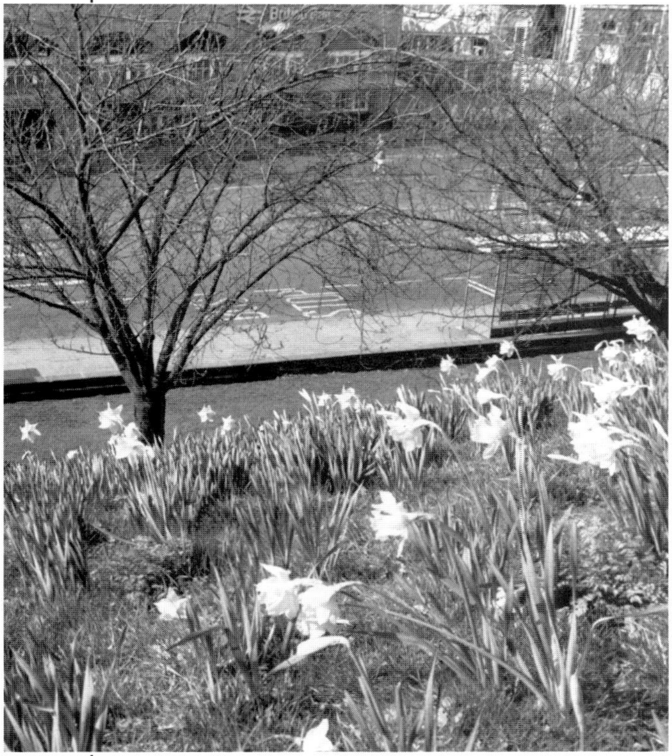

❧ A very dear friend of mine was terminally ill with cancer and I was trying to keep up her spirits by telling her what was going on in the outside world. One afternoon I happened to mention I would be going to York at the weekend. Tears filled her eyes, "Oh, how I love York, those beautiful daffodils on the hillside near the castle walls. I wish I could see them once more before I die." I tried to console her by telling her she would, knowing in my heart this wasn't true.

The day of the visit to York was very cold and windy, but for a few minutes the sun broke through and there were the daffodils just as my friend had described them. I snapped from this angle and that, in fact almost a whole film on daffodils. The results were wonderful, the look of joy on her face said it all.

PUTTING YOURSELF IN THE PICTURE.

The problem of how to appear in your own photographs is by no means a new one.

In the days of relatively insensitive glass plates, before cameras were fitted with shutters, it was possible to remove the lens cap, move quickly into position, stand motionless while the exposure was made and then go back to the camera to replace the lens cap. The movement of the photographer would not be recorded in the photograph.

The introduction of dry plates in the 1880s - plates sensitive enough to record movement and for exposures as brief as a fraction of a second - meant that for the first time cameras had to be fitted with shutters. Many of these had pneumatic releases, triggered by a puff of air sent along a tube from a squeezed rubber bulb. If you wanted to include yourself in your photograph all that you needed was a long enough piece of tubing.

By the turn of the century the first cable releases appeared. These offered an alternative to the rubber ball and tube. Cable releases up to thirty feet long were manufactured. It was with a device of this sort that Captain Scott and his colleagues photographed themselves at the South Pole.

Tubes and cables worked but they added to the clutter that photographers had to carry. Devices that could be fixed directly on to the camera were more convenient.These released the shutter after a short delay - time enough to get into the correct position. Clockwork powered devices of this sort first came on the market around the time of the First World War and continued to be made until comparatively recently.

Timers actually built into the camera did not appear until the 1930s.

The introduction of electronics into camera technology has made the provision of auto-timers almost universal.

❧ When my sister and I were in our early teens my dad was friendly with a Polish man who worked at the same firm. I remember Dad inviting him to visit us for the day. Jan, as he was called, had just bought himself a fancy camera. It gave a few seconds lapse before the shutter released so the taker could nip into the photo if so desired. At dinner, Mum being true to her native Yorkshire, served up Yorkshire pudding. Real Yorkshire pudding at its best is always eaten immediately it is out of the oven. Jan had other ideas. He wanted to record every aspect of his day with us. We spent several minutes at the table, mouths watering at the anticipation of the Yorkshire puddings while Jan took photos. I think Mum was a bit mad at this slight delay but she never let on and we do have a lovely photo of all the family from that day - fortunate really because it wasn't long after that visit that my dad became ill with cancer and died. Soon Jan went to Germany to live. We kept in touch at Christmas. The last memory I have of him is rather sad. He sent a photo of himself by his Christmas tree; he looked so alone. I imagined him with only his camera for company. I expect he set the time lapse and then moved to sit by his decorated tree.

One year we didn't hear from him and I think Mum's letter was returned. We presumed he had died.

POST MORTEM PHOTOGRAPHY

Today we have reservations about taking photographs at a funeral. The Victorians, however, had a totally different attitude towards death. Death was no stranger to the Victorian family; most lost at least one member prematurely as a result of the high level of infant mortality or the limitations of the medical knowledge of the time. It was by no means unusual for professional photographers to be asked to take a portrait of a deceased loved one.

In 1878 a photographer explained how he tackled this sort of commission:

'On being called to make a photograph of this kind I make it an invariable rule to agree as to price, and obtain a payment before setting out. If I cannot do so, I at once refuse it altogether, and for this reason : it is very rare that one can make a pleasing picture of this kind, and then, if they are not previously paid for it is a great chance indeed if they are accepted. To attempt to force them by law to pay is not worth the trouble, risk and loss of time. But having done this, it is a duty to obtain the very best possible result circumstances will allow. Where the subject is already in the coffin, then the head should be raised, or the edges of the coffin covered with a sheet to hide that as much as possible; for if this be not done a most ghastly picture is certain to result. It is best so to arrange as to make the subject appear like a person asleep; but the least portion of a coffin being seen at once dispels any illusion to all beholders of the picture.'

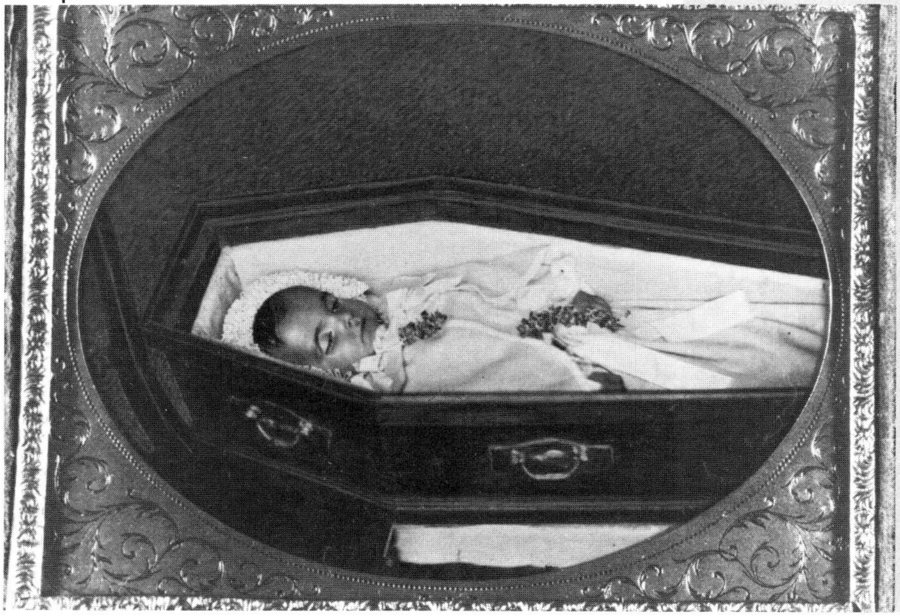

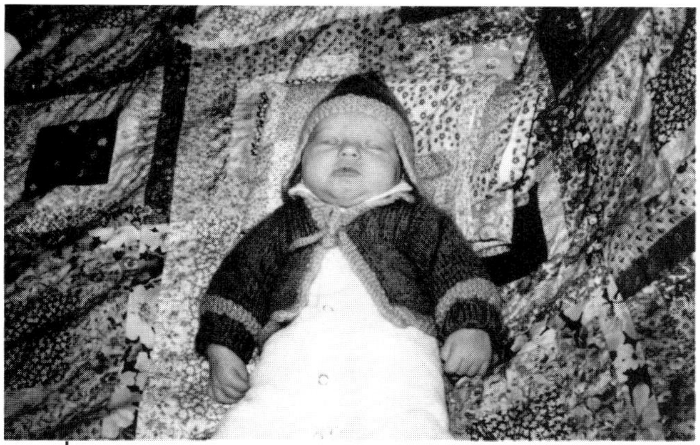

❧ This looks like a real rehearsal for the death bed job: its got everything - the sunken eye sockets,the hands clasped on the chest, the open mouth, close to which you put the mirror, trying to get the last faint breath. Even the brocade in the background, heavily figured and strong in its pattern, carries with it the hint of the grave. You can almost hear the relatives whispering; 'He looks at peace at last' or 'It was a good life' or 'He would like his ashes scattered at Kings Cross Station, platform eight'.

You may think that I have passed over but really that is not the case. This picture is the result of over - indulgence. The aftermath of a heavy Christmas dinner and too much hock. Ten minutes later I was up dancing the hokey-cokey.

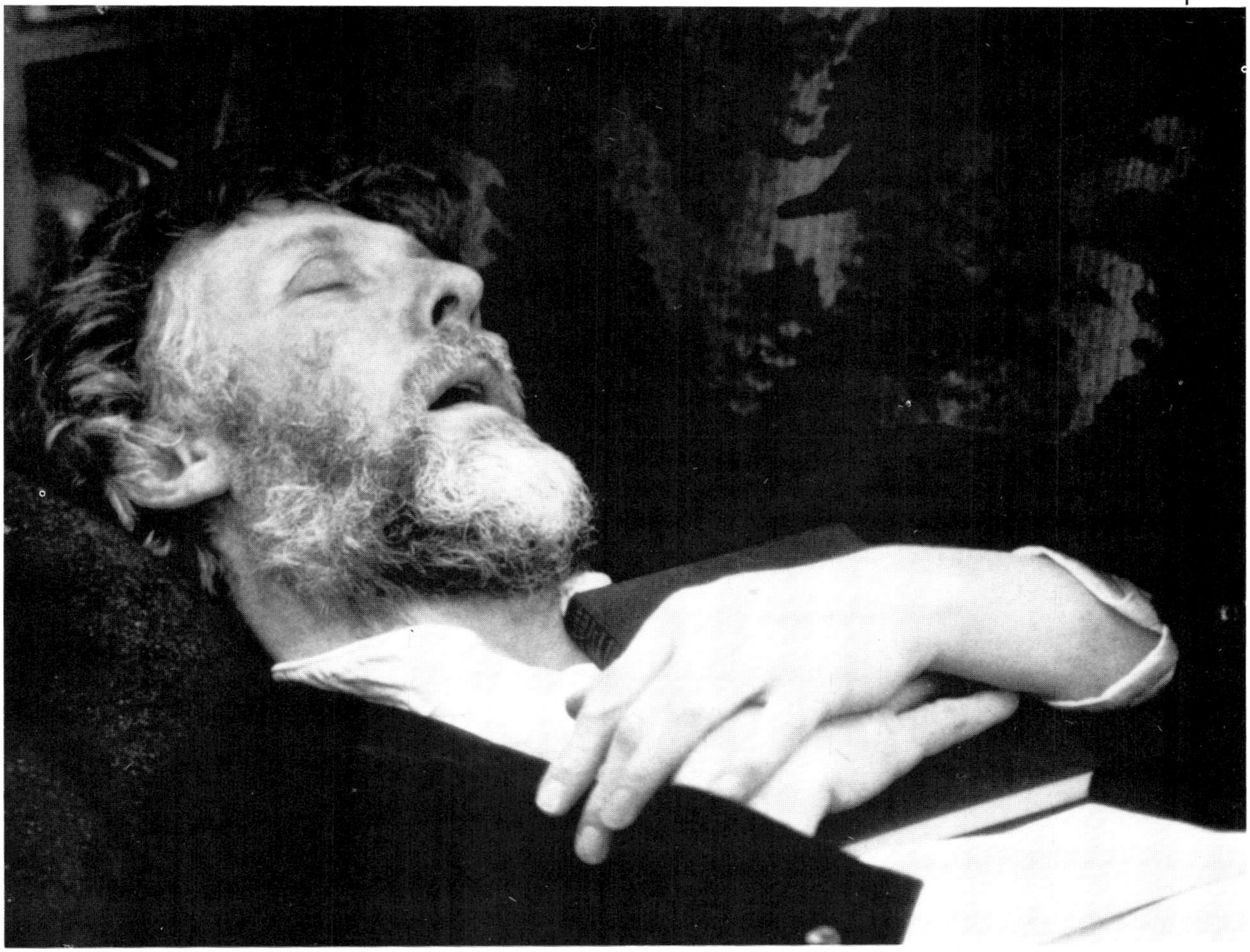

❧ Photographing weddings is very easy. The click of camera shutters is an expected part of the ritual, but it's much more difficult to photograph funerals. Curious. Funerals are as much public events as weddings, they create just as much on-the-street nosiness, but people don't want to remember them with photographs.

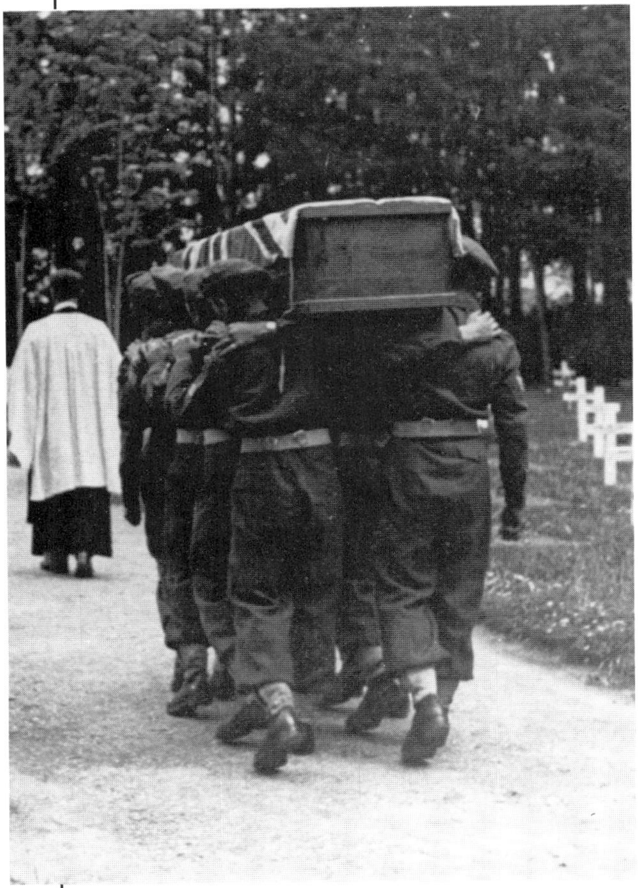

Unless it's a state funeral, photographs are taboo. If you were close to the deceased, you should be too upset to photograph; if you weren't close, you're intruding into grief. You're always supposed to smile on photographs - and people don't, on the whole, smile at funerals.

I confronted all this a couple of years ago when Jack Hulme, the photographer, died. Jack had photographed every aspect of life in the pit village of Fryston near Castleford. It seemed a pity he wouldn't photograph his own funeral, a major event in village life. So I thought it would be an apt tribute to take the pictures for him. I asked his daughter Christine for permission and she agreed. I lurked around the corrugated iron church photographing the procession and the burial across the desolate churchyard. It was very unnerving because even though funerals tend to be relatively slow and stately affairs you have to move fast. And there's not much scope for asking people to 'do that bit again'.

I leapt over gravestones feeling like the very lowest of paparazzi. A camera gives you a protective screen from reality.

❧ I know of very few people who have photographed a family funeral. When a good friend of mine died I asked his widow how she felt about me photographing the funeral, something I wanted to do to mark his passing. With her permission and cooperation I photographed the whole ceremony: leaving the house, arriving at the church, the interment and the meal afterwards when friends and relatives gathered to celebrate his life as much as to mourn his passing.

Taking the photographs was a delicate task; how to make good pictures which summarised the day whilst remaining unobtrusive. As I felt the photographs didn't really belong to me, but more to his widow, I passed over the negatives and prints for her to keep and incorporate in the family's visual history.

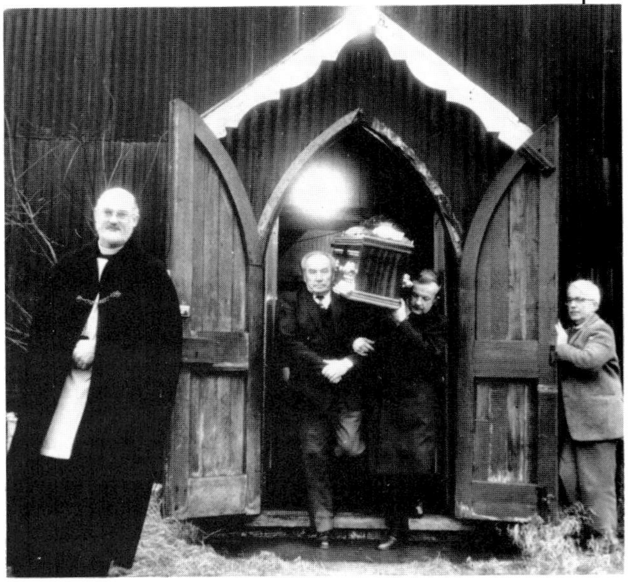

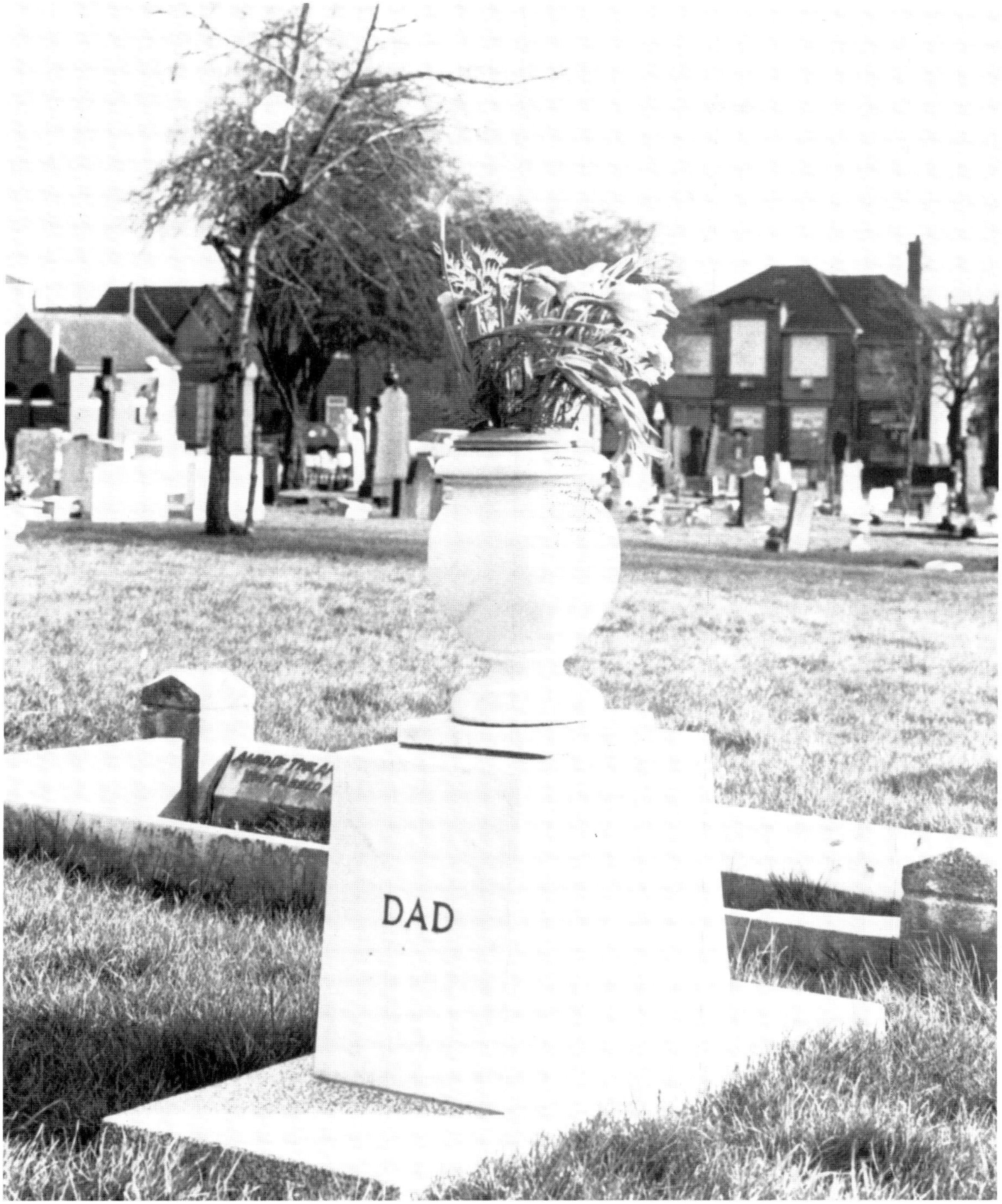
DAD

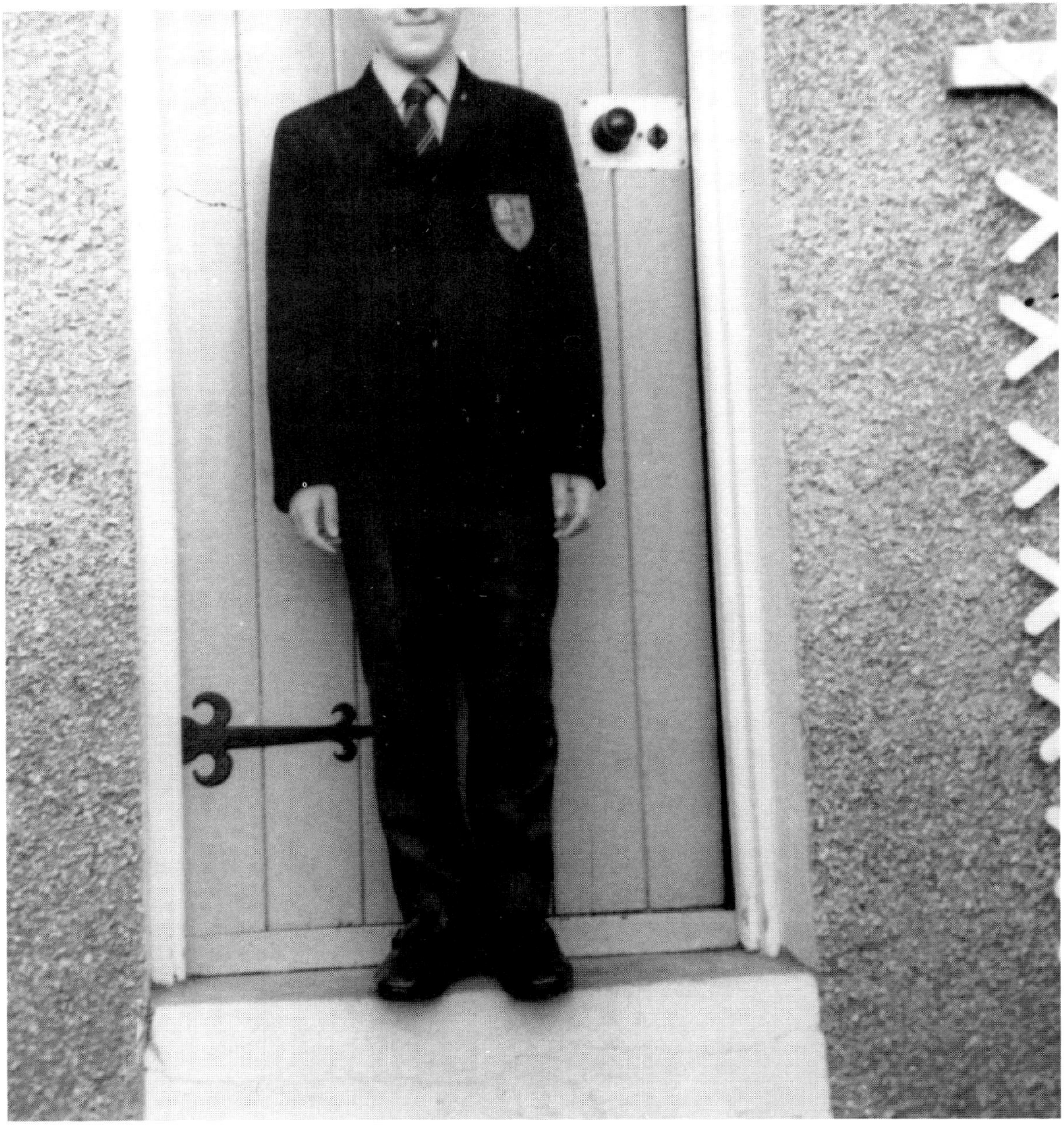

'Taken on my first day at
Grammar School.
Mam must have been happy with it,
she's kept it for twenty years.'

CHAPTER THREE

TODAY SIMPLE SNAPS TOMORROW PRICELESS TREASURE

Kodak advertisement 1934

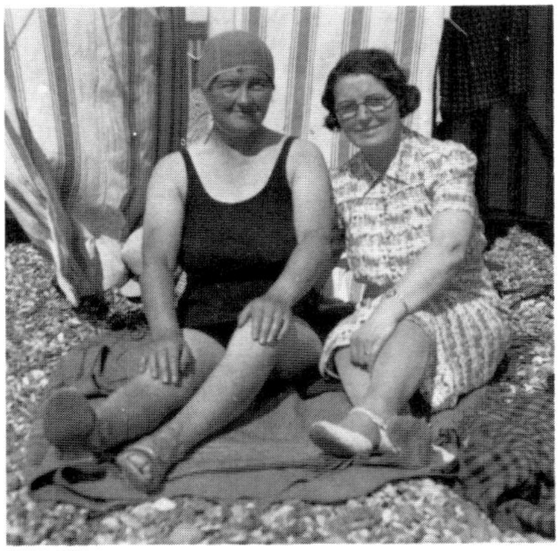

❧ It was just after the war, probably 1946, and the black-out curtains were still up, when one bright summer afternoon the physics master instructed us all to climb onto the desks and lie down. When we were all settled he went over to the central blind, told us to look up at the ceiling and cut a hole in the fabric. Using a mirror to reflect the light, there appeared on the ceiling a panoramic view of the streets below: traffic, trees, houses, people, everything. There was even the image of a boy having a crafty fag in the bicycle sheds. It was magic.

That year I bought my first camera, a Kodak 1A, and made a dark room in the corner of my bedroom.

CAMERA OBSCURA

The principle of the camera obscura (Latin for dark room), in which light passing through a small hole into a darkened room will form an inverted image of the scene outside, was known to both the ancient Greeks and Chinese.

In about 1500 it was described by Leonardo Da Vinci. At some time during the sixteenth century, lenses began to be used to produce brighter, clearer images and, during the seventeenth century, cameras obscurae were in general use by artists as an aid to drawing. Large enough for the artist to sit inside, they were carried around like sedan chairs Later, smaller versions were made that could be carried in the hand. It is from these that the modern photographic camera has evolved.

❧ When I was a swede-basher living over the back of Maltby, I somehow got my hands on this book about scientific experiments for boys. It was filled with matchstick men doing things and one of the things was to make a camera. To do all the things it said I had to improvise. I took a large piece of paper, rubbed it with bacon fat, made a box, placed the paper over the back, set it up in the fork of a plum tree and looked through. I was amazed. There, coming across the field, in the strong sunlight, yet upside down, was the woman who looked after the evacuees. I was very naive for a ten year old and this was a magic carpet.

❧ I decided to get into photography. First and foremost I wanted a camera, any sort of camera. Our next door neighbour came up with a little beauty. It was a very small Kodak box camera which used 127 film. It had single shutter speed and a fixed lens. The viewfinder was a wire oblong which pulled out of the side. If you put your eye close enough to it, you could see the whole world.

❧ My first experience of practical photography came when I was ten years old. The local toy shop was selling a small paper case which contained a negative of a footballer and a piece of contact paper. You pulled out the covering paper and left it in the window to get the sun. After a time, if the sun was strong you could take out the contact sheet and find a brown picture of your footballer on it. Unfortunately, after a few hours in the daylight it had disappeared. It was not fixed, as I found out later.

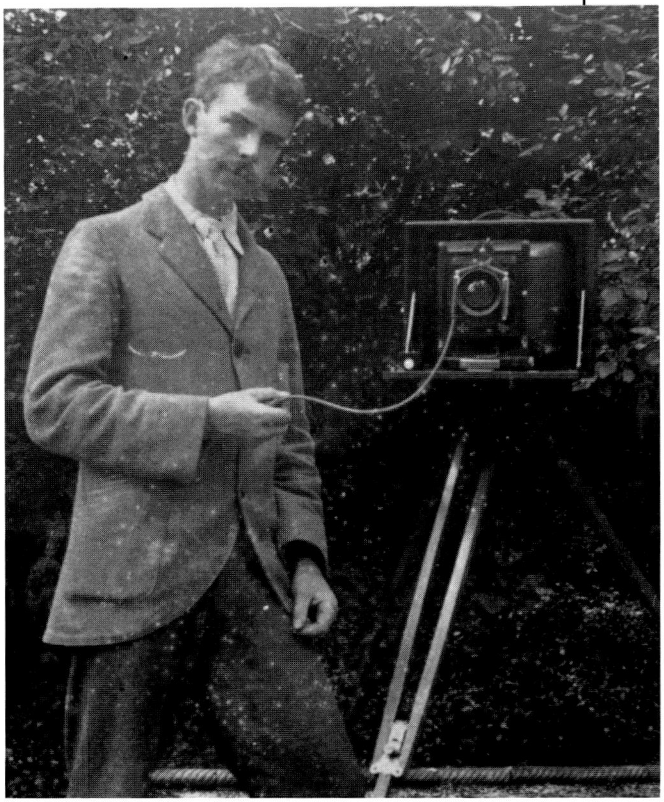

❧ I got my first camera in 1955 when I was sixteen. It was a folding camera with a little black metal plate on the side with silver lettering reading, "The Kodak Company Inc., Rochester, New York, USA, 1918". I inherited it from my Great Uncle Fred, a retired police sergeant who had put his head in his gas oven less than a year after his wife, Aunty Bella, had died from a stroke. Upright and secretive as he was, we had no idea how depressed he had become. There was also a box of snaps of family and friends standing looking at the camera, in the park or on the Promenade at Whitley Bay in their best clothes. People always seemed to get dressed up for the camera. Uncle Fred was always in a three piece suit with a silver watch chain across his ample belly. He stood stern and unsmiling with the slight nervous figure of Aunty Bella at his side, she in a long coat with a fur collar. I used this camera for the next five years. I took it to teacher training college and snapped my friends in studied poses at Stratford, Lichfield and Great Malvern. It then went round the cathedrals of England one August producing some passable pictures of fine architectural features and on to Paris, Brussels and Cologne. Eventually it developed a tiny pin hole in the bellows which came out on the negative as a triangle of white. The man at the camera shop said it could not be economically repaired.

It was replaced on my twenty-first birthday with a flashy little German number, a Balda Baldessa 1b which cost the princely sum of £14. I have had several cameras since, but have regarded none with the affection of that first one, already forty years old when I got it.

❧ My father, a greengrocer, was also an avid photographer. He visited Covent Garden market early one morning and found on sale one of the first 35mm cameras to be imported into this country from Japan. Dad bought one and was so excited he jumped up on top of his lorry and was scanning around, framing up, when a fellow yelled over to him, "Get bloody down! Why d'you think they're so cheap?" It turned out that two suitcases of them had been stolen from the docks.

❧ I use a late 1940s bellows camera which my father bought from the Co-op to photograph my childhood. It cost him £10 and it was recently revalued at £8. It has an unusually good lens, but is otherwise lacking any sort of sophistication - no rangefinder or exposure meter - and I never bother with flash as it kills atmosphere. As a result, I estimate exposure and, if I'm photographing people in poor lighting, have to ask them to hold a tape measure to the end of their nose. If nothing else, it breaks the ice and gives the impression they're being photographed by a half-wit. The camera needs regular repairs - the bellows have been patched up four times - but I'm so used to it that it's like an extension of myself. I sometimes photograph instinctively and wonder afterwards if it was right.

❧ I find other cameras alarmingly complicated. It may be a bit of a fogeyish gimmick, but there's an issue here; so many amateur photographers are obsessive gadget collectors. It's not photography, it's consumerism. They lug great bagfuls of gear around with them and by the time they've sorted it all out the picture has gone. The great Henri Cartier-Bresson used just his camera and his skill. Mind you, he did use a Leica.

JAPANESE CAMERAS

Cameras have been made in Japan since the 1840s. However, it was not until the after the last war that they made a significant impact on the European market.

At the time of the Korean War, many servicemen were suprised at the quality of the cameras they were able to buy in the Far East. However, the first Japanese cameras were not imported into Britain until 1957 when the Board of Trade allowed a £15,000 quota. This amounted to less than five hundred cameras and included just twenty Minoltas and six Nikons.This trickle was to eventually turn into a flood.

Most Japanese cameras are now no longer made in Japan. The trend within the industry is to move to countries where production costs are lower, such as Taiwan and China.

❧ It is probably true that a great composer can work with an old piano, but a good one is better. It is true that fine pictures can be taken with simple cameras, but versatile ones are better. With a viewfinder camera I learnt to compose, but my single lens reflex made imagination possible; the paralysis of parallax vanished. I could hold it to my eye or look down to my waist. I could shoot a man at right angles, or fill the frame with a flower. Its ground glass screen showed me instantly how blurred spots could change into sharp green leaves and harsh rectangular concrete blocks fade to an inoffensive grey blur. This was real composing. With a 1.9 lens almost all light was available. With a 135mm telephoto, I could compress space. Unlike a gunman, I could see the effect before I fired.

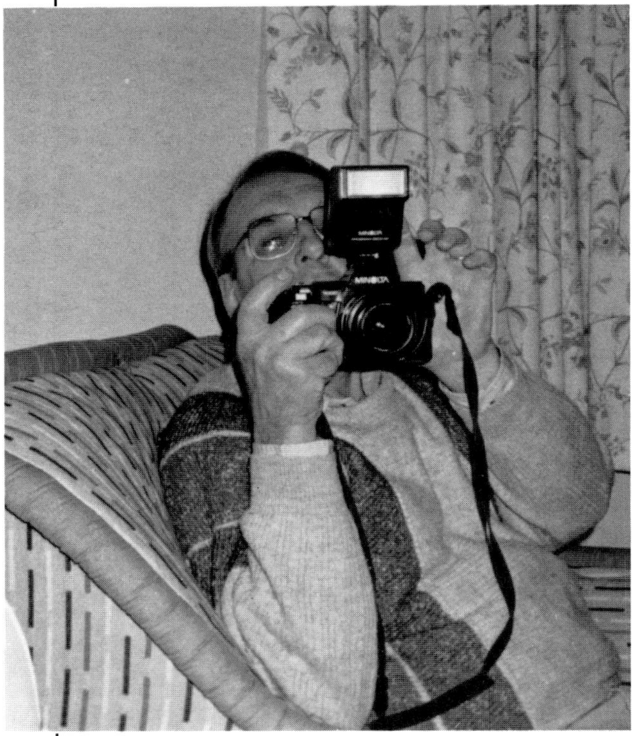

❧ I bought my first camera in 1948 while on holiday in Guernsey - it cost me £3. The name of it escapes me, although I know it was some sort of bird. I had never heard of the make before or since for that matter. It didn't take me long to realise it was not that good a camera so I decided to trade it in. The shop I took it to was in a street which no longer exists in Sheffield. The window was full of second-hand cameras. The chap could hardly wait to get his hands on my nice new camera and he gave me £6 for it. He then sold me a Zeiss, a folding camera for £9. It had a F3.5 Tessar lens and a sports viewfinder, a very useful facility which I'm surprised they don't have now. It made a moving object very easy to centre.

WHAT'S IN A NAME?

The camera referred to in this story was one of a range produced by the Leeds firm of Kershaw and Sons Ltd. A number of their cameras were named after birds: Myna, Raven, Peregrine, Penguin and Curlew. The reason for this was simple. Some of the directors of the firm were keen bird spotters and this was a way of combining their interests.

Over the years, many pieces of photographic equipment have got their names in similarly imaginative ways.

The Kodak range of Brownie cameras was named after characters in childrens' books invented by the Canadian author Palmer Cox. Hektor lenses for Leica cameras were named after the lens designer's pet dog and Canon cameras are named after the Japanese Goddess Kwanon.

❧ An enthusiast will think nothing of spending £700 on a camera. But what is the enthusiast enthusiastic about? Is it the camera or the pictures he can take with it? I've heard of someone who buys the latest electronic marvel with anti-red eye, auto-focus, infra-red flash, LCD readout and an embarrassing electronic female voice that declares far and wide, "You are overexposed." Six months later he'll trade it in for the Mark 2 version, never having taken a single picture. Photography! What's that? It's the technology that fascinates him. There must be some bargain second hand buys around near where he lives.

POLAROID PHOTOGRAPHY.

The first satisfactory method of 'instant' photography was invented by an American, Dr Edwin H Land. He is said to have been inspired by his young daughter's impatience to see her photograph. She could not understand why she had to wait for the film to be processed and printed.

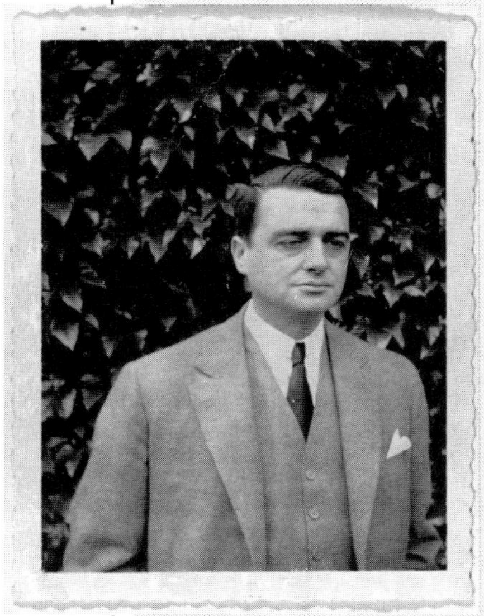

Land announced his discovery in 1947, and the first Polaroid cameras went on sale the following year. In one minute they produced a sepia-coloured photograph. The one millionth Polaroid camera was sold in November 1956. By this time, improvements had reduced the development time to about fifteen seconds. In 1963 the first colour film was produced.

The first Polaroids worked on the 'peel-apart' principle. After waiting for development to take place, the photograph was peeled away from the 'negative'. This was a messy and fiddly process. In 1972 a new camera appeared using a different method. The SX-70 automatically ejected the picture after exposure, development taking place outside the camera. There was no litter and no chemicals to get on your fingers.

❧ Not many people had Polaroid cameras. When my boyfriend acquired one we decided to enjoy the freedom of instant photos without having developers looking at them. One was a perfect study of his erect penis. For some reason, probably not wanting the children to see it, I put it in a book on a high shelf and forgot about it. Years later, after I remarried, my new husband took down Gray's Poems because he wanted to check something and found the photo. Luckily he believed me when I said I hadn't kept it for any particular reason. He knows that I cannot bear to throw anything away.

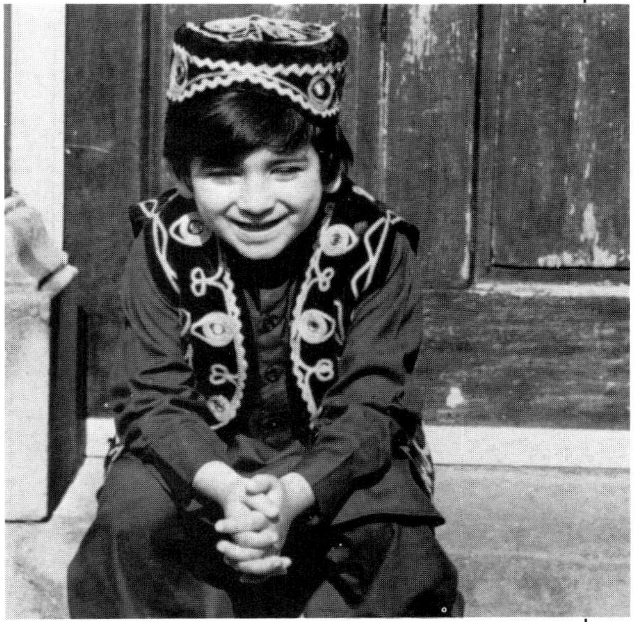

❧ In 1983 I was on a trek in Nepal with my girlfriend. It was stunning, there was so much to see and we took photographs everywhere. My girlfriend realised one day that she had left her camera behind somewhere on the trail. We went back but could not find it so we continued with our trek.

A few days on we found a police station and decided to report the lost camera. We were sitting outside telling the officer our story, when the officer's wife came out to hear what was going on. She asked how much the camera was worth. When we told her its value in Nepalese currency she fell off her stool. It turned out it was worth the equivalent of a year's income for them.

❧ I'd been taking pictures with an old cheap camera bought in the Leeds Tatters' Market. It worked fairly well outside in bright sunshine but was much too slow to use indoors and I wanted to take pictures of my mates playing cards. In 1949, chemists just about held the monopoly on photo processing and chemicals, so I asked for advice in a shop in Beckett Street. The man suggested flash bulbs, but my camera only had time and instantaneous settings, so he suggested magnesium flash powder and I bought a tin for a shilling. The instructions on the tin said that the quantity that would cover a sixpence weighed ten grams and would give enough light for f15 at five feet on film of 32 Scheiner, whatever that meant.

We set it up; Billy Bowskill, Bateman and me. I fixed the camera to a stool with string only to discover that we didn't have a tanner between us so I used a penny and poured out the magic powder. Into this I stuck a sliver of home-made touchpaper, to diffuse the light. Duce, the fourth member of the team, held a piece of tracing paper about 2.5 feet square just in front of the magnesium. I opened the shutter on time exposure and Duce lit the fuse. It spluttered down almost to the powder and appeared to go out. By now the film had been exposed for about 8 seconds. In desperation Duce bent down and blew on the touch paper. There was a blinding flash and a huge cloud of white smoke filled the room, Duce lay on the floor coughing his ring up, his face covered in white powder and eyes like onion rings. The tracing paper, still clutched in his scorched hand, was the size of a small burnt chapatti. The negative, when developed, was grossly over-exposed.

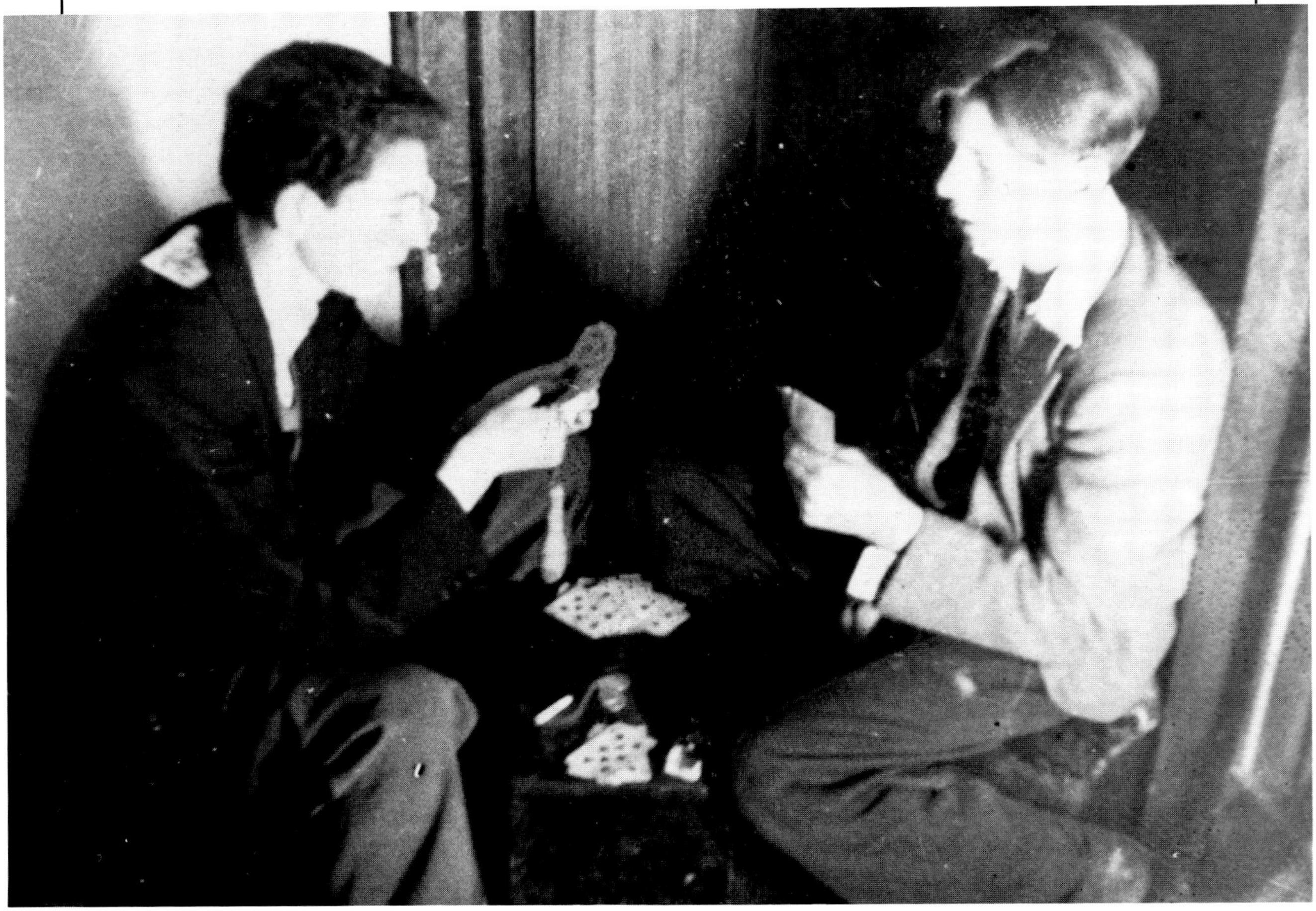

FLASH PHOTOGRAPHY.

Magnesium burns with a very bright white light. As early as the 1860s, it had been used as a source of artificial light for interior or night photography. In 1865 Piazzi Smythe succeeded in taking photographs inside the Great Pyramid using magnesium light. There were several problems associated with its use. Magnesium was comparatively expensive; it produced huge amounts of smoke and it was potentially dangerous. Some photographers lost their fingers through the careless use of magnesium powder.

Contrary to popular belief, magnesium was not used widely for portrait photography. Photographers preferred to use natural light. Even with the most basic snapshot camera it was possible to take indoor portraits if the sitter was near a window.

The first flashbulbs were introduced in 1932. 'Sashalite' bulbs resembled ordinary domestic light bulbs filled with aluminium foil. They were used in the same way as magnesium ribbon or powder. The bulb was fired by hand after the shutter had been opened, By the late 1930s, devices which allowed the flash to be synchronised with the shutter opening had been developed. At first confined to professional cameras, these were soon to become standard on all popular cameras. By the end of the 1950s, all but the cheapest cameras could be used with synchronised flash.

As flash bulbs became smaller they became an integral part of the camera.Today's compact cameras use rechargeable electronic flash instead of flash bulbs.

❧ Until they brought out the little flash squares, some form of magnesium powder was used for interior or night shots. It was lethal and really stank. To get experience I would work with anyone. I once went, with an old man I sometimes helped, to photograph a banquet in Leeds. He took an interminable time setting up the equipment. Everything had to be perfect, but as soon as he had taken the picture he quickly made for the door with me following in hot pursuit. We knew that seconds later a residue of white ash would fall like snow and settle in the soup.

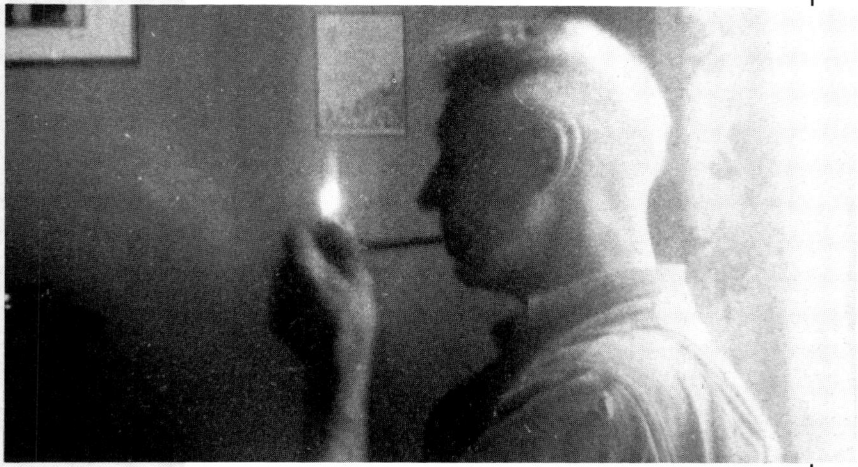

❧ This was my father-in-law taken at about 6.30pm in October 1949. I only had a cheap box camera but decided to try and get a photograph of him indoors. Instead of a flash gun, I used another type of flash - that from a Swan Vestas match. There weren't many flash guns around in those days. If I'd have bought one it would have cost me more than the camera. Considering the camera I used, I don't think it turned out too badly at all. It's a bit grainy, but I quite like the effect since it makes it arty.

Having set up my subject, I instructed him to light his pipe on a given signal. Had I discovered a way of creating cheap flash photography by using an ordinary match? I doubt it because shortly afterwards I purchased a new camera complete with a very large fan-shaped flash unit. So much for one's dreams - I still couldn't seem to get the perfect light and shade shot I was aiming for, even with the large and expensive flash outfit. Eat your heart out Lord Lichfield and three cheers for the simple household match.

CELEBRITY PORTRAITS.

Photographic portraits of celebrities are by no means a modern phenomenon. In 1854 a Parisian photographer, Disderi, patented a new method of portrait photography producing small mounted prints approximately four inches by two. These, because of their size, became known as 'cartes de visite'. After photographs of Victoria and Albert went on sale in 1860 a popular craze developed for collecting celebrity cartes de visite. These were placed in albums alongside those of one's family and friends. Royalty, politicians, writers, actors and actresses, sportsmen, even famous criminals and courtesans, all found their way into family albums.

The production of these portraits was a large-scale business. Thousands of copies of the most popular ones were made. Over seventy thousand cartes de visite portraits of Prince Albert were sold in the week following his death in 1861.

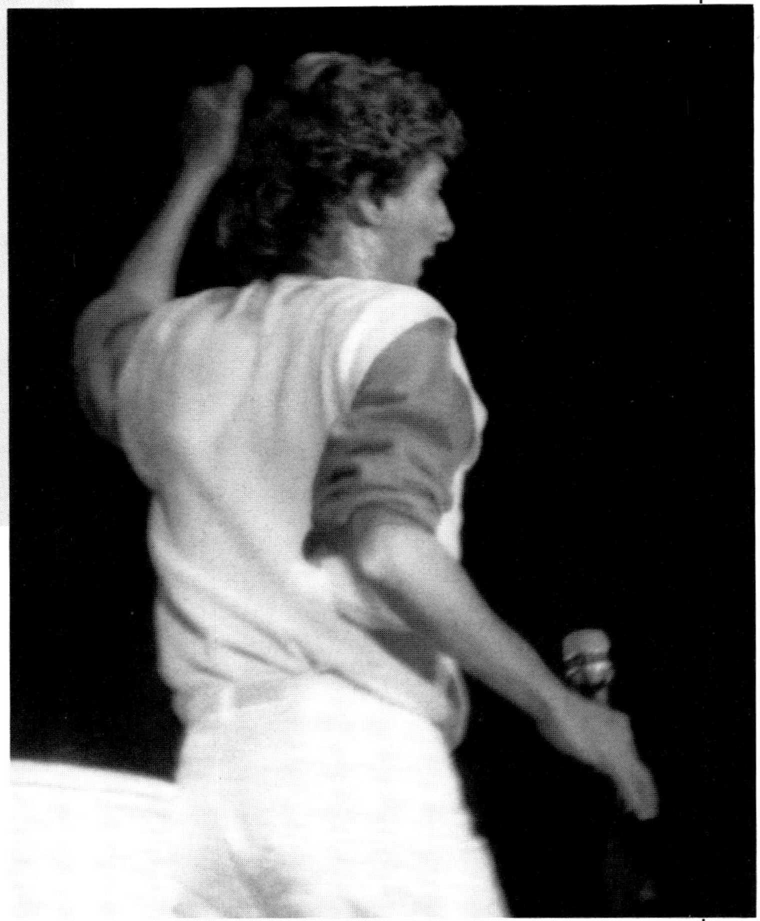

❧ I spent a large percentage of my formative years being in love with this or that pop star or actor and spent an incredible amount of money indulging my passion in trips to concerts and plays. Using a little point-and-shoot camera with built-in flash, there was never much hope of getting good shots of my heroes in action from Row ZZ of Wembley Arena. You needed decent binoculars even to see the show! The constant frustration of going to the chemist and picking up envelopes containing strips of blank negatives caused me to start looking into the techniques of low light photography. I learned that taking a flash photograph from Row 36 of the stalls would only result in a nice shot of the backs of the heads of rows 35 to 30. I bought a 35mm SLR camera and a second hand 135mm telephoto lens. I read up on what speed film I should use, with what shutter speed and aperture. I've had some reasonable successes, particularly of my last heart-throb, Barry Manilow.

I don't take many photographs these days. The Russian camera I bought is really heavy and I can't be bothered carting it round. I don't go to many concerts anyway, it's expensive and I get irritated by the constant popping of flashes from the fans who haven't yet learned their lesson.

❧ When I first started courting Geoff he had three serious hobbies; cycling, ballroom dancing and photography. He had a decent bike and patent leather shoes for dancing but, to his regret most of his photographic equipment was make-do-and-mend. He wasn't content just to take pictures; the object of the game was to develop and print his own. I remember being introduced to this craft. After the film had spent its required time in the developing tank and had been washed and fixed, we retired to his dark room to do the printing. The room in question was actually the windowless staircase that ran between the kitchen and front room at his mother's home. On the call of "Now!", I would stick my hand out of the door at the bottom of the stairs holding the frame up into the daylight and count however many seconds it took to imprint the picture onto the paper before rapidly bringing it back into the darkness, shutting the door quickly behind me.

As the years passed, his passion for photography grew. Now he could afford a decent camera, a proper flash gun, an enlarger and, number one priority at our new house, a darkroom. He only had it for twelve months before our daughter was born, then it was back to the old routine of blacking out the bathroom.

❧ Bathroom processing, which many photographers have to make do with, can be a far from satisfying experience. You know for certain that as soon as you go in and lock the door every member of the family will want to use the toilet. Papers away, lights on, out into the bedroom and wait for your recall. As you re-lock the door, the pleasant aroma of developer is overpowered by the smell of the last toilet user. This smell can last a long time as your darkroom is not only

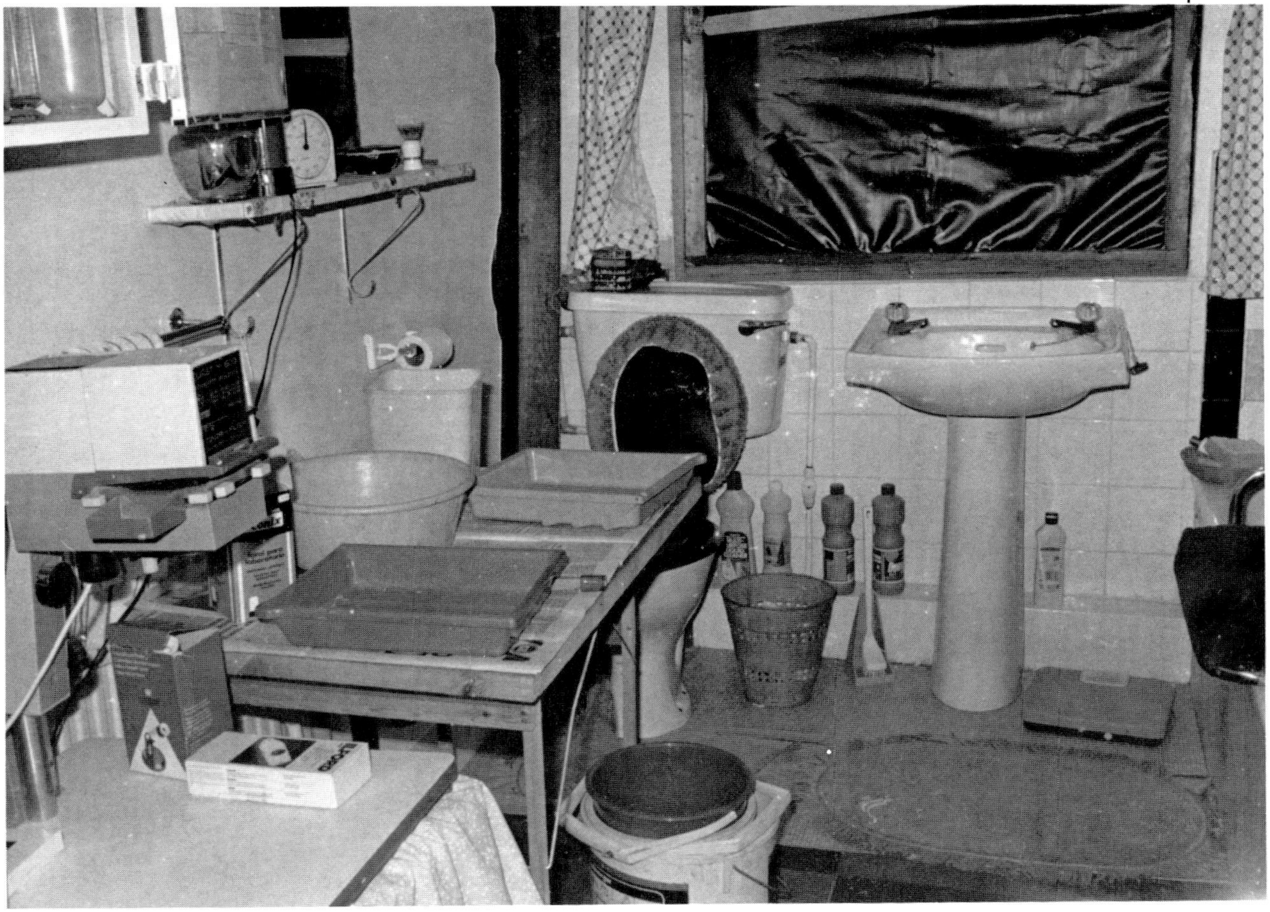

light-proof but the vents are also blocked. Starting again, your eyes getting used to the dark, you look up at the window to see a square of light all around your light proofing. Opening and closing the door has sucked the light board slightly, causing the light leak. More drastic action to block the light is needed. Off again, a quick bucket of cold water for print washing, bucket under the tap in the bath and - hello? only a trickle. Someone has decided to wash downstairs and the machine is taking all the water. Eventually, after a few door knocks to answer totally irrelevant questions, you may be able to produce a few prints.

❧ Looking back at 1941 and Castleford Grammar School, I have distant but pleasant memories of being in the Photographic Society. Then as now I liked long and unusual words, so the name of a chemical used to avoid stains on contact prints has remained in my mind. The name of that chemical was Phenol Phthalein. Imagine my surprise when I came across the name of that very chemical again. Where? It is the main component of chocolate laxatives. I often wonder if, during my photographic days, I was more regular with the help of Phenol Phthalein than I normally would have been.

❧ Although Leeds Camera Club was filled with chemists and solicitors and I was a sixteen year old living in one of the more ragged-arsed districts of Leeds, I took to going to their meetings and lectures. It was the 1950s but in some way there was a backward drag and the photography they were talking about was locked into a 1930s pictorialism based around exotic chemicals and heavy papers. I first heard ideas expressed there that I am still playing about with forty years later.

❧ There is no doubt that joining a camera club is one of the best ways to learn about photography and I have been a member of my local club for many years. I am not one for entering competitions as I am not naturally competitive. I can never come to terms with how a certain print can get full marks from one judge and in another competition, with another judge, can be criticised and marked low. I realise that it's all a matter of taste but I find it embarrassing. There is no doubt that there are prints and transparencies which will always cause a gasp in the camera club when they are shown, but there are hundreds of prints, both colour and black and white, which are really run-of-the-mill and only become perfectly composed or exposed when the owner points out the perfection.

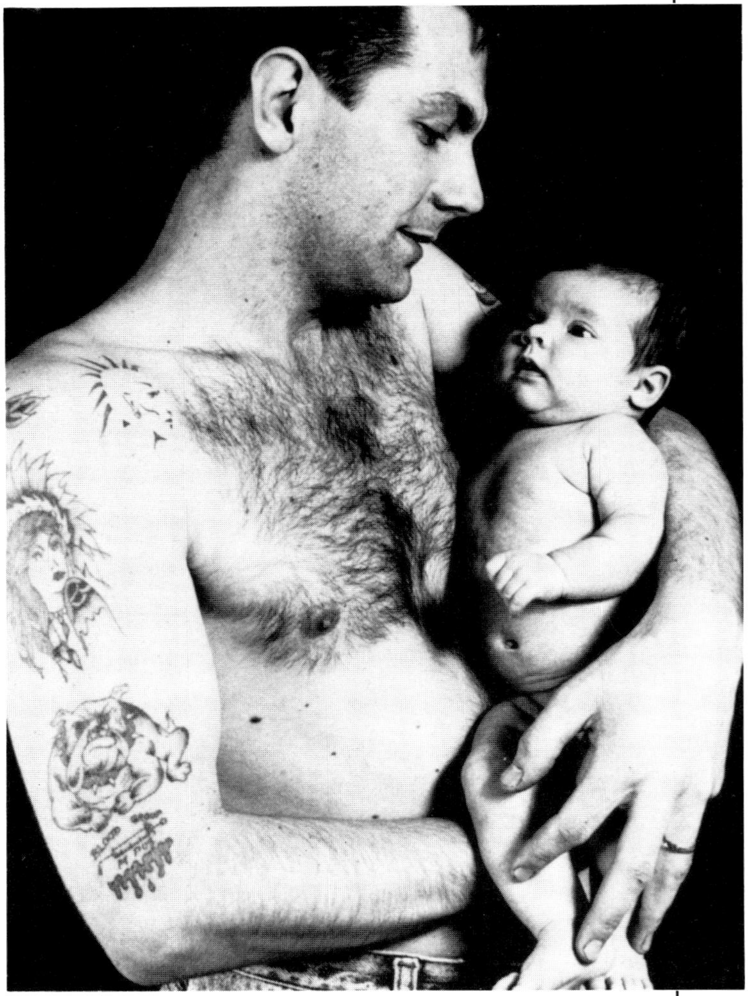

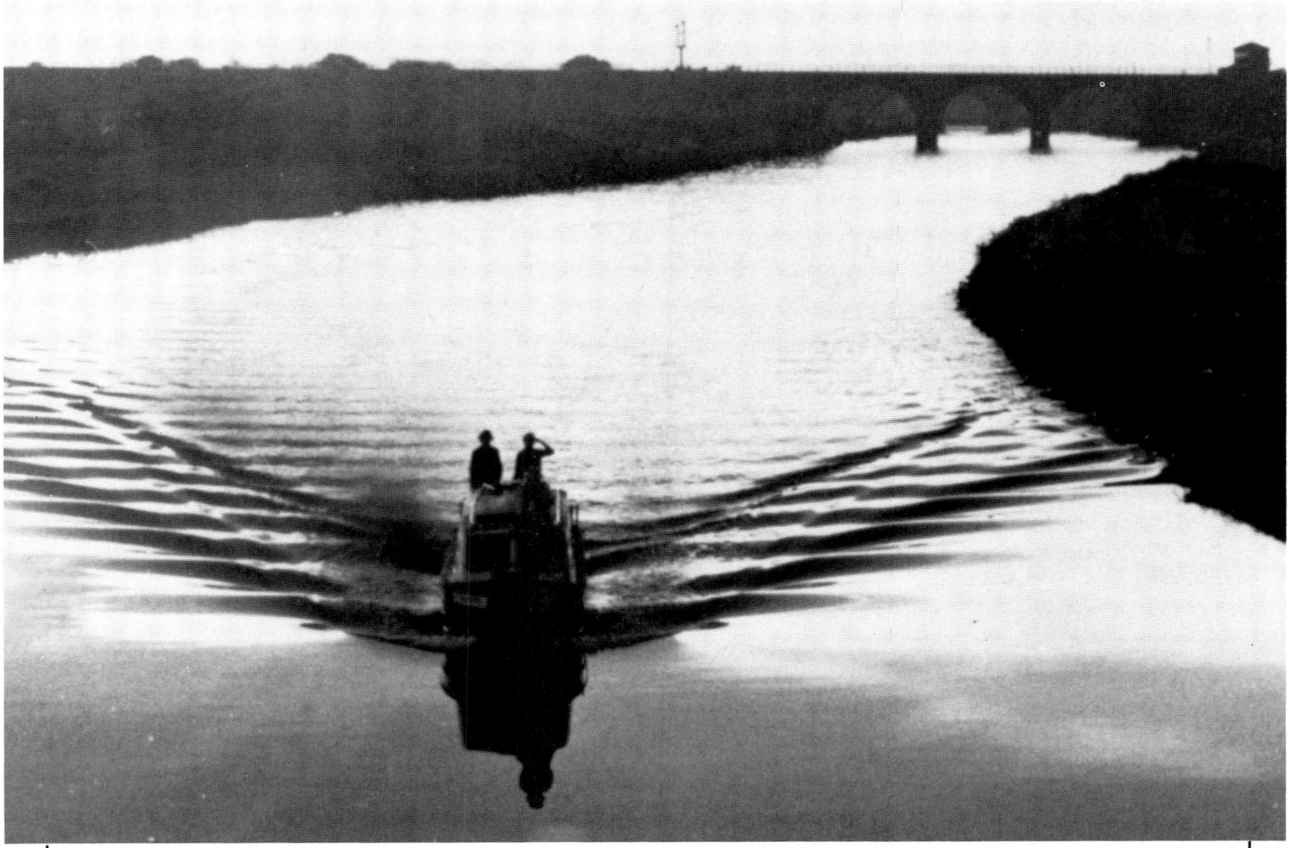

❧ Some of the modern stuff in certain photographic magazines really does defy belief. When the experts advise you to smear Vaseline onto a lens or to move the camera to get an out-of-focus effect, after lens makers have spent thousands of pounds on making pin sharp lenses, the world's gone crazy.

❧ Look around you. We're white, middle-class, and middle-aged. It's not just us. Nationwide, camera clubs are finding life difficult. Its not just the young who don't come - we do have some women members, but not enough.

There's a lot of members who want to recruit, but they are frightened of getting the wrong sort of people; they want more members but the same as themselves. Membership is expensive at £25, soon it'll be £30 each; that's a lot for a couple. We probably could make provision for those who couldn't afford it, the unemployed and so on, but we don't bother. Members don't want to recognise that things have changed.

There was a suggestion of a combined rate for couples, and they were very surprised when I said, "What about me and Eddie? We're a couple too."

Yet they're going to have to change. I've been suggested as President for next year and, if I am, they'll have a come-out gay president. They've accepted having the non-competitive section, even though some of them don't like it. I think everyone realises they couldn't go on the way they were, with some people going into all 37 competitive categories trying to win everything, and some just entering in one tiny specialised thing, like black and white butterfly. More and more just want the social side and to look at slides. We have to face it, the dark room in our premises is getting less and less use and yet still they say, "We've got all these cups and they've got to be competed for."

Some of us who didn't want a competition got together and picked out the most striking things for the show. "You shouldn't judge yourselves, there should be an outsider judge," they said. They couldn't see that would destroy our point. The thing is, we've got to escape from a 1920 vision of photographic pictorialism, from the time when the rules were fossilised.

❧ I once knew a young chap who taught photography evening classes. He used to teach in such a manner that he frequently needed a nude model. The easiest solution was to hire his wife, in that way he kept the fees in the family. For some reason he never wanted his students to know she was his wife so, when students asked if they'd be having a model next week, he used to say, "Oh, yes, I'll be able to get that ginger bit to come in again." I really don't remember much more about the intellectual content, but I do remember that facially she had a look of the Queen!

❧ In the 1950s I was working down in Soho. The big expansion of the porn market had not taken place but this was a traditional red light area and there were a number of dodgy operations going on. One enterprising operator,

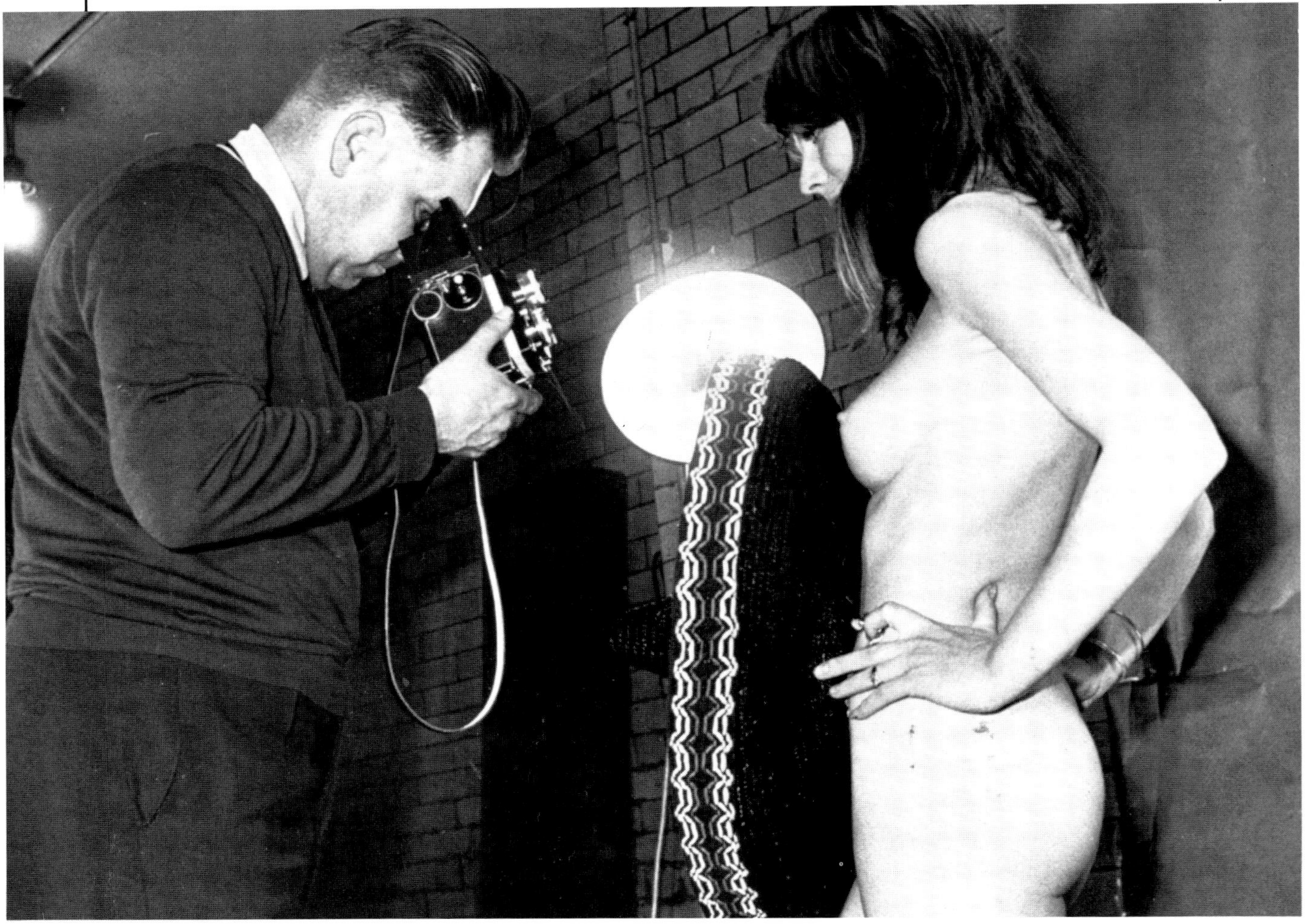

OVER-EXPOSURE.

It is not known who took the first photograph of a nude but there are examples from as early as 1841.

Throughout the Victorian period there was a steady trade in such photographs. Discreetly referred to as 'Academies' or 'Etudes', they provided a useful tool for artists and illicit pleasure for voyeurs. As the names suggest, France was one of the major suppliers.

In Britain the forces of law and self-appointed moral guardians such as the Society for the Suppression of Vice waged an unending war against the peddlers of such material. In 1874 police raided a photographic dealer's shop in Pimlico and seized over one hundred and thirty thousand 'obscene' photographs.

What is one person's art, however, can often be another's pornography. As recently as 1933 customs officials in New York refused to admit a portfolio of photographs of Michelangelo's paintings in the Sistine Chapel because they were 'shocking pornography'.

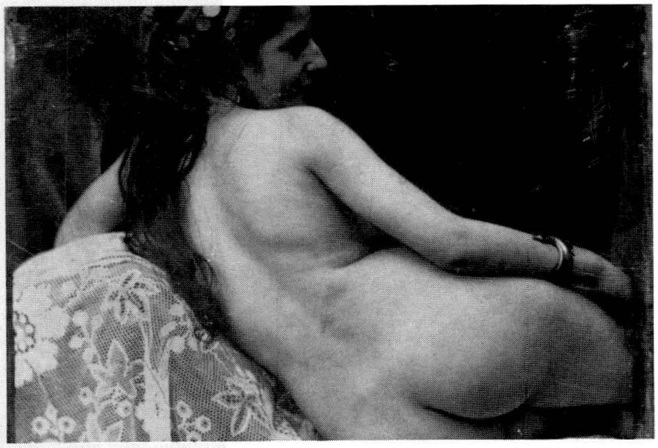

sadly no longer with us, hit on the great idea of renting a room, employing a model, a tart really, charging £5 a time and inviting photographers to come along to make artistic studies of the human form.

They came in droves. A whole range of the dirty mac brigade - lads of seventeen right through to octogenarians. And what a collection of cameras; Box Brownies through to state-of-the-art Swiss jobs. I suspect that few of them contained film. I once saw one old fellow going in with a cardboard box painted black which hung from his neck on a string.

❧ In the early 1960s, when we were newly married and quite poor, we probably would take two rolls of film a year. Times have changed. Now not only do you think of getting a replacement camera each year but I reckon that I am more likely to take two rolls of film a week than not.

Working at a developer's you meet all sorts of people. One day I served an old lady who wanted her film developing but when she gave it to me it was completely unravelled. I tried to explain to her that it couldn't be developed because it had been exposed. "Oh, no" she strongly pointed out to me, "I know it will be alright.I took the film out of the camera in my handbag, it was quite dark."

On another occasion I processed a whole film of twenty-four close-ups of a woman's face. The lady had obviously used the camera the wrong way round every time. Of course, she realised when she collected the film that she had made a mistake but she just seemed to be surprised and not at all embarrassed. She was quite an elderly lady and was most probably blinded by science. I only hope she hadn't been photographing anything of earth-shattering importance.

❧ I was really into photographing motor racing and motorcycle racing. In fact it was a motorbike accident that put me in this chair. Afterwards I tried to carry on, but it wasn't the same. In a wheelchair you can't duck and dive, get round spectators who are in the way, be in a position to take a risk to get the perfect shot and then get out of the way. The accident changed everything. I just couldn't get into the good spots to take photographs. Even if I could tell other people to take the picture for me I couldn't tell them just when and have them react in time; everything happens so fast in racing. Anyway, it takes the control and pleasure out of it. Like somebody said, "I hate the situation where the specific bit of equipment you need is other people."

I did try a way round it by taking pictures from a distance. Someone codged me up a release using a piece of pneumatic tube 60 feet long with the camera set up on a tripod, but it didn't really work. The cost is another problem. When every picture on the roll is important it's even more annoying when one goes wrong. If you're on a pension you are not like a pro who can run off reel after reel and not bother.

I thought I'd try subjects that didn't move about, and where there wasn't a crowd standing up to get in the way. They're reclaiming an old tip at the back of here and I started doing a series of pictures to show how it got gradually tidier and greener but I gave up. I got disheartened because I couldn't get up to different places to show the changing skyline properly, and the pictures were boring because they were all from the same level. When you're in a wheelchair you can't get a higher or a lower viewpoint. It's hard work

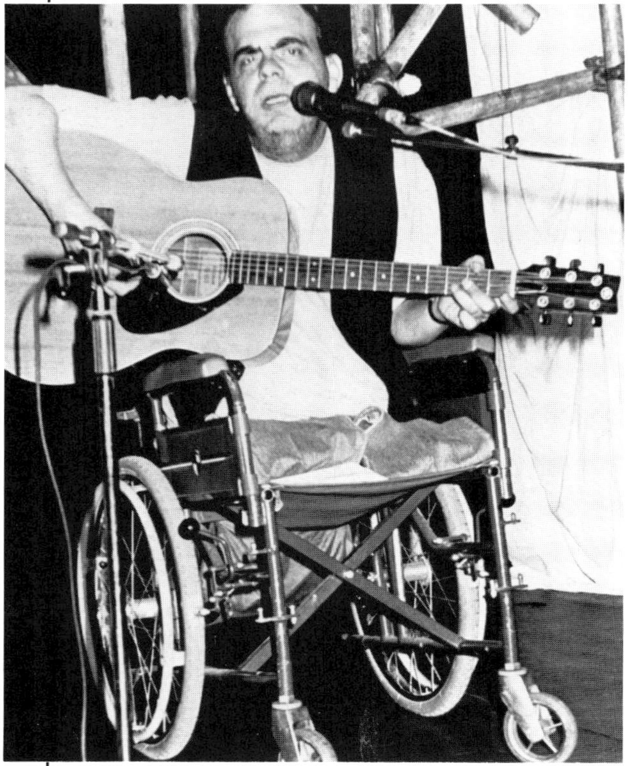

to set the camera up on the tripod then you can't get up to the viewfinder to see what you're going to get if you want a higher view. Also, I haven't really got the strength to push the shutter release; using the delay timer is fiddling; really it needs some sort of attachment to fit on my hand to increase the pressure. And all the time it's money.

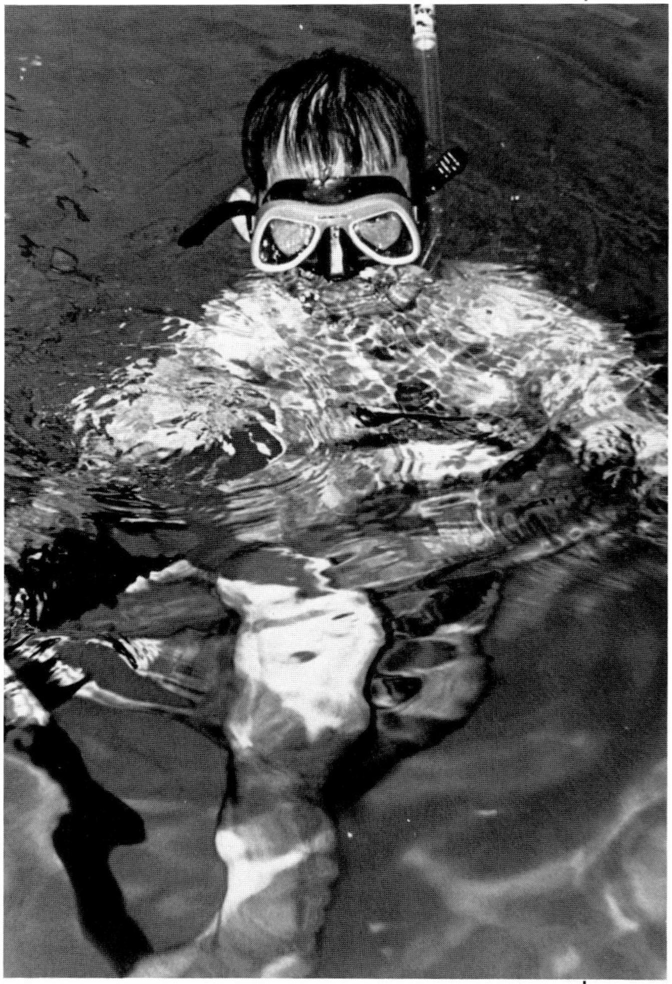

❧ I got interested in doing photography because I was able to create a picture. I like to find something simple and make a picture of it. I realise that doing photography makes me have less epileptic attacks. I helped to form a club to let disabled people participate in photography and exhibit their work. I have also begun to take photographs for a number of charities.

❧ I was in Nigeria when I noticed a large lizard of quite startling colours, bright orange with a purple head. The creature was quite unconcerned and allowed me to shoot off a few frames. I like to caption each picture accurately so not knowing the name of the animal I asked one of the house boys if he knew. He didn't but assured me his brother, who was at Ibadan University, would get the name for me. Two days later the lad came running over waving a piece of paper. "Mr Cryer, I have the information you asked for. We in Nigeria call the animal a leezard."

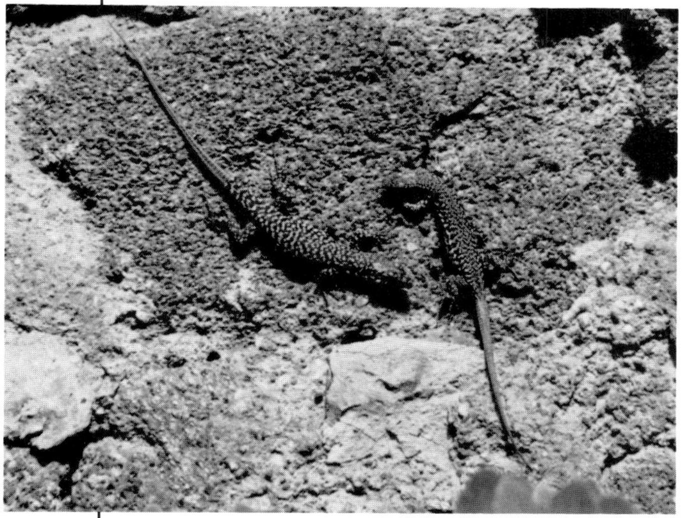

❧ I found it very difficult to accept the fact that my parents were thinking of selling our home, even though I had moved out the previous year. Each time I went home I thought it might be my last visit, so I would take loads of photos: the view down the hall, the telephone, I even took a photo of the bathroom ceiling, remembering the times I'd spent contemplating it whilst having a bath.

❧ And this is Linda doing some varnishing and this is a pile of plasterboards being delivered. This is Paul and Robert putting the walls up. This is me painting the windows. This is me painting the door. This is me varnishing the floor. And this is me....

Fascinating? Riveting stuff? Well, we think so. It has taken us fifteen months to renovate the place - in periodic intense bursts of action. Well, what else can you do when the house you are renovating is in southern Brittany and you live 600 miles away in Yorkshire? No scenic views or quaint photos of the local natives posing self-consciously in authentic Breton hats intrude in our photograph albums. About five hundred photos tell the story of the search for our house, the ones we rejected; the one with a house, four acres, two barns, an outbuilding and a church all included in the £25,000 price; the one with the tramp in the attic, the one with ivy-covered interior bathroom walls; the one chock full of solid, old French furniture up tothe ceiling; and the one we finally chose.

Sometimes we take out those albums illustrating our progress for just the two of us to look at. We don't need to share them with anybody else. There is tremendous satisfaction and pleasure in recalling our progress and the fun we had with the friends and folk who helped.

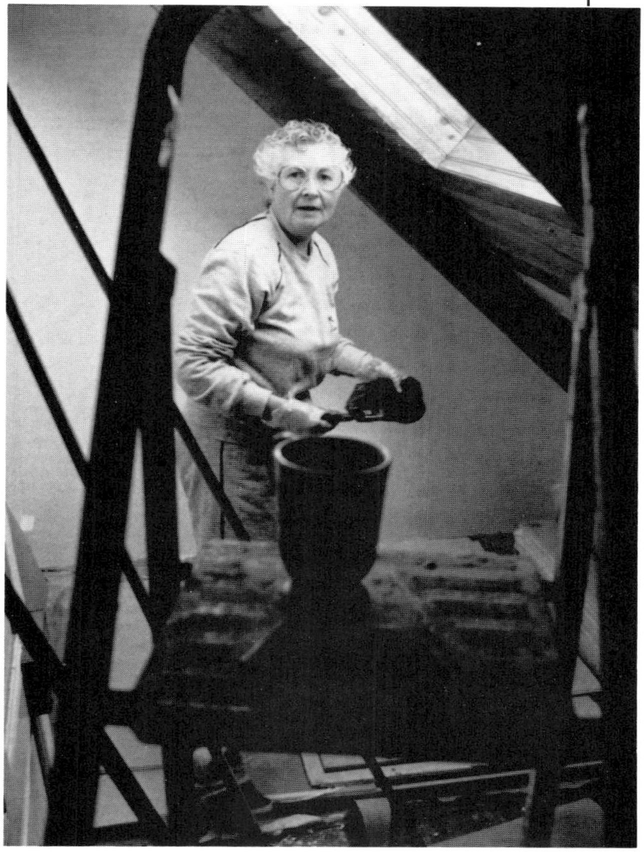

❧ I was in La Rochelle when along a path came a woman in a donkey cart holding a baby. It was a lovely image and totally unexpected. After she had passed by I thought, "I wish I'd taken a picture of that," but on reflection I am glad that I didn't because it would have been out of context. In any case, what would I have said to the people who looked at the photograph back in my living room in Canada? I'd have said, "It's a French woman in a donkey cart," and they would have said, "How nice." But they wouldn't have known about the atmosphere; the small path, the smells and the trees which I knew were just around the corner.

❧ Although we usually take cameras with us, the first time I went to Paris I didn't take one. This was because I wanted to remember the occasion but wasn't bothered to have an accurate picture. Usually I take pictures of places I do not expect to go back to but I did expect to return to France. Therefore I didn't take pictures.

❧ Photographs are necessary only to trigger second-rate memories. You do not need a static, two-dimensional representation of an instant in time; if something is worth remembering, you will remember it. If you want to forget something, on the other hand, the last thing you need is a time-bomb planted in one of your drawers.

Photographs can only degrade memories, they wrench them out of context and trap them for decades. Photography is partial. Just think of all the important things never 'snapped' by our camera; divorcees leaving court, family funerals, the student who did not graduate.

Photographs mean memories, and by extension obligations. They represent the past and all the baggage that stops you getting on with living your life the way you want. For years I was looking for a function for photography. Although I had cameras from the age of twenty I had used them just to take holiday snaps and the like, but never systematically. They weren't required in my job and, because I was a scientist by training, I could not see any way in which I could bridge the gap between my search for something new and my training.

Then I saw that the close-up lens could open up the world by allowing you to concentrate your attention on the small things that are found in nature. Not only could you photograph the flower but you could take pictures of the hairs on the petals. Ivy-leafed Toadflax is found on a lot of walls and is not recognised, but blow it up and you see it contains great beauty. You learn about nature, but you also can learn precise scientific facts.

❧ I've never been one for just taking holiday snapshots so I usually set myself little projects to help further my photographic knowledge. At first these were simple, like restricting myself to the use of one particular lens for all my shots. This taught me a lot and tested my ingenuity at shooting interesting compositions.

Once I was showing my photos to an artist friend. He thought they were good as far as they went but there were no people in them. I've always felt that pointing a camera at someone was an invasion of privacy and fought shy of this. After my friend's comment though, I set myself the task of including at least one person in every photo I took on my next holiday. This was a good project and I was freed to some extent from the inhibitions I had of using my camera in public.

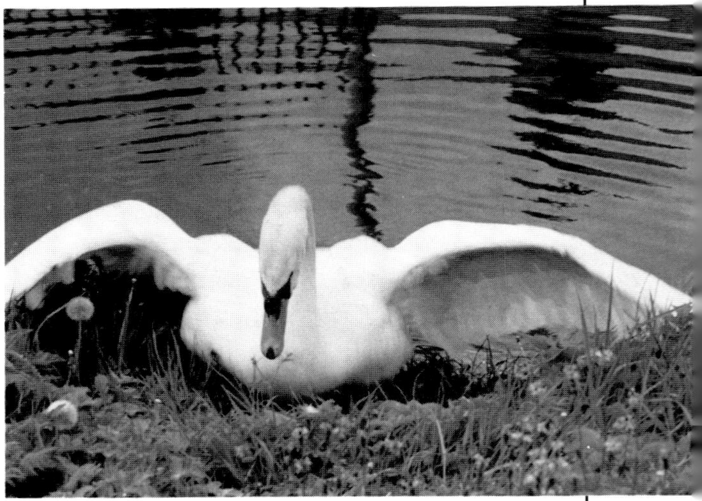

❧ I have always had a passion for birds and have been a member of the RSPB for years. On holiday I try to combine a bit of birdwatching with photography. Sadly, my attempts so far rarely seem to live up to my expectations. I sit patiently until a half tame sparrow comes up to me, really close, and I snap it. On the photograph all I get is loads of background and this tiny little brown blob in the middle. I suppose what I need is a telephoto lens. Every year I say I'll get one and every year I keep on taking really disappointing photos.

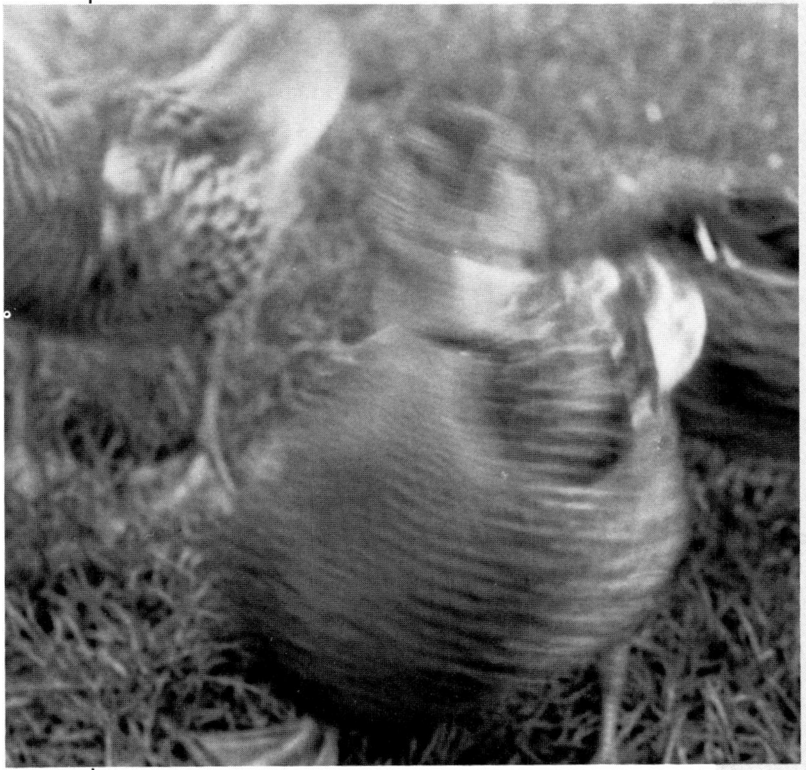

❧ My father is the world's worst photographer. Although he had been to Art School he never seems to have mastered the camera. He misses everything. He misses the tops of heads, feet, the view. On the other hand, he's very good on floors. We've got pictures of floors from all over the world taken while he's winding on. There's a nice one, for instance, of a Turkish floor, all tiles. It should have been of my mother. As you see, there's no great tradition of photography in our family.

THE IDIOT-PROOF CAMERA.

In 1888, George Eastman invented a camera that was to revolutionise photography. The name he gave it has now become synonymous with popular photography - the Kodak.

Taking a photograph with the Kodak required just three simple actions :

1 Turn the key (to wind the film on)
2 Pull the string (to set the shutter)
3 Press the button (to take the photo)

The wide angle lens meant that no viewfinder was needed. You just pointed the camera at the subject. The shutter gave a set exposure of about one twenty-fifth of a second. When the film was used up - the Kodak was sold already loaded with enough film for one hundred exposures - the entire camera was returned to the factory where the film was removed, developed, a set of prints made and a new film loaded, before it was returned to its owner.

Eastman coined a brilliantly simple sales slogan for the Kodak, 'You press the button, we do the rest.' For the first time everybody could enjoy the pleasure of taking a photograph. Photography, previously confined to professionals and knowledgeable amateurs, had begun to be transformed into a popular pastime.

The Kodak was the very first 'point-and-shoot' camera. Today, thanks to electronics, many of the decisions involved in taking a photograph are taken out of our hands. Developments such as DX coding, automatic focusing and exposure make it easier than ever to take sharp, correctly exposed photographs. George Eastman would have approved. But even the most advanced technology, cannot replace the eye and the imagination of the photographer.

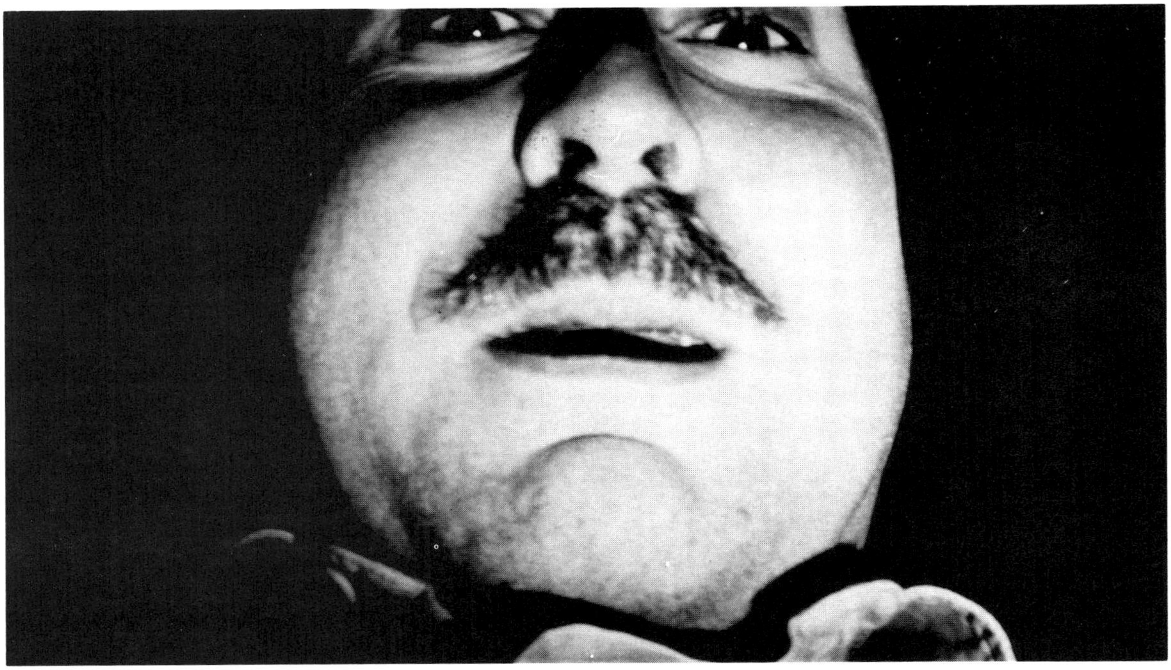

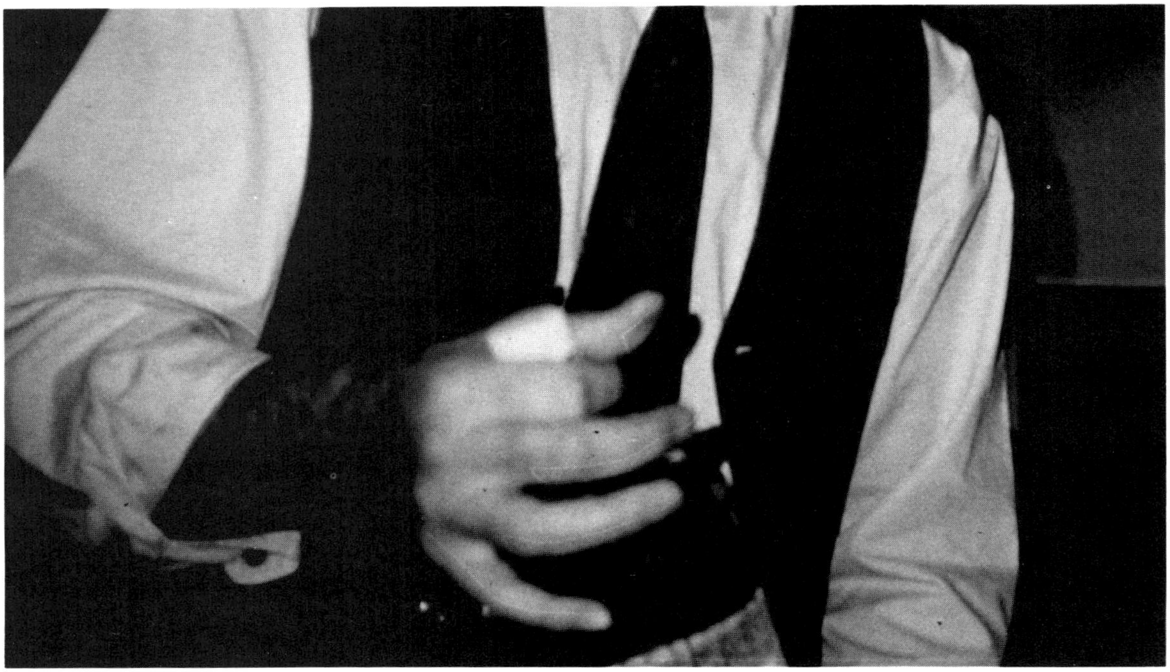

❧ The Barnsley Women's March Against Pit Closures in 1984 had everything. It was the greatest march by working class women this country had ever seen and it took place in brilliant sunshine. A row of chanting Barnsley women led the way and then came female delegates from all over the north. Arthur Scargill, holding the hands of small children, followed them. Then there were more women and, coming up in the rear, were the men of the coalfields. There were banners, drum majorettes and slogans, and standing, as I was, on the corner looking towards the Police Station, I could see everything.

Not many people had cameras, so few images of that great historical occasion exist, but I did have one. It was so exciting. Unfortunately I was too excited, I moved the camera, took photographs too quickly and instead of getting the pictures of a lifetime I have a sleeve full of blurred, out-of-focus shots. Arthur Scargill is just about recognisable in his black hat, but he's the only one who is.

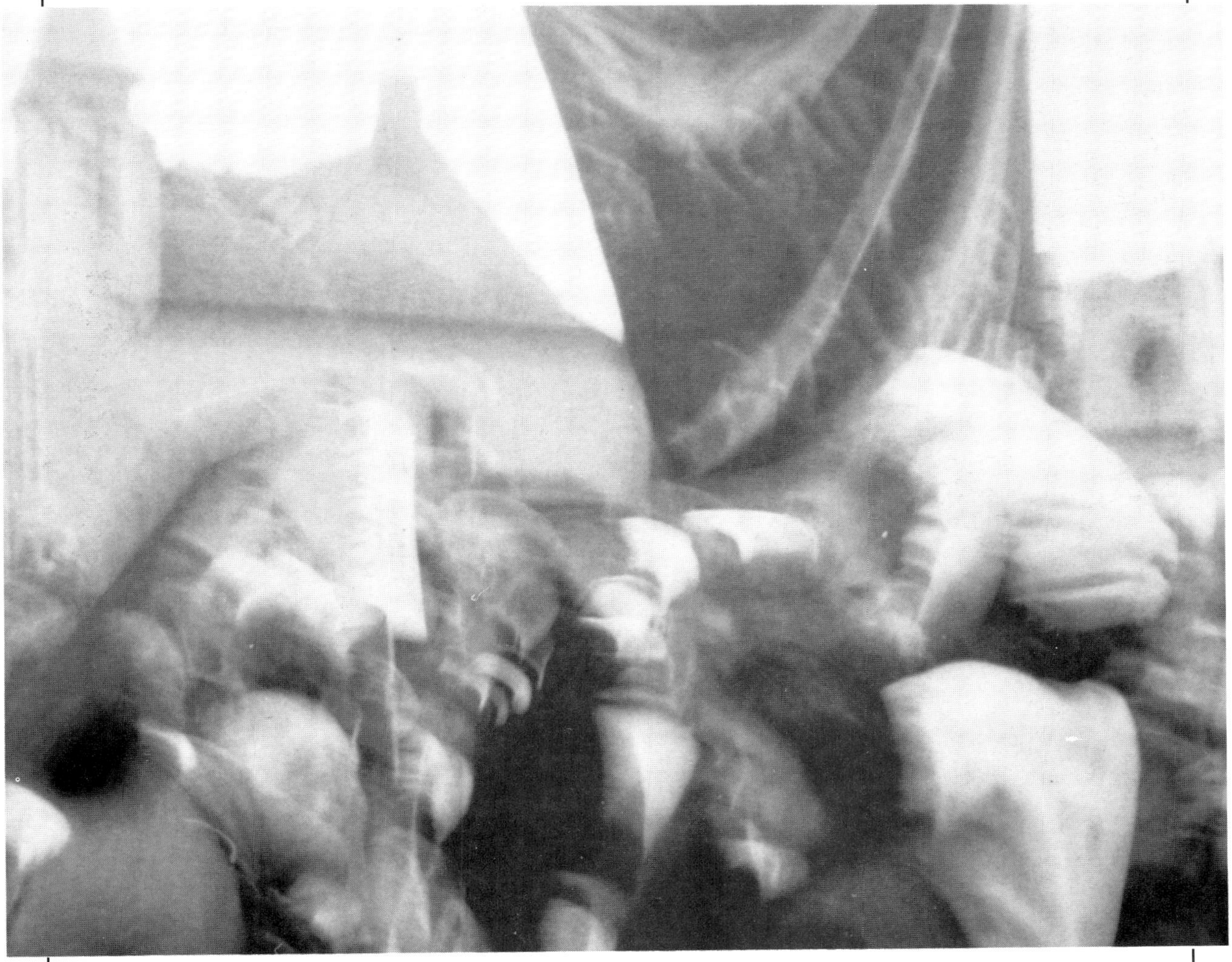

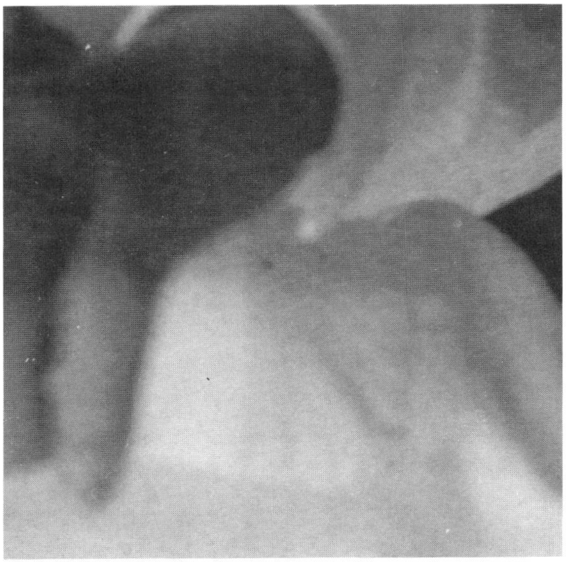

❧ Dean is good at mending things, which is handy because I'm great at breaking things.I dropped our new camera at Agios Nickolaos and again, when I slipped on the road to Kritsa. Dean inspected the camera carefully and pressed the shutter release to establish that the flash still worked. This is the resultant snap.When we got home Dean superglued all the loose bits back into place.

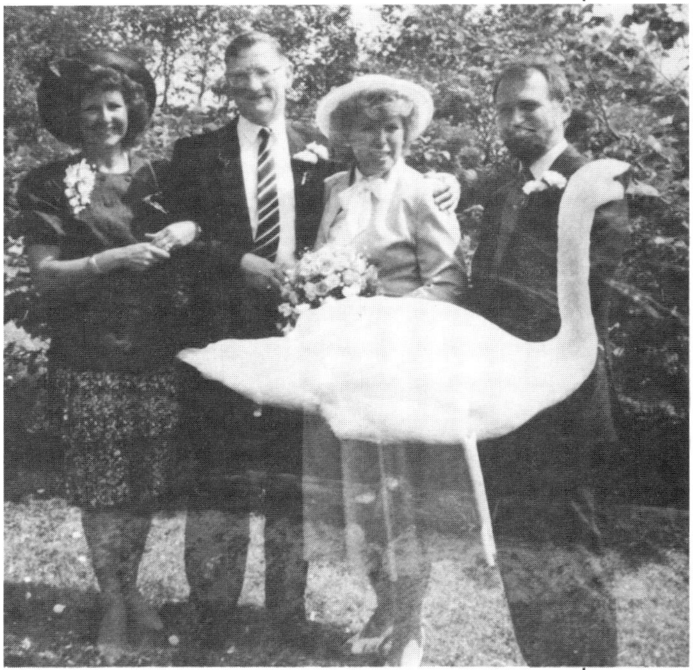

❧ Just before we were married, I was all over Bradford taking pictures of the scenery. At the wedding I asked my friend to take pictures of us using my camera. The photographs that came back were spooky. One shows my grandson's head appearing from a lake. Another is of my other two grandchildren who had emigrated to Australia just before the wedding and there they were, guests. Very strange. The best one is of me and Donald outside the church with a beautiful white swan on our arms.

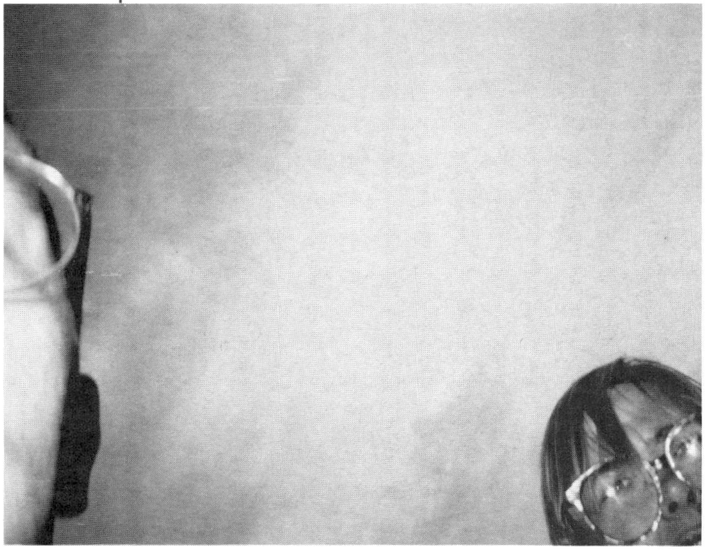

❧ A close friend whose family is very religious had an uncle in Italy who died. It is tradition that photos are taken of the coffin inside the church. When the photos were later developed, the film had not wound on properly and so one photo was superimposed onto another. This produced a picture where we see the altar and wreath-covered coffin with all the mourners standing around, and then in the top left-hand corner above the cross, three faces in a line as clear as can be. It was obviously just a photographic mistake but the old auntie was so scared that she called the priest to exorcise her house!

❧ My brother invited us to visit him at RAF Church Fenton for the annual air display. I took my little 127 point-and-shoot camera and spent the day happily snapping the breathtaking highlights of the many aerobatic displays. There are two snaps I particularly treasure from that day; one of a headless policeman mounted on a most beautiful chestnut stallion and the other, my 'piece de resistance', the photograph of The Red Arrows which everybody in the world must have taken - a grey, cloud-laden sky with not an aeroplane in sight.

❧ A photographer I knew years ago started to take an interest in astrology, graphology and Tarot cards, things on the fringes of the Dark Arts. He'd come across a technique for photographing the aura of people and objects, I think it was called Kirlian photography. Before he changed jobs, he built himself a magic box - it worked on the principle that the electric discharge field around a person or object would create an image. In his early experiments he got his work-mates to put their hands into this box, and got the image of the aura around their fingers.

Once he borrowed my wedding ring and got a good aura from that. I still have a copy of it but at that stage he wasn't interpreting the prints so I don't know any more about myself or the ring! Presumably, there is money to be made too, for shortly after this he left his photography job and set up in the prediction business. As far as I know, he's still making a living that way.

❧ This was a fluke. I was photographing a Salvation Army rally in a park. I came to the end of the film, started changing it, and then noticed a woman SA officer about 20 feet away carrying a child under her arm. It was nice enough in itself, so I hurried the new film through, intending to follow her and take a picture. Then, heavens, there was the banner in front of me proclaiming "Suffer Little Children". There was no time to think, I just aimed and pressed the shutter. That is why the woman is slightly blurred. I like to say it enhances the impressionist movement.

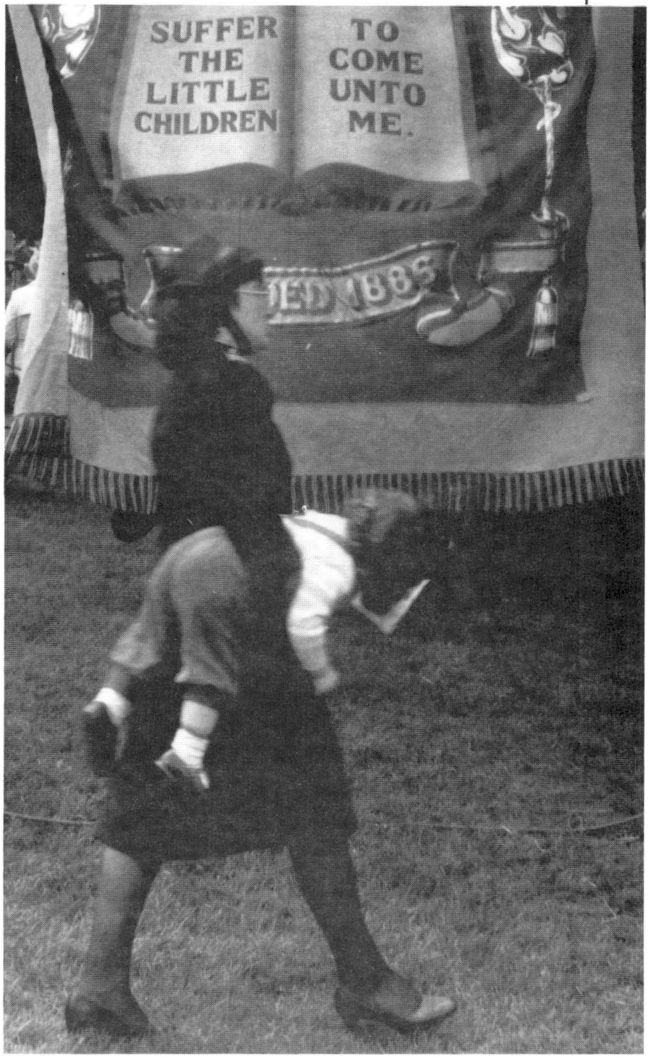

❧ Years ago my sister worked for a home shopping agency. Her job was to visit customers to collect their weekly payments and deliver new orders. One of her customers in Royston was a very old lady who was a medium. She and her husband were very frail and rarely left the house. I once visited her with my sister and she proceeded to tell me all sorts of things about myself. Her conversation was eerily punctuated by remarks thrown over her shoulder to the spirits who were hovering there filling her in with the details of my neck complaint, "You should try sleeping without a pillow" and my eyesight, "Your right eye sometimes feels like it's closing up - it's nothing to worry about."

She asked to see a photograph of my sister's children and, looking at it, proceeded to tell my sister what my nephews would do in later life. The youngest lad she said would be a good chef. He was at that stage still at the local comprehensive and showing no great inclination towards cookery. However, four or five years later he started a course at Barnsley Technical College in catering and now works as a chef at a local restaurant.

I reminded my sister about the fact that this had been predicted. She'd forgotten all about it.

PHOTOGRAPHY AND RELIGION

At first, many devout Christians believed photography to be sacrilegious, especially if it was used to capture a representation of the human face. A German newspaper, the 'Leipzig City Advertiser', roundly denounced photography ;

'Man is created in the image of God, and God's image cannot be captured by any human machine. Only the divine artist, divinely inspired, may be allowed, in a moment of solemnity, at the higher call of his genius, to dare to reproduce the divine-human features, but never by means of a mechanical aid.'

However, such ideas were soon overwhelmed by that other deity - commerce.

❧ Although we are followers of Islam we are not fundamentalists, as you can see from my cousin's High School graduation photograph. In Trinidad the races are mixed up and everything is relaxed - I didn't know what racial meant until I came to England. Being in a melting pot, you take things from other groups. Every girl likes to be sexy and although she wore a bolero for the ceremony itself, when she got into the photographer's studio that came off and she showed her shoulders.

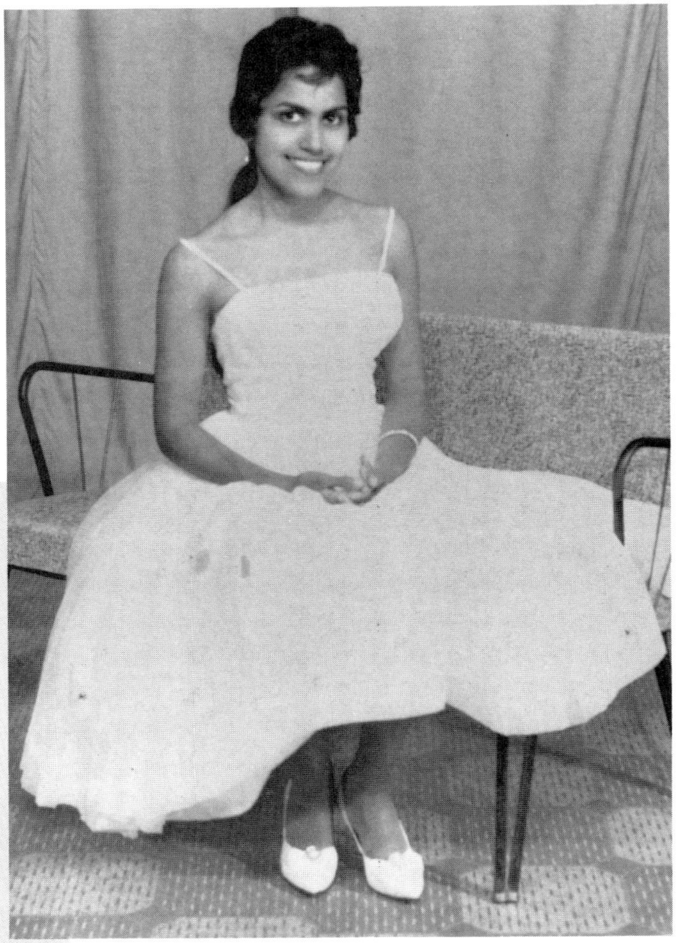

❧ My cousin got married in 1988. It was a traditional Muslim wedding, and only photographs were allowed to be taken, videoing was forbidden. There was a large turnout of friends and relatives, some of whom we hadn't seen for years. One particular cousin had changed so much that I hardly recognised her. In that time she had become an Orthodox Muslim, and so the taking of photographs was forbidden. Because my cousin wouldn't allow anyone to take a picture we decided as a group to take a photo anyway.

A large group of us chased her around the house, each with a camera, and in the end we all got a photo of her from really funny angles trying to hide.

❧ In Cairo I saw a crowd. I went to have a closer look and saw that there was a man taking photos of soldiers with an old wooden camera on a tripod. It was painted in green wood preservative-varnish melted in the heat. The photographer was dressed in full uniform with his Colonel looking on. It turned out that they were taking ID shots. On top of the camera was a copy of the Qur'an. The soldiers used this to swear on oath that it was actually them in the photo. This struck me as strange because the Qur'an comes down hard on image taking.

❧ This is real sleaze; the sort of thing you see on the front of really nasty videos. It was taken at Nora's fortieth birthday party. What you can't see is the crotch. Fortunate really because the little popper things which kept it in place were always popping.

Look carefully though and you might pick out the Pirelli slippers with pompoms, I wear them all the time at home. What makes it worse is that I'm a teacher. Can you imagine it. Mothers saying, "This is Kevin's teacher."

Ugh! All that meat and no potato.

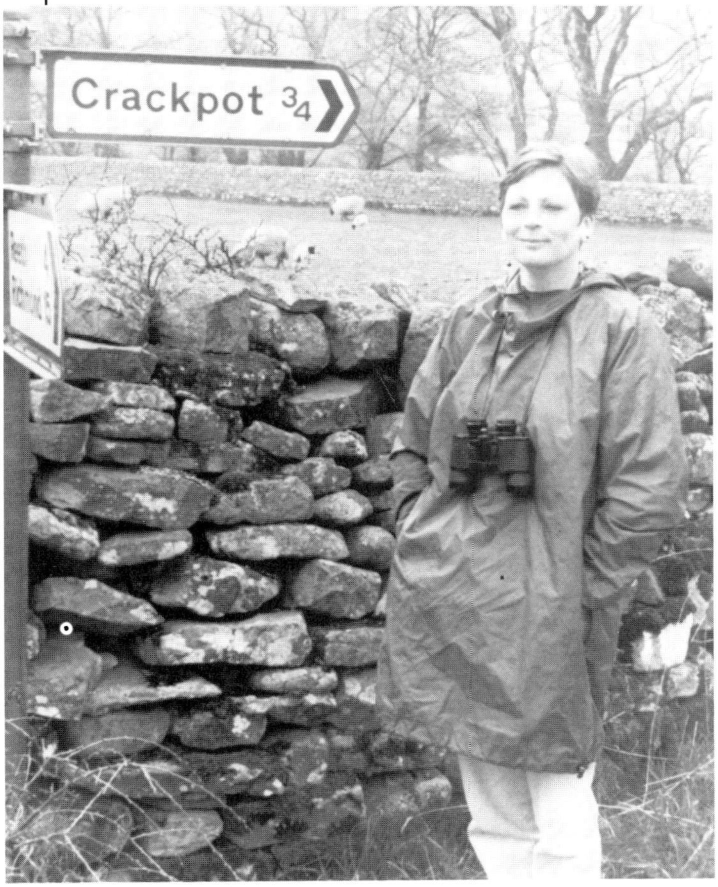

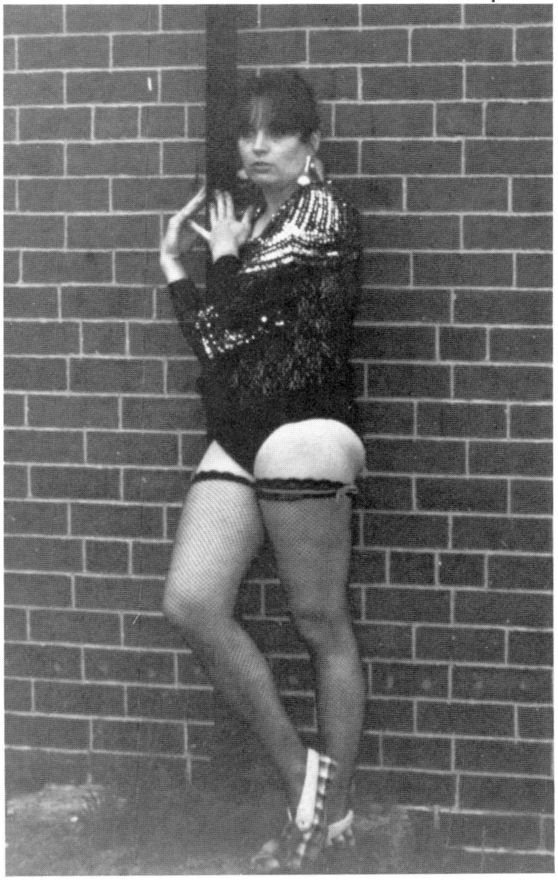

❧ I've really hated going to collect snaps from the developers ever since I saw a programme on telly a few years back on film developing and realised that every packet is actually checked - looked at - by the people in the shop for quality or whatever. It had never occurred to me before that the people I handed over my little yellow slip to would have seen part of my life. So consequently I have very few shots of my lover and I hugging, or looking romantically at each other over a candle-lit table or any of that stuff, and certainly nothing naughtier - like kissing or sitting up in bed together.

I just couldn't stand the thought of the sniggers of the shop staff and pictures of us being handed round.

❧ When I was about ten I remember coming across this photograph of two little girls and not recognising either of them. I was astonished when Mum told me it was me and one of her friend's daughters. My immediate assumption was that I was the slim dark haired serious one on the left. I took a lot of convincing that I was the tubby blonde with the fringe having difficulty hitching her knickers up!

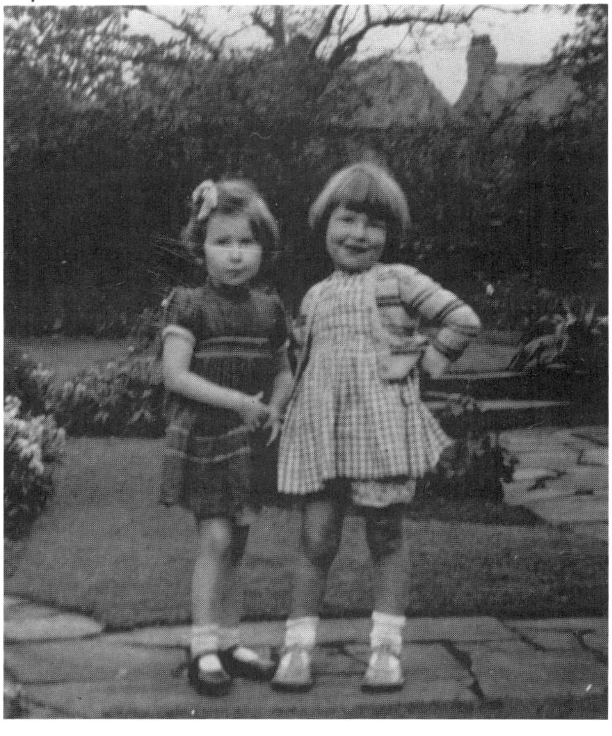

❧ The two best shots I have of me as a seventeen year old were taken on the same night. In one I am dancing with François in Paris. The other was taken from the side and you can see that I've got next to no breasts. Conscious that I am being photographed, I am pulling my mouth in to disguise what my dad used to call my Hapsburg lip. The other shows me to advantage. I'm smiling with my mouth open. My father said I looked like Sophia Loren.

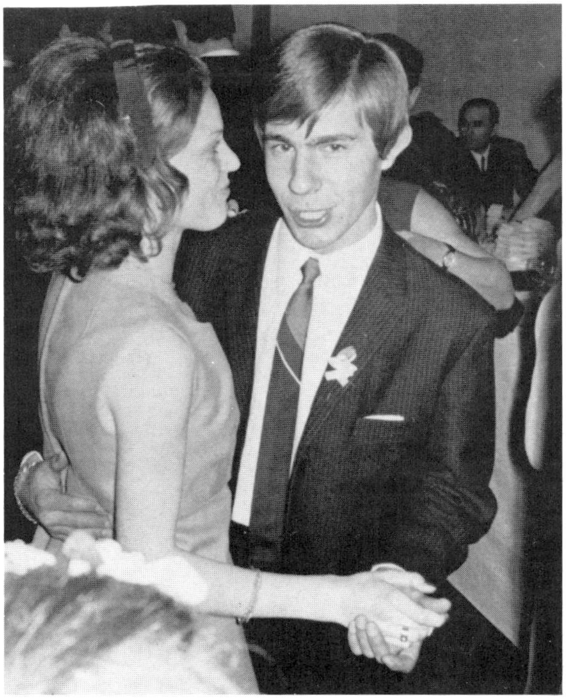

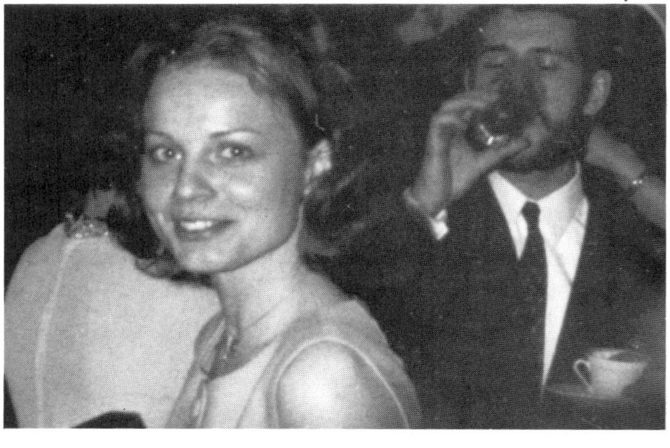

PASSPORT PHOTOGRAPHS.

The usefulness of photography as an aid to identification was soon realised.In 1871 an Act of Parliament, under the Prevention of Crime Bill, made it a statutory requirement that all arrested persons should have their photographs taken.

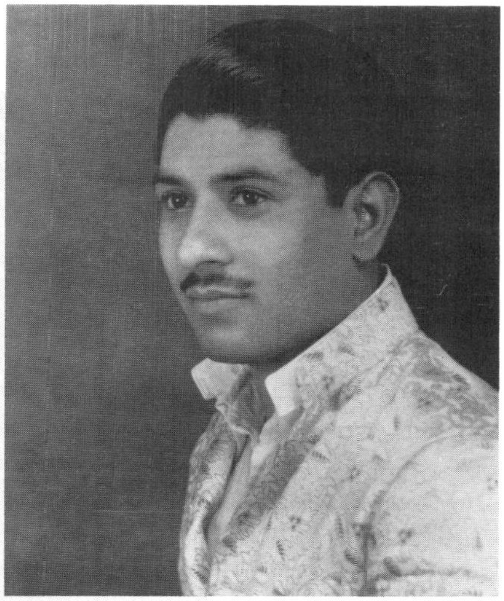

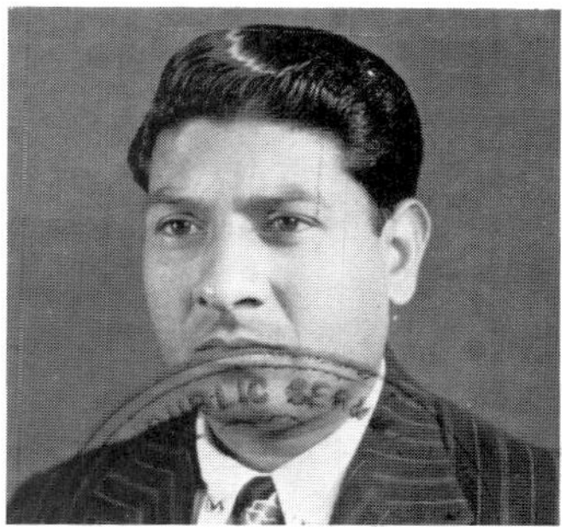

Passports date back as far as the sixteenth century - one signed by Charles 1 is still in existence. The passport photograph did not appear until the outbreak of the First World War. On February 1st, 1915, a new one-page passport folding into eight with a cardboard cover was introduced. In addition to a signature and a physical description of the bearer this also had to carry a photograph of the passport holder.

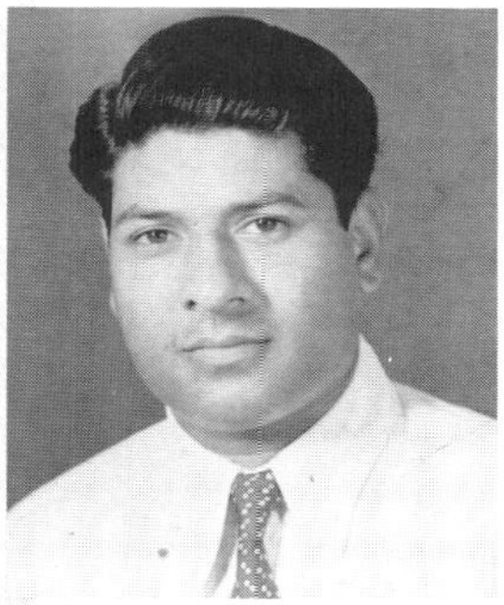

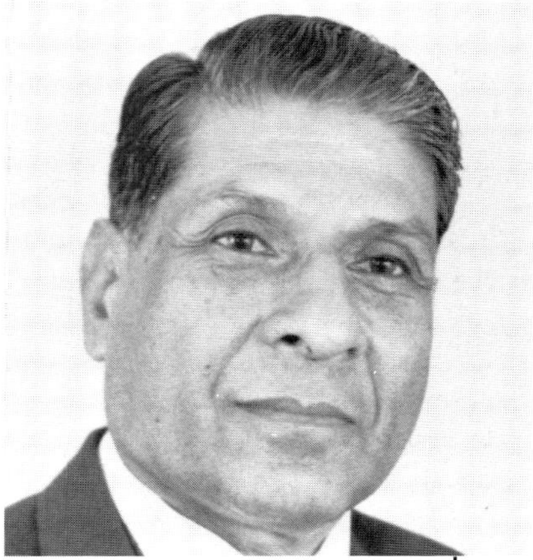

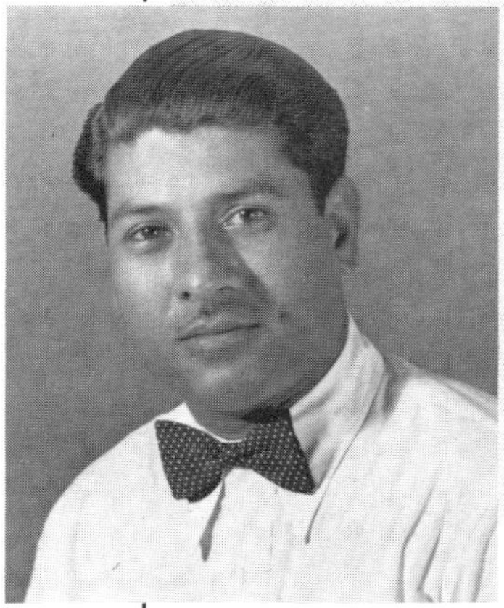

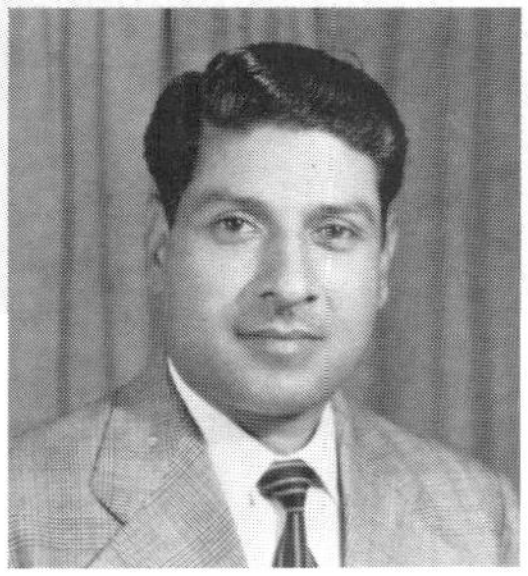

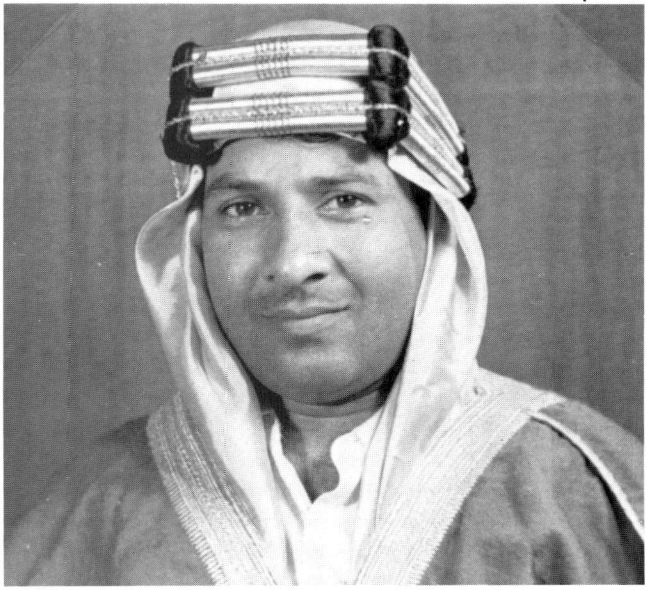

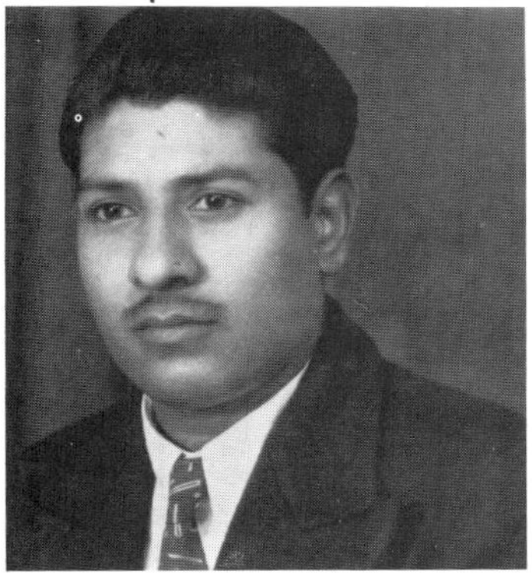

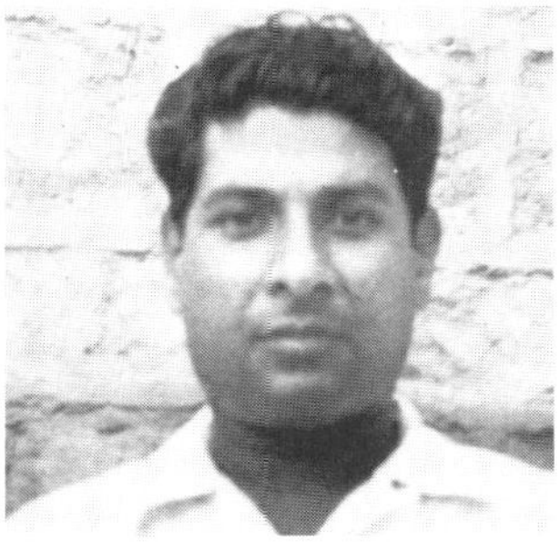

❧ We were once visited by a well spoken old lady. She wanted six passport photos so we took her downstairs. Before taking the photos, she began pulling jewellery out of her shopping bag. She had everything, diamonds, rubies, necklaces, earrings - she must have had millions in that shopping bag. She insisted that she wore it all while she had her picture taken. The reason she wanted the photos was to see which pieces of jewellery looked best on her.

❧ A man came into our photographic shop to have some photos taken prior to going on holiday. He had glasses and also a very large black moustache and beard. However, three weeks before he left on his holiday he got some contact lenses and shaved off both the beard and moustache. This made him so unrecognisable that he had to come back and get some more done.

❧ When I was pregnant I had no washing machine so I had to wash big things in the bath. I'd got some wool sheets to do but found they were quite difficult to wash by hand as they were very heavy. I took my shoes off and got into the bath. Well I'd seen a programme about treading grapes and I thought it would do just as well with wool sheets. Bill was always taking pictures and before I knew it he'd snapped me treading the sheets. I looked a real mess and I made him throw it away.

❧ A year or two ago my photograph used to appear in the local press from time to time. Irrespective of whether a press file copy was used or whether the photographer came for a special snap, the results were uniformly depressing. Determined to improve matters I decided to supply my own photographs for future occasions.

Visiting the town's best portrait photographer, I explained my problem and had several photographs taken. When I saw them they were if anything worse than the press versions. I was appalled. "But these are awful," I protested to the photographer. She smiled sweetly. "Yes. That's because they're a good likeness."

❧ My dad advised me to buy that car. It's a Skoda Coupe and I've since found out that they are quite rare. Its pseudo-sporty lines were at odds with its sixty mph top speed. When the windscreen wipers worked, they crossed over in mid-sweep and got stuck there. The draught blowing around the driver's legs was unbearable and unstoppable. The back of the driver's seat collapsed unpredictably, unnervingly and dangerously. My mates dubbed me the Czechoslovakian Playboy.

I was lying in the bath chortling over all this when I came up with the idea for this photo. Digging out some old glasses, a nasty anorak with fake fur round the collar and smarming my hair down, me and my wife went on to the drive and got this picture. Friends and family don't believe it was me, thank God. I tell new friends that it's Malcolm, my father's love child.

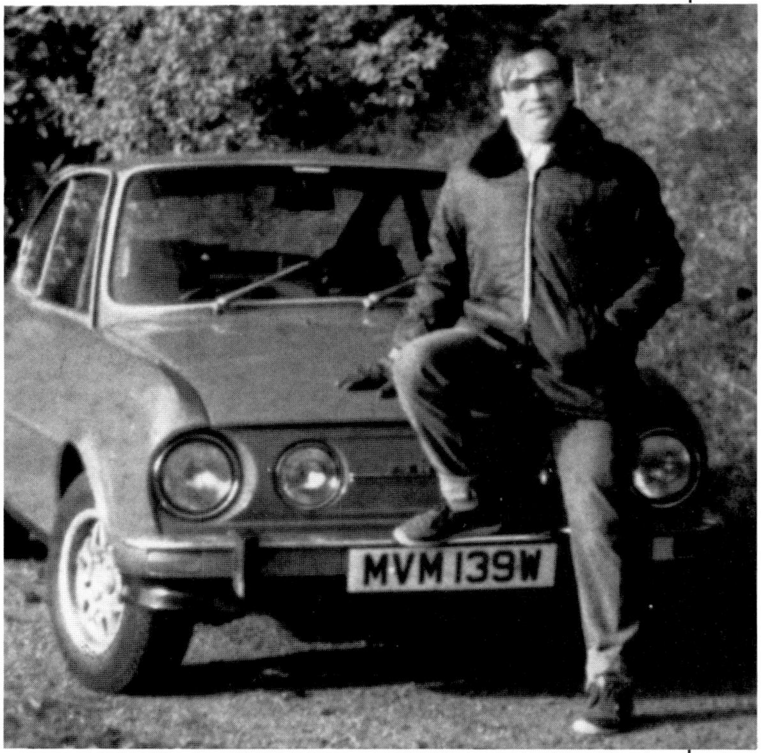

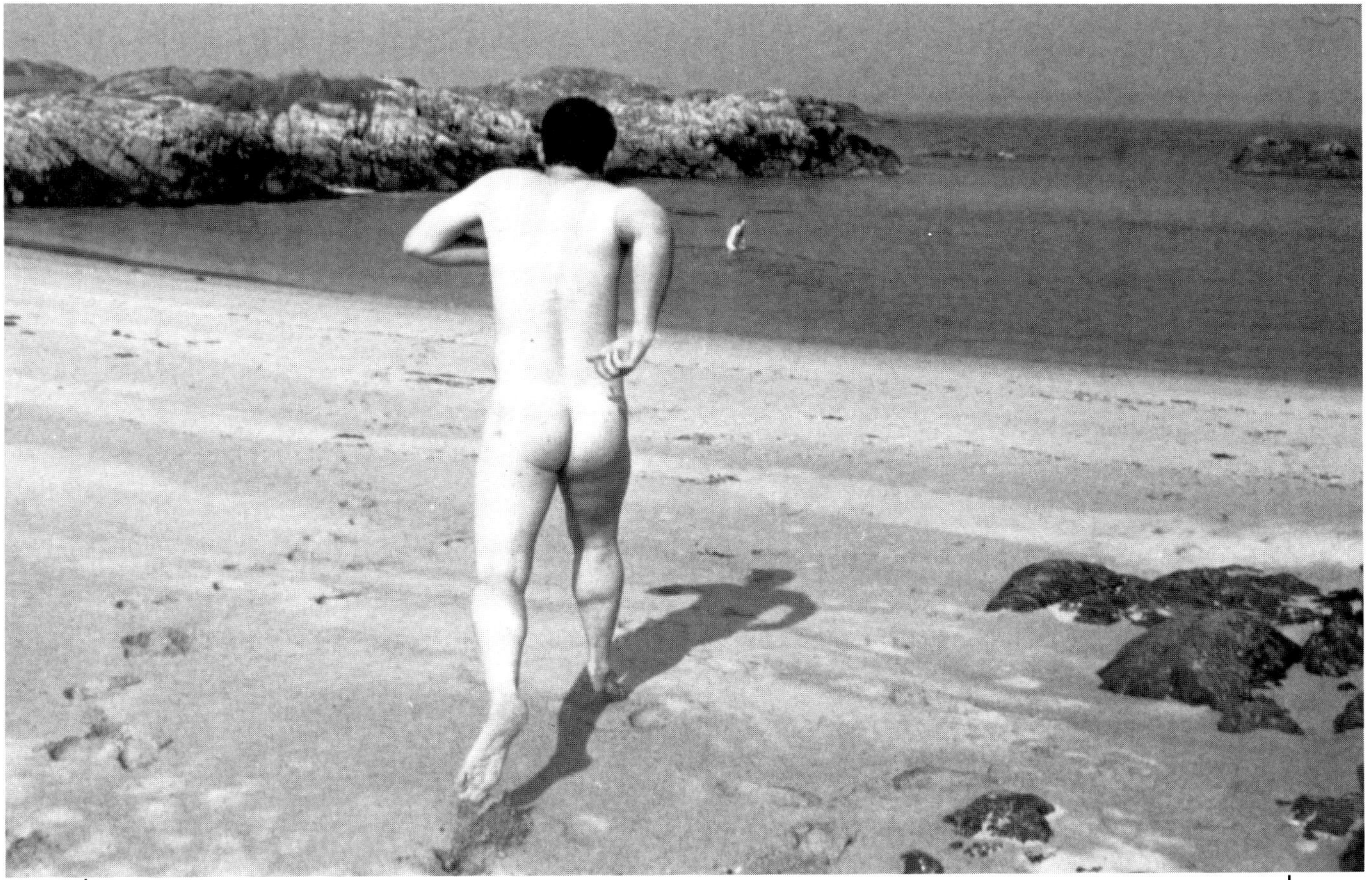

❧ I went on holiday to Tenerife with a couple of my mates. One night we went out to a posh cabaret. One of the turns was a pickpocket who needed volunteers. When he got me on to the stage I didn't know whether I was coming or going. He said to me, "Have you got a belt on, George?" "No, I wear braces," I replied. "Are you sure?" asked he. When I looked down my trousers were round my ankles. To make matters worse I wasn't wearing any underpants.

There must have been a thousand people in that audience. I was almost blinded by all the flashes coming off those cameras. For the rest of my holiday, total strangers kept coming up and saying, "Have you got your underpants on today, George?"

I laugh when I think there's people all over the country with photographs of my wedding tackle in their albums.

❧ It always amazes me what it is possible to take and what has to be censored. When I was a lad you could see pictures of a naked girl in the Health and Efficiency magazine, or Health and a Fishing Book as we called it. Pubic hair was air brushed out.

Now, young people's albums are filled with images of themselves naked or topless on the beach and only the middle-aged turn a hair when they glance through the photographs.

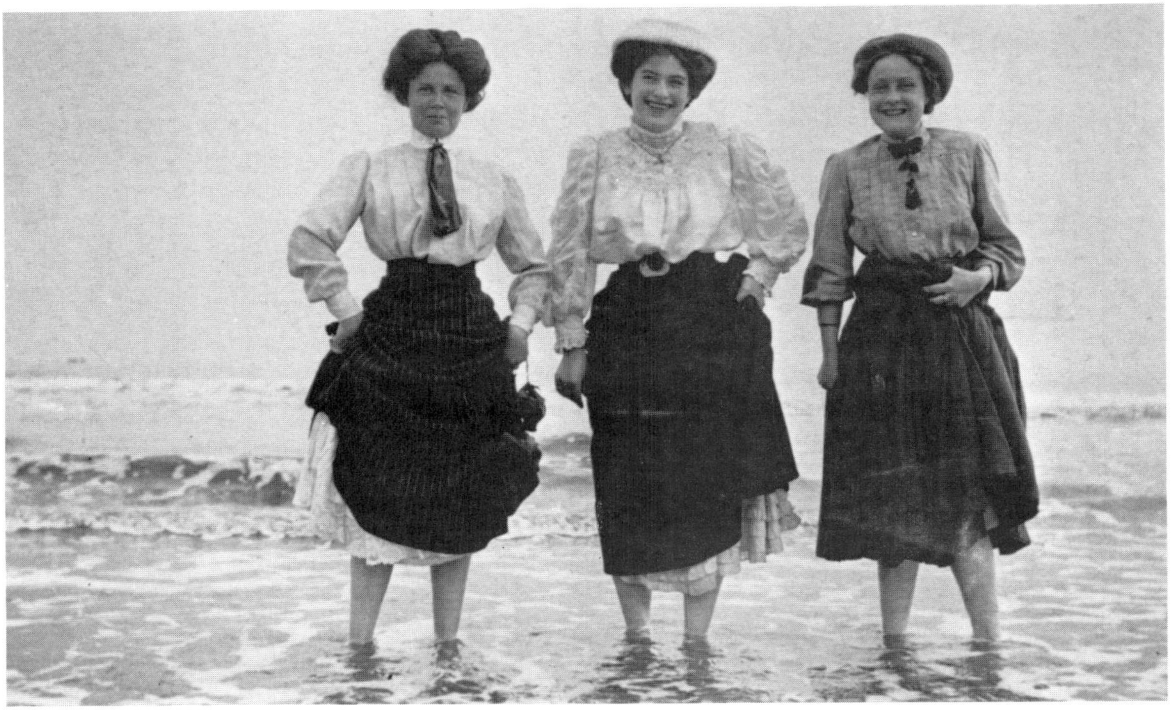

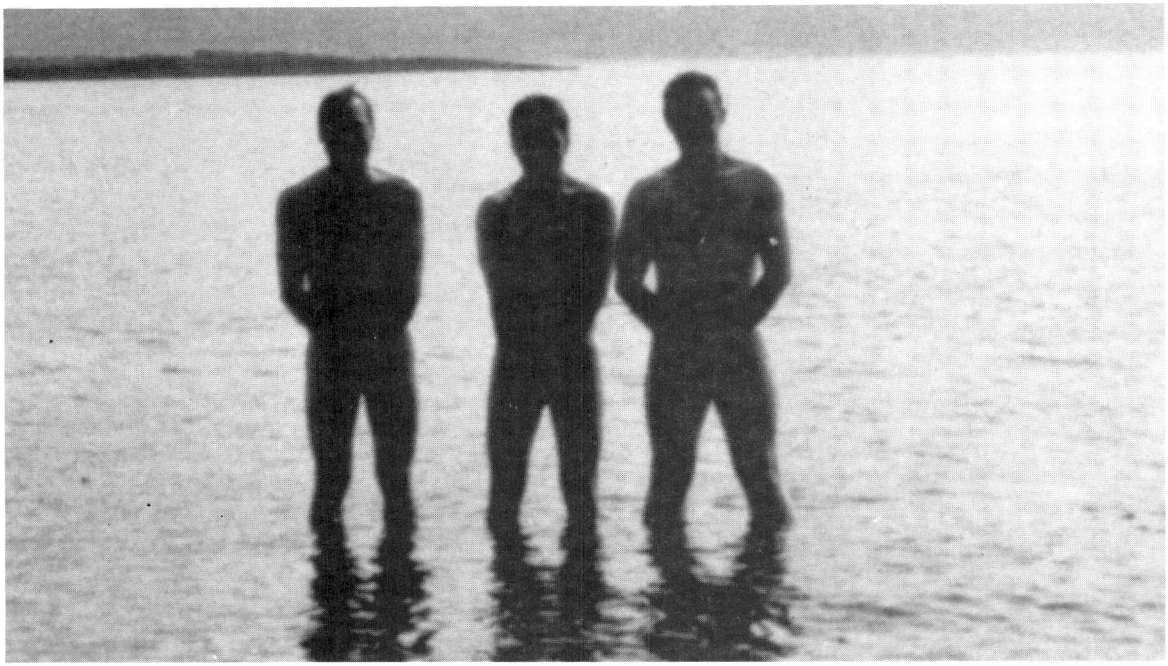

❧ I cannot clearly explain the power this picture has over me; all it shows is a girl of about twenty with strong arms, small breasts, bracelets and dark hair looking directly into the camera. It is a studio shot, there is a lightly washed sunset canvas in the background, and she is sitting on what looks to be a piano stool. The singlet and shorts suggest the late 1920s.

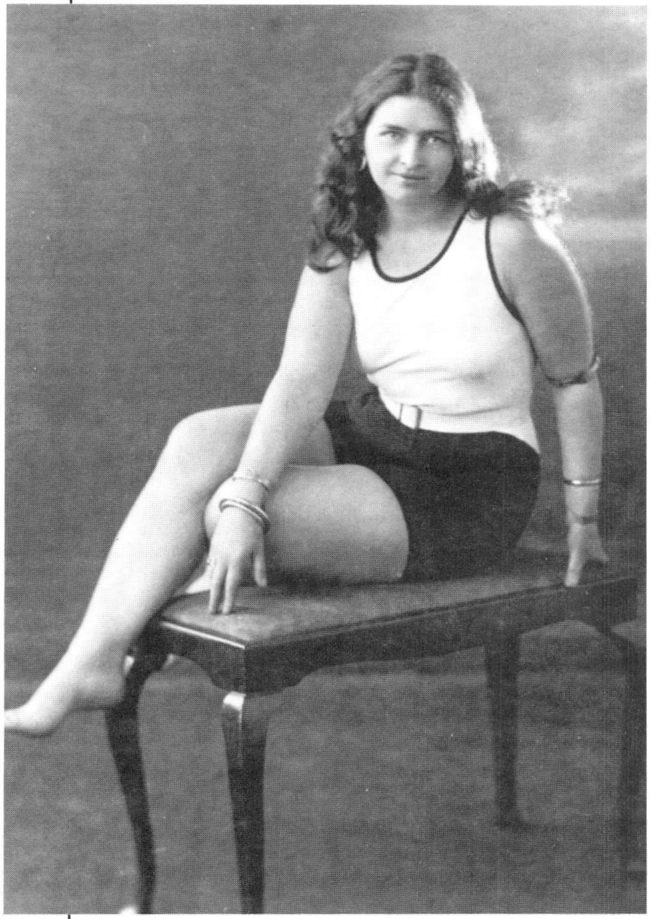

The emotions it arouses are erotic, yet mixed in there somewhere are - and I don't want to sound too cloying - echoes of another theme; she is physically beautiful but that beauty has now faded. What I am responding to, at the best, is the youthful charm of someone who is now an old woman or someone who is dead.

❧ My portrait photograph was stolen from Rochdale Art Gallery. I was interviewed by the police at the time because, thinking that some pervert was after me, they needed to ensure that I wasn't in danger. The Observer, the Rochdale Observer that is, did a long article about it. The photograph was taken after Mr and Mr Yates, four doors down, asked my mother if I would pose for them. I said I would so they took photographs of me in profile or resting my cheek on my hand, and submitted them to a photographic committee. All went well, they won a prize of some sort and one was put on display. Then came the day when it disappeared, frame and everything. That's when the police called. I was worried, I can tell you. The ink was still wet on the newspaper when a boy I hardly knew - I was going out with someone else at the time - came round and presented it to me. It was very awkward. I had to pretend that I was still mystified when actually I knew all that had happened.

Eventually I married him. Much later we got divorced.

❧ If you are in an acting profession then you are always conscious of how your photograph can be taken and used. You have to be particularly careful.

I'll give you an example. When my partner died I was required to attend a press conference and there were, as you would expect, batteries upon batteries of cameras. It was part of the job, yet I have to say it was rather weird. I had some experience and was particularly wary of how I presented myself. Half way through the interview I scratched my nose with the side of my finger. Next morning all of the tabloids carried the picture and suggested that I was wiping tears from my eyes.

❧ On fine summer days the benches outside John Street Market in Bradford are always occupied by a good cross-section of humanity. Many is the time I've sat there thinking that a photograph of each bench taken at regular intervals throughout one day would make an interesting picture book.

On the day in question, I was sitting watching the world go by when I noticed a man with a camera around his neck. I kept my eye on him. He was hovering at a discreet distance, weighing up my bench. I guessed by the telephoto lens he had on his camera that he wasn't just taking broad street scenes. He had that over-nonchalant air about him that I've seen in myself when in a similar situation. Eventually it was obvious to me that he was going to take the photo. So just at the point I thought the shutter was released, I looked straight into the camera and winked! With a bit of luck, when he printed up the negatives, he'd realise he was the watcher being watched.

❧ If ever you're feeling flush and bored, try amusing yourself with this little trick. Go into one of those photograph booths then pull your eyes down and nostrils up for one shot. Do something ridiculous with your mouth for another, push your fingers behind your ears and stick them out for another. Remember to keep your fingers as far as possible from the particular feature you're interfering with. When you get home cut them up with scissors and make some grotesque identikit pictures of yourself. When I had a go, it didn't matter how repulsive the composite picture was you could still tell it was me!

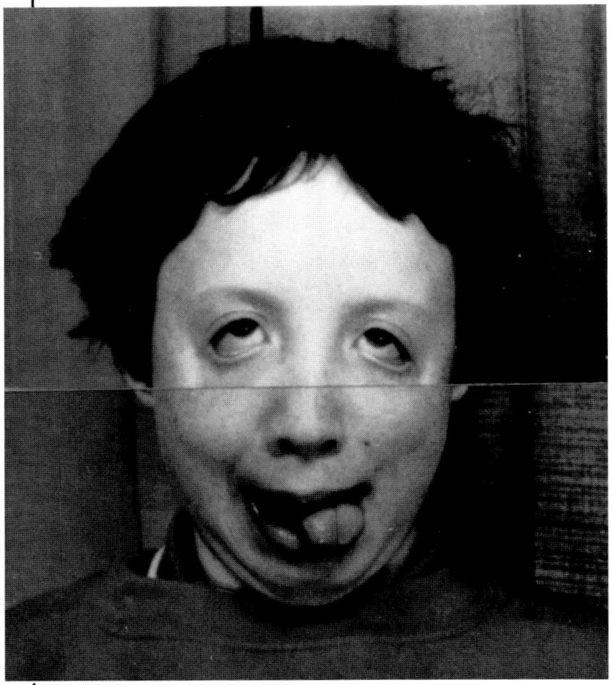

PENNY-IN-THE-SLOT PHOTOGRAPHY.

Automatic photo booths have been around for a lot longer than you might think. In 1891 the Automatic Photograph Company Limited first put its machines into public use. 'The Photographic News' commented: 'at most places of public resort the automatic machine may now be noticed. In appearance a cross between a parish pump and a pillar letter box - a thing not of beauty, but one which seems to arouse much curiosity.'

'Amateur Photographer 'magazine described how the machine worked;

'The victim gets on a stand two or three feet from the machine, puts a penny in a slot, and looks intently in a small mirror just above the lens. the exposure lasts for a couple of seconds, when a small bell rings to indicate that "all is over". A noise of clockwork is then heard inside the machine, which indicates that the plate is passing through the developing, fixing and washing baths. then something is heard to drop into a small box in front of the machine, and on lifting the lid a portrait on a sheet of thin iron is seen - a "tintype", in fact'.

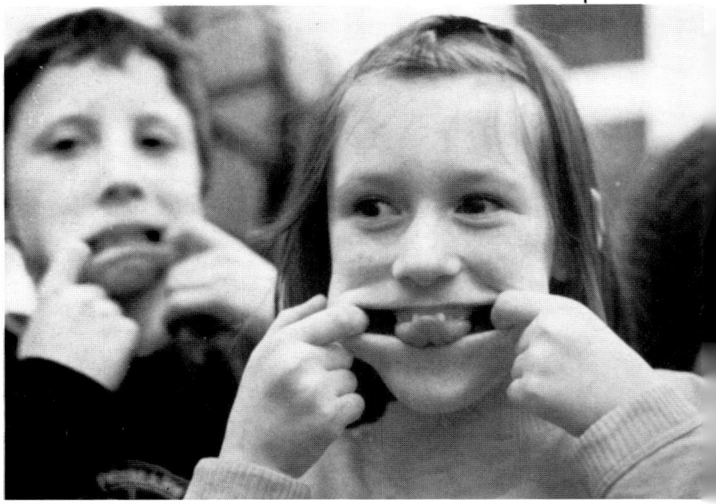

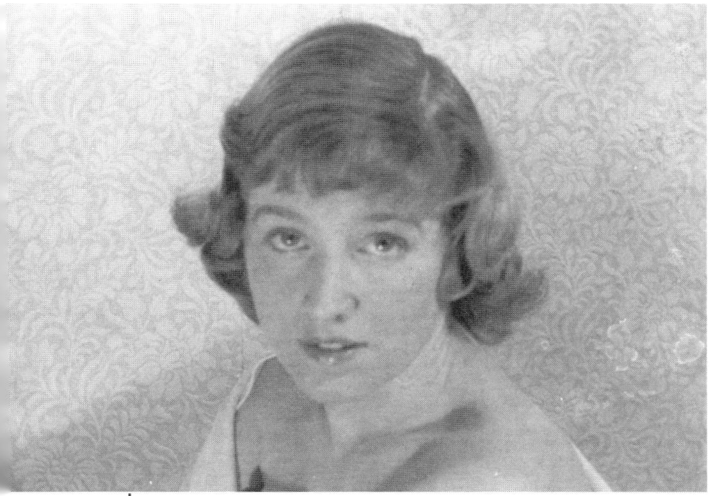

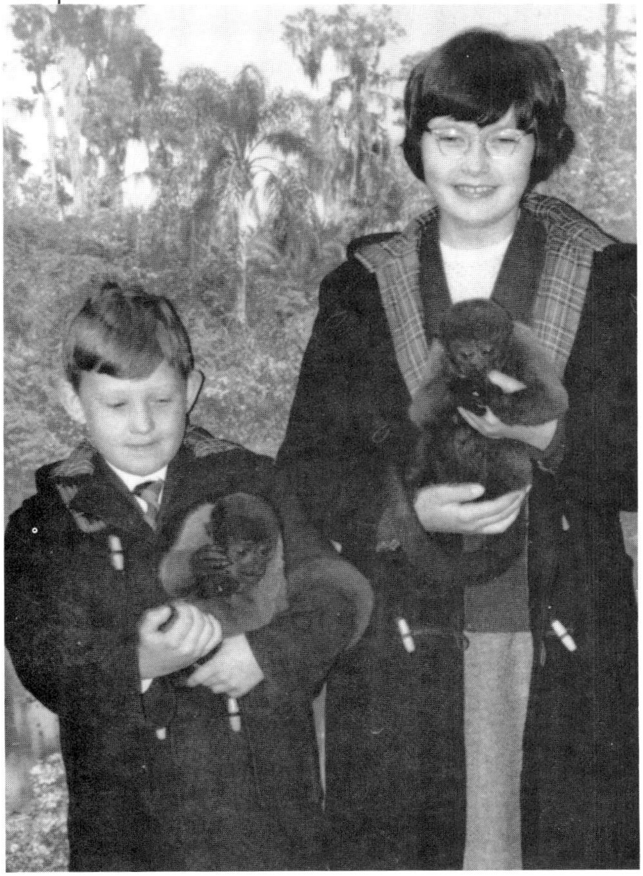

❧ When someone in the billet got a Dear John letter - you know the sort of thing; a note which starts in a formal way and goes on to say how she can't wait any longer or has found someone else or wants her freedom - then it was the tradition to hang it on the wall so that the rest of the National Service lads could write ribald comments alongside it. If a photograph existed then this was hung up alongside, the darts were produced and we all got down to serious target practice. When it came to sensitive responses we were a bit lacking in that department.

❧ Many people don't like the idea that their image could be kept forever by someone they do not know. It's more than intrusion, it's close to the idea of having the evil eye put on you. I've met the objection in Malaysia, also in Moslem countries and once in Yugoslavia on the road to Greece. I had taken the picture of a teenager when his mother approached us and began remonstrating. She spoke German and managed to communicate to my father that the picture in itself was an evil thing and she would not allow one of her children to be photographed by a stranger.

❧ When I was about eight and my brother was ten, we went on holiday with our mum and dad to Cleethorpes. While we were there we had a photograph taken of us both holding a tiny monkey. Every time I see it I don't remember the holiday, what I remember most is that a dead body had been found in the swimming pool the day before we arrived.

❧ Although I had been refused permission, I sat down and, as any half-decent photographer would do, I took my camera out of the bag. We were about fifteen rows from the stage, dead centre.

Using 400 ASA film and setting the camera speed to 1000 I hoped it would be enough to compensate for the lack of flash. With a 200 telephoto lens I might just be able to get a decent shot.

Chuck Berry appeared at exactly eight, fortunately the person in front of me didn't appear at all and I was able to rest my elbows on the seat and steady myself. The lights on Chuck were flashing wildly. One second a decent exposure was there, and the next it was gone. However, I stuck to it. Needless to say I had to be careful not to be spotted by

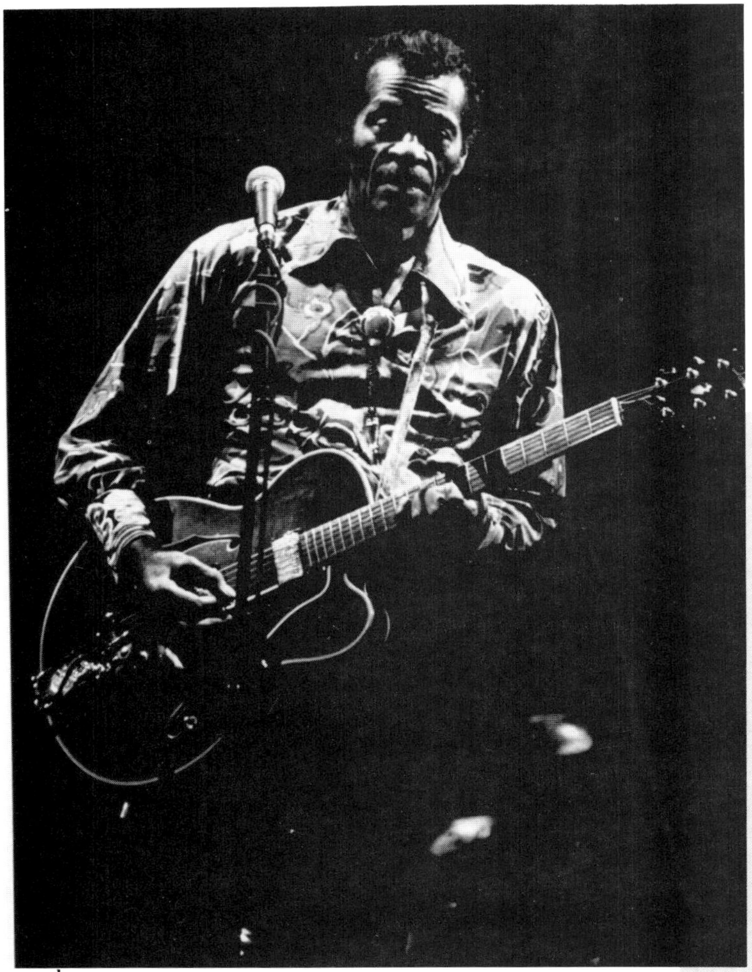

security, who although quite friendly when we chatted in the foyer, looked as though they would throw out Mother Teresa. Two films are shot, when Chuck takes a break and tells a story about a dog. Fairly still, with this beautiful light on him I get what I believe are some great shots. Two minutes later all hell breaks lose. Three bouncers are at the end of our row gesticulating wildly for me to give myself up and come out. I do. Two of the bouncers drag me through a door, and the third is despatched to get Dave.

Nothing. Fortunately I'd removed the films from the camera during the concert and passed them to Dave - just in case. So now I'm more than worried - I'm being searched and bollocked and Dave is on his way for the same treatment.

My camera bag is looted, the unopened boxes of new film are confiscated and two empty film cases are found in my jacket pocket. They ask me to remove the film from the camera, I do. They stamp on it and rip the film out and throw it against the wall. Dave is brought in, spread-eagled like some hoodlum in Miami Vice and given the treatment. No film is found.

Dave had passed the films on to Geoff and Les. The bouncers had just thought there were the two of us. The other two had gone to the bar so fast they didn't know we were a foursome. Thank God for alcoholics!

THE CAMERA FIEND.

The appearance of the first hand-held snap shot cameras was a cause of great consternation amongst certain sections of society. For the first time it was possible to photograph people surreptitiously so the camera now represented a threat to personal privacy. No one could call their face their own.

' The Amateur Photographer' magazine observed in 1895; 'We are gradually beginning to think that when a man gets hold of a hand-camera he loses some of his moral balance. He degenerates into that worst of all photographic types - the snap-shot fiend.' A sure method of dealing with these photographic nuisances was suggested; 'There is but one remedy for the amateur photographer. Put a brick through his camera whenever you suspect he has taken you unawares.'

As the number of snapshot cameras increased, the novelty of candid photography diminished. However, the early years of snapshot photography raised issues relating to personal privacy which are still to be satisfactorily resolved. It is not just the famous who suffer from the intrusive nature of photography.

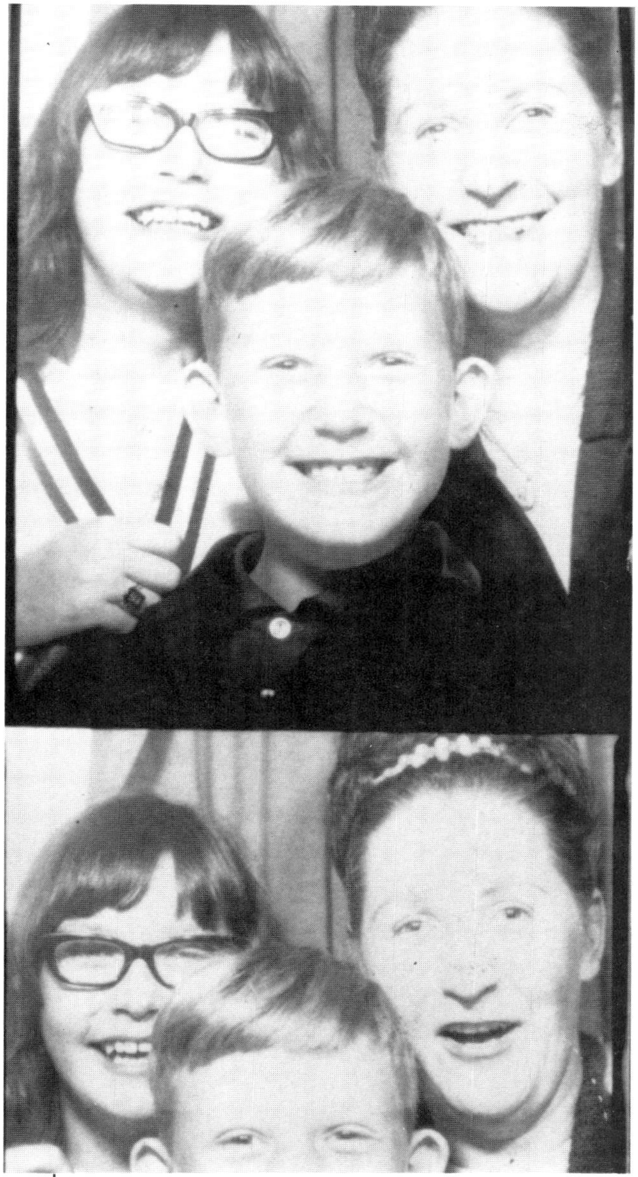

❧ If you ever need a passport photo, give the Woolworth's photo booth in Dalkeith a wide berth. I've never suffered a flash like it. For the first picture I was just limbering up my features. I literally felt the heat of that flash, so by the second picture I'm looking very worried. On the third photo tears are streaming from my eyes. I didn't hang around for the final shot. As I staggered out of that booth half-blinded, a middle-aged shop assistant stood, arms folded, smirking. "Aye, hen," she said, "It gets a lot of 'em like that."

❧ We pulled into this rather smart German service station and I went to get coffee whilst Reini settled down to breast feed Jessie. When I came back I found a Japanese man sitting at a nearby table was taking pictures of her, clicking away, photo after photo. When I saw him I was very angry and glared. He seemed oblivious; he was taking in the local colour. I moved between him and Reini. Would you credit it, he got up and moved to another table to get a different angle. "In a minute", I said, "I'm going to take that bloody Nikon and shove it up his arse".

"Don't be childish," she said, buttoning up. "It's been done before. He wants to photograph the natives."

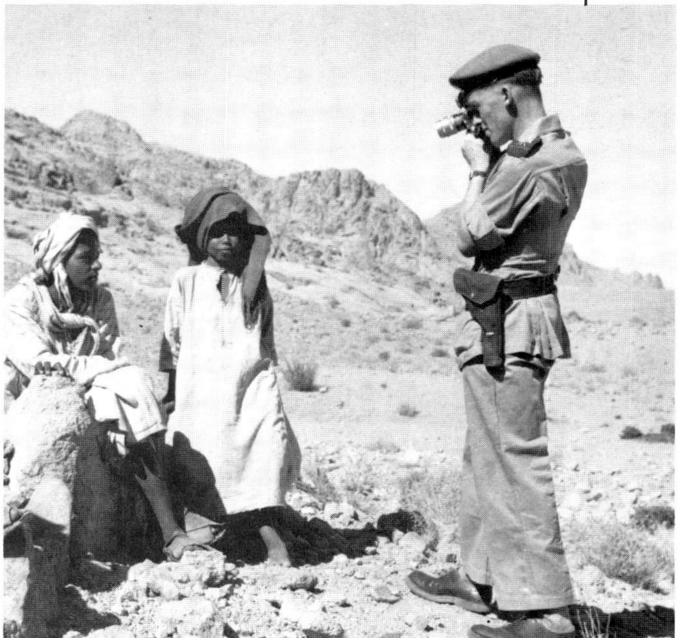

❧ I worked for a pittance as a waitress in Scarborough during the school holidays. I wasn't at all keen to be snapped by the inevitable photographer with the monkey who stopped me on the prom. I was doubly annoyed when one of a group of lads muscled in and put his tattooed arm round me for the shot, but I was too shy in those days to tell him to 'piss off!' I had to buy the photos after that to keep my reputation - I didn't want my mates to see them in the photographer's window. I was sixteen.

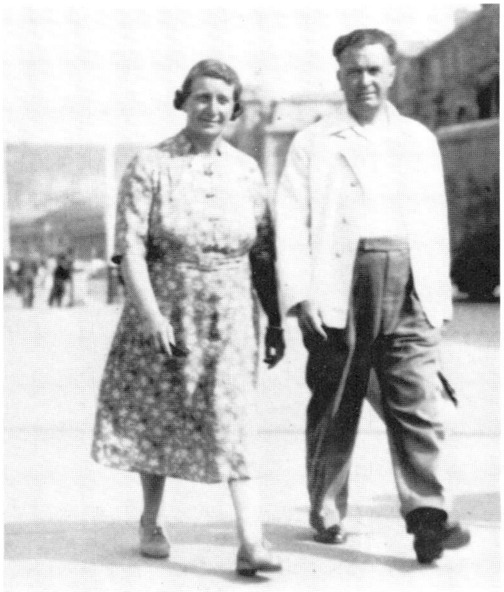

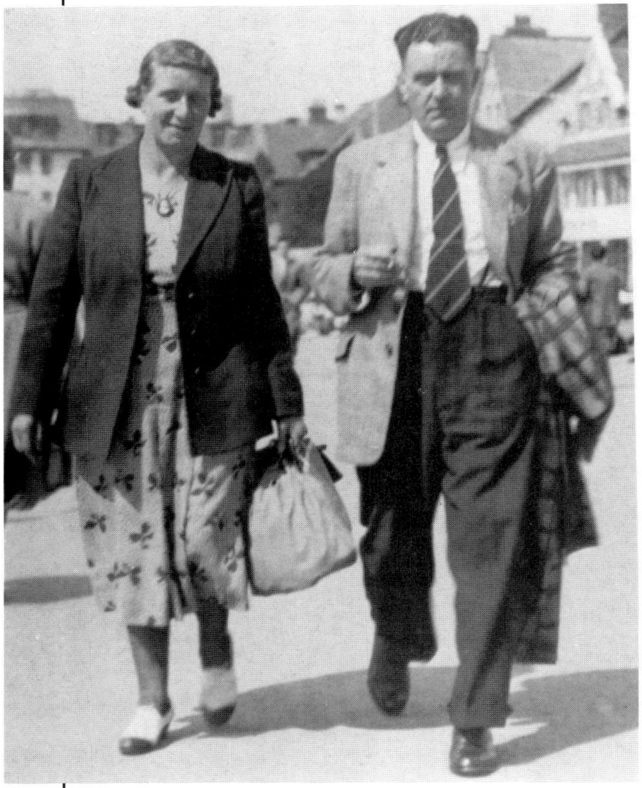

❧ By the look of it you would think we were off to see a show on the South Pier. We went to Blackpool every year, we've had some wonderful holidays there. This photo was taken by one of those chaps who walked along, snapped you and gave you a ticket to collect the photo later on.

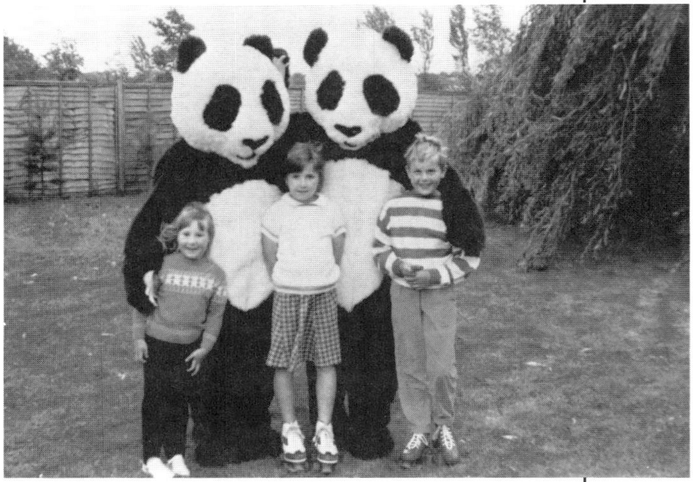

❧ I have a couple of photos of my sister and myself dressed as pandas. We were working for a carpet company in Harrogate at the annual fair held in the exhibition centre. I feel a bit embarrassed when I look at them and wonder how I managed to get myself involved. It was a few years ago, September time and in the middle of a heat wave. Everyone kept on saying, "I bet you are hot in there". My sister said to me, "If one more person says that I will hit them!" Luckily, we were well paid.

❧ Grandma Lines was forever dressing up. She lived a drunken, but essentially dull, life in a yard in Fazelly Street, Digbeth and did a spot of cleaning for a woman who she called Madame. I suppose that dressing up was a form of escapism. The most intriguing costume is the one taken in the studio, but the dress I know most about is the crinoline. This was purchased from a sale at the Birmingham Rep and was used as a prop on club outings to Blackpool. On these occasions, although well into her seventies, she would carry a sign which said 'Just Married'.

I wish I had a photograph of how I best remember her in the 1940s; a little woman, not five foot tall, sporting a tailored suit covered in costume jewellery and wearing a fox fur and white tennis pumps. I do not have such a photo so these theatrical pieces have to do.

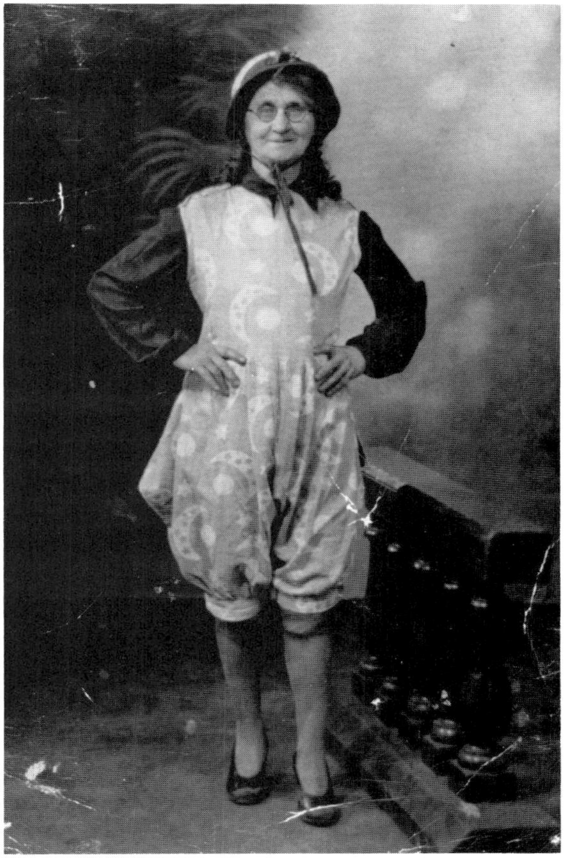

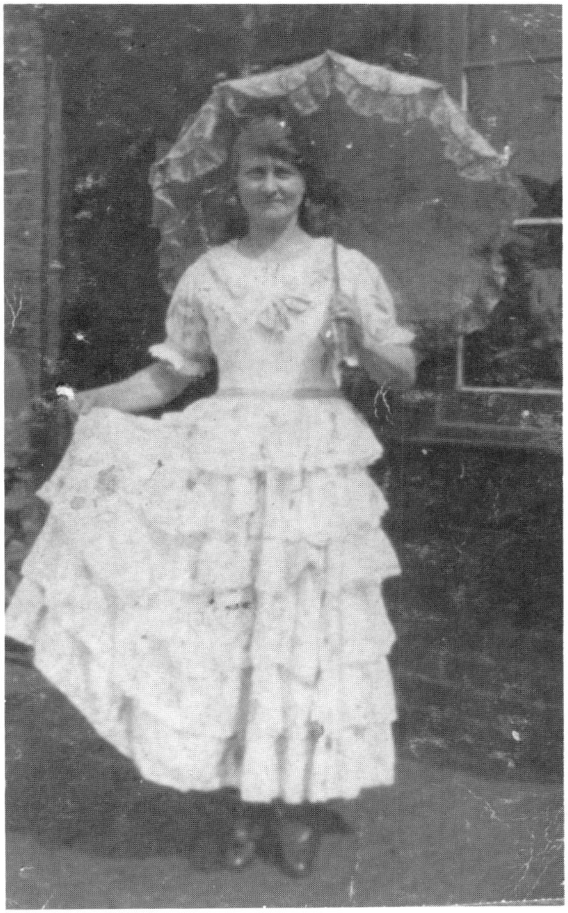

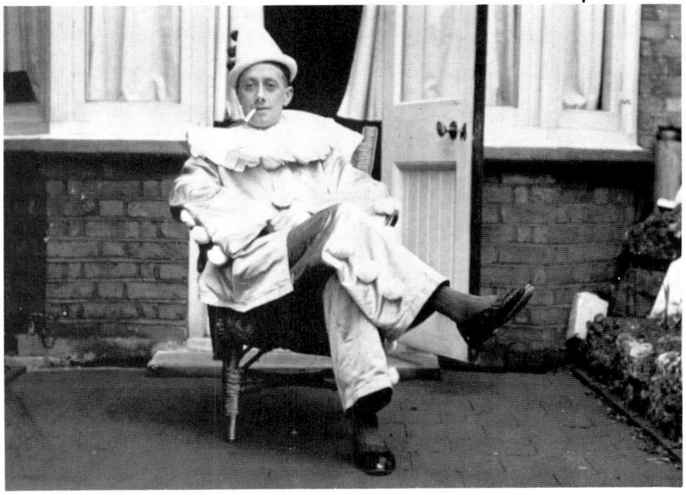

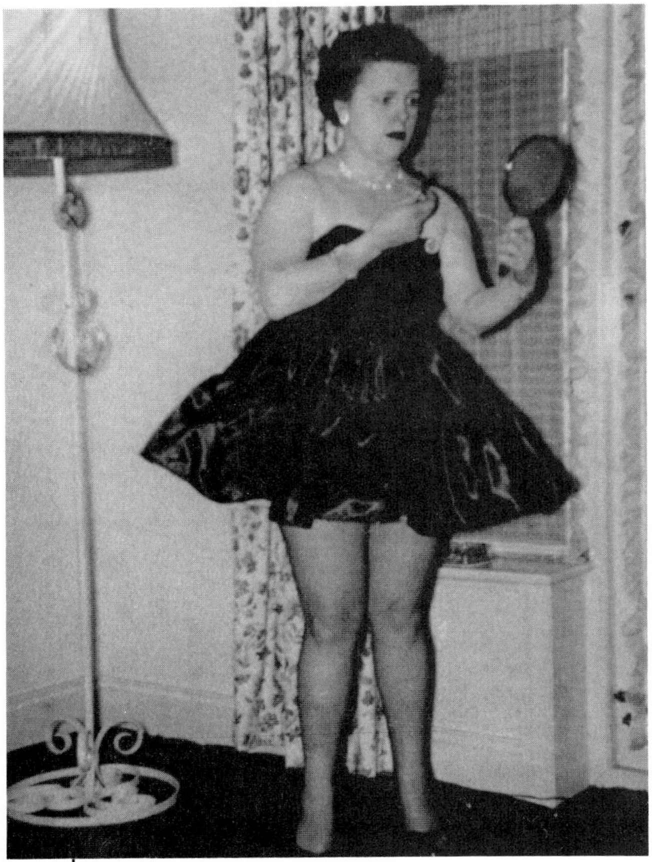
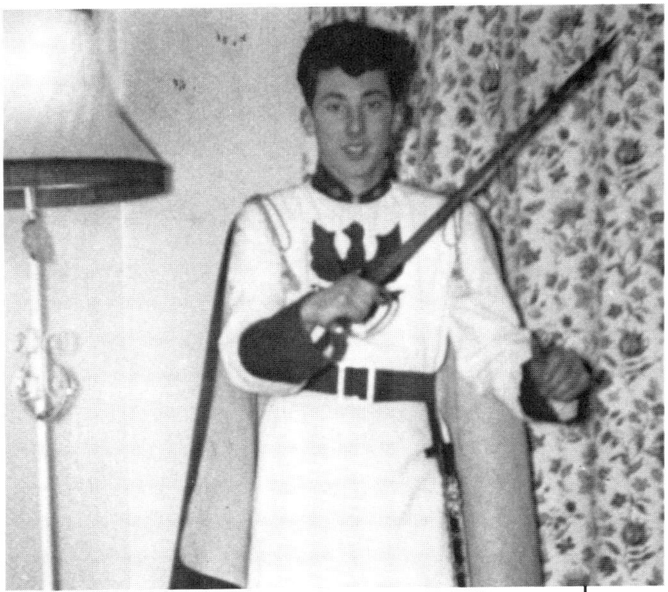
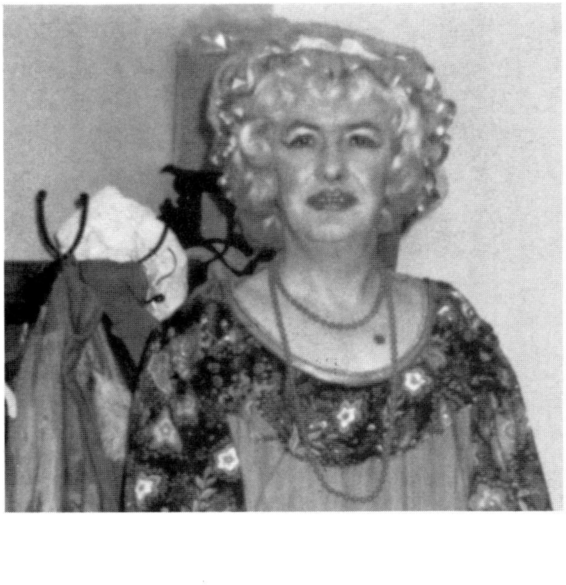
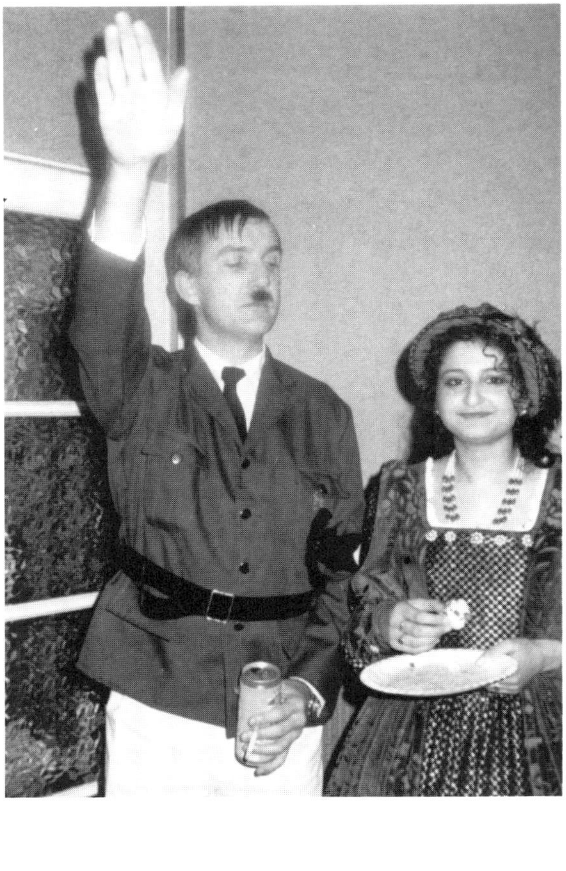

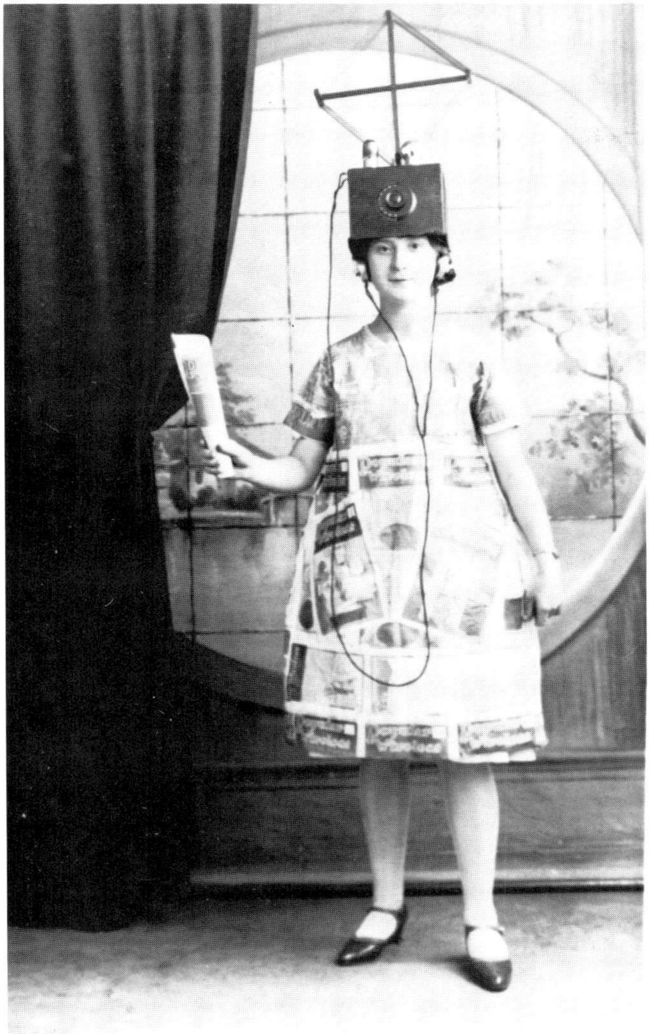

❧ My parents have never been ones for tradition. For that reason I have always enjoyed Christmas. All their single friends and general waifs and strays always end up at their house for Christmas dinner. Every year one of their closest family friends, Jim, arrives on the dot of six bearing mince pies and the rest. He's a big man although his weight is up and down like a yo-yo. We all usually gather for the feast at about 7pm and Jim always eats more than everyone else put together, munching his own and everyone else's dinners.

As soon as dinner is over, Jim heads straight for the living room and collapses on the carpet for his post-prandial nap. As soon as his head hits the floor a great snore begins. At this point every year, my sister and I get out the make-up and set about his wobbling features whilst tape recording his snoring. At the moment of completion, we get out the camera, and snap the sleeping beauty before collapsing into fits of giggles. We then rewind the tape and place it on his chest with the volume set at maximum. Again the camera comes out as we press the play button and wake Jim up with his own snores. This game has never ceased to provide us with amusement.

❧ Before we were married I used to go on holiday with my wife to her auntie's in Penarth, South Wales. Being a photography nut, I was always looking for unusual subjects. One year I photographed my bare foot next to my wife's on the sand. Auntie, on hearing about the photograph, thought this very odd. About three days later, my feet came up in giant blisters and were too painful to walk on. The doctor was called and I spent the rest of the holiday in bed. Auntie thought there was a moral in this somewhere.

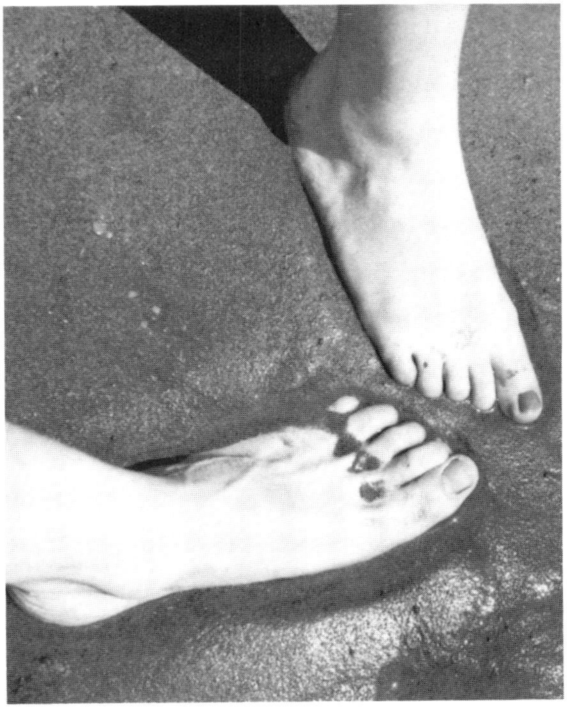

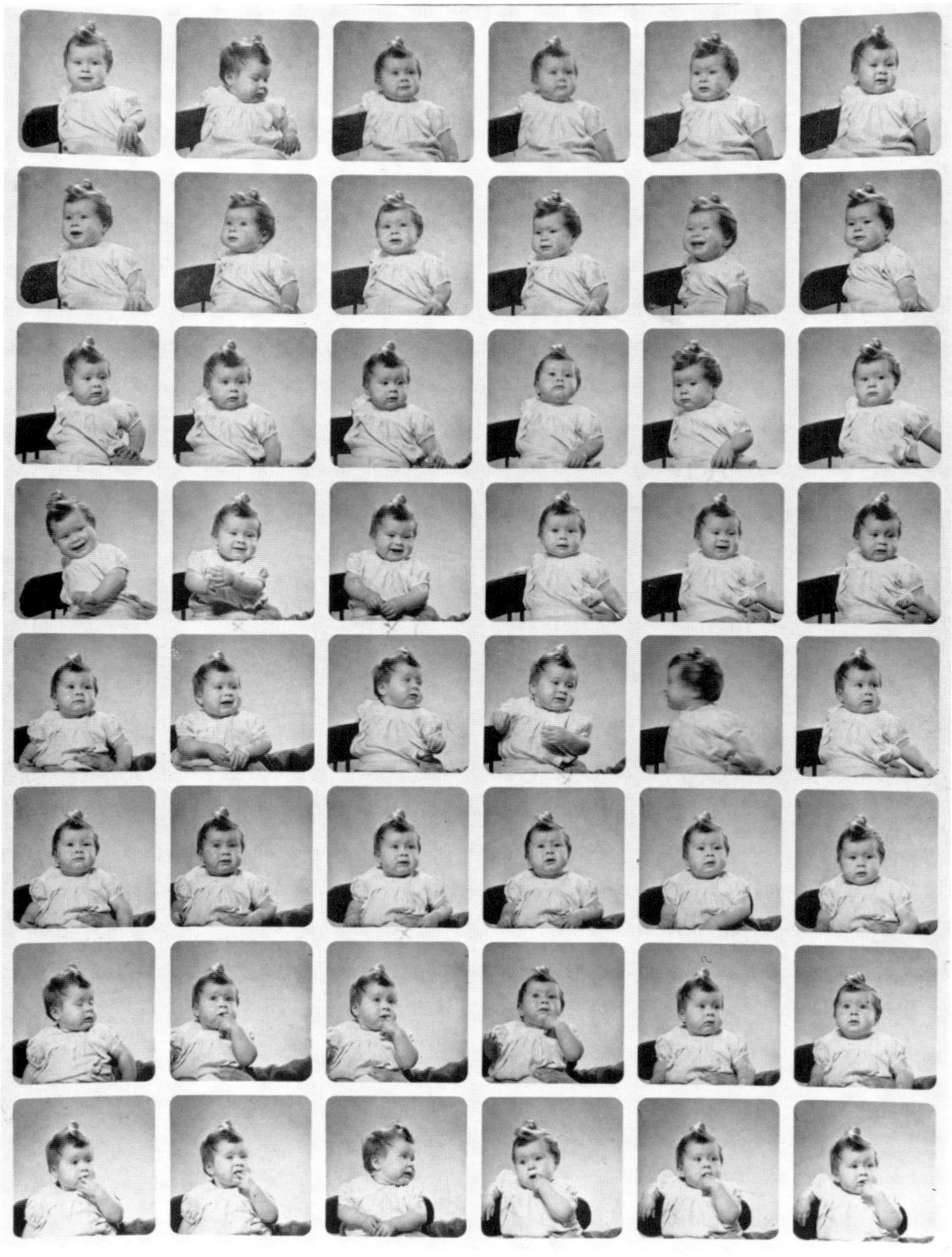

❧ I don't know if all major cities had a polyfoto studio. Leeds did and I know that Birmingham had one. It was a very small shop opposite the trolley bus stands in Union Street. The earliest photographs of me were taken there sometime just before the war. The background is very Art Deco, you know the sort of thing, plywood surfaces and a couple of lines of thin white piping following a curving corner. I am in a coat with shiny buttons, wearing a beret and sporting patent leather shoes.

The normal fare though was the sheet of inch-high portraits which you purchased so that you could have an enlargement. These images often survive in tins up and down our family, usually in groups of three of four. The groupings have irregular shapes presumably because these are the dross which was left after the others had got away.

POLYFOTO.

Introduced in 1933, Polyfoto was a totally new concept in photographic portraiture. Special polyfoto cameras produced forty-eight separate poses in quick succession on a single glass plate. The sitter was provided with a proof sheet of forty-eight individual portraits, each little bigger than a postage stamp. From these they were able to select their favourite pose for enlargement.

The first demonstration studio was in Selfridges in London's Oxford Street. As the company expanded, studios were set up in most major cities and towns, usually located in department stores. By 1939, there were twenty polyfoto studios in London alone.

Over the years, millions of these distinctive little photographs found their way into wallets and handbags.

In 1969 the company went into liquidation. The Sunday Times commented on the news;'How can a company with a household name like that fail to make money?'

❧ I know what you're thinking. "What the chuff's he got on his head? Well, if you must know, they're Deeley Boppers . I bought them from one of those rip-off merchants on the South Shore at Scarborough. "C'm on folks, get your Deeleys, one fifty for stars. two pounds for balls, only a few left." Bloody liar! He had another five thousand in a van round the corner. Anyway I let him con me into buying two pairs; stars for my daughter, balls for me. We sauntered off along the front licking expensive two-tone ice-creams. I saw a bloke in a shop window and he looked a right prat in his sawn-off Levis, red and white sneakers, his face smeared in insect repellent and a pair of balls bouncing on his head. Then I realised it was me.

'Yes, this is all well and good,' I can hear you saying, 'but why has he got his daughter's thingy boppers on in his own back yard?' Well, the simple answer to that is that mine broke and seeing how this was the last exposure, I had to pose for it, didn't I?

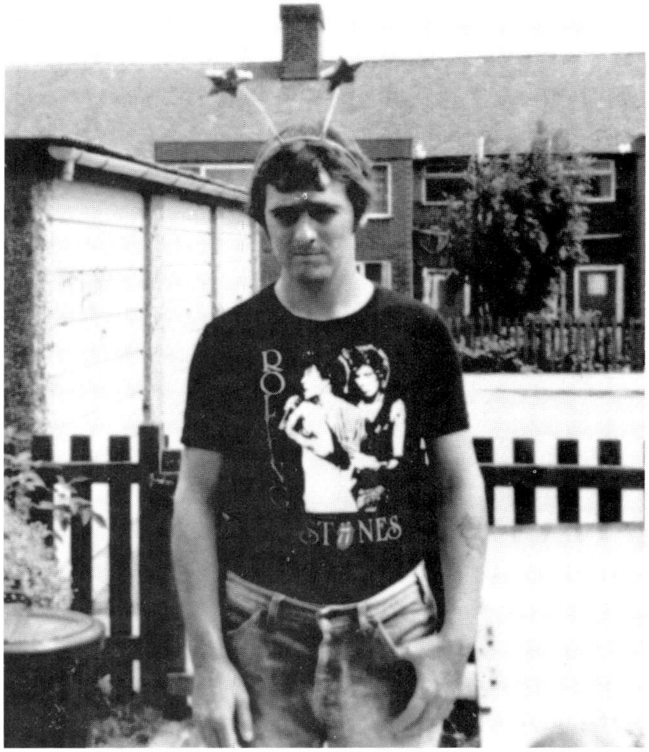

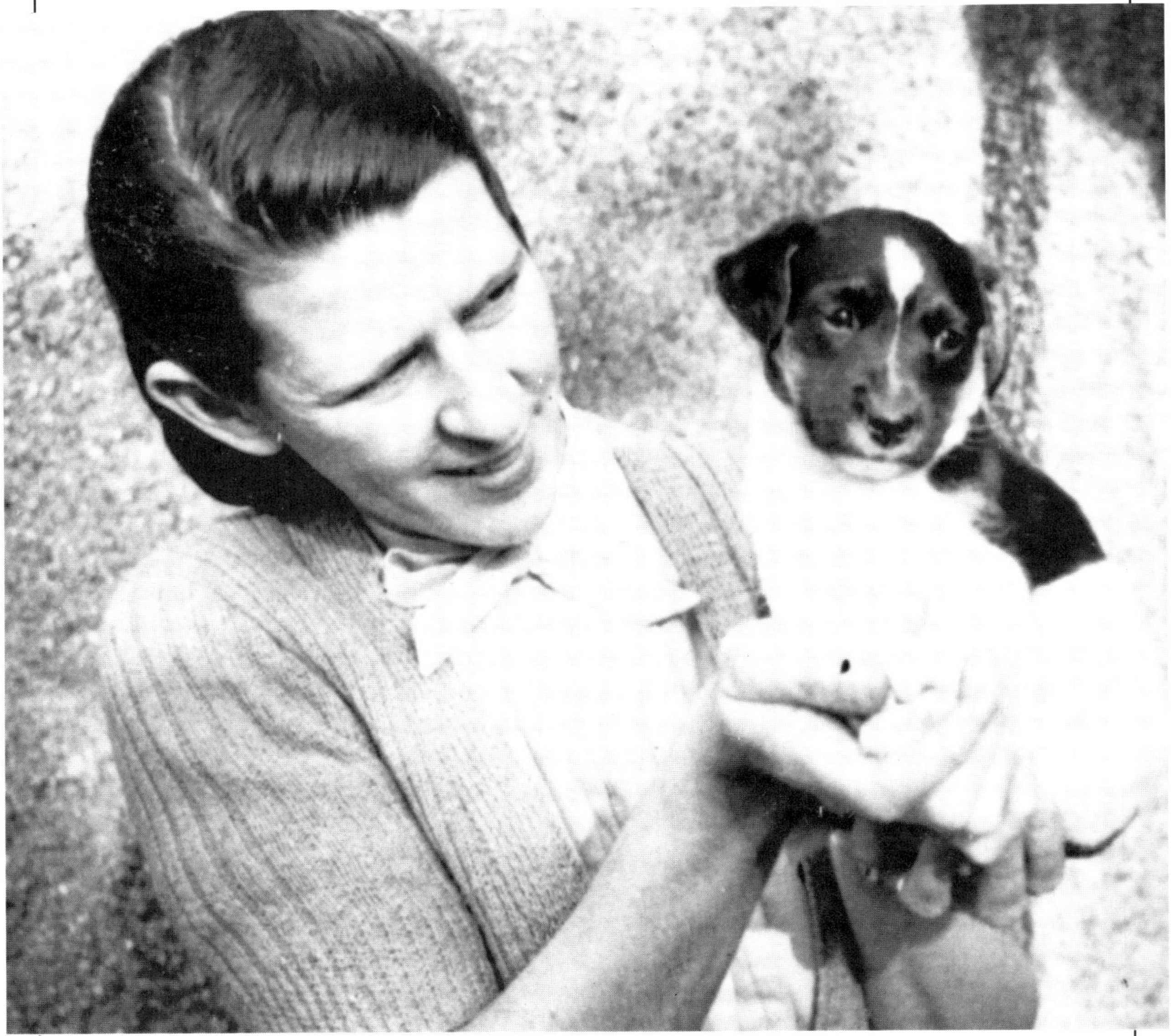

❧ I always felt my dog Bob was talented. He would jump up on the gate and release the latch and get out. Bob would then go for a quick walk before returning home. When my mother was told she did not believe it so, armed with a camera, I decided to get evidence. I took a photograph of Bob opening the gate, then decided to take another.

By this time Bob was in the middle of the road. A big Thurston truck suddenly stormed past, knocking him over. So now I have two photographs - one of Bob opening the gate, and one of the truck that killed him.

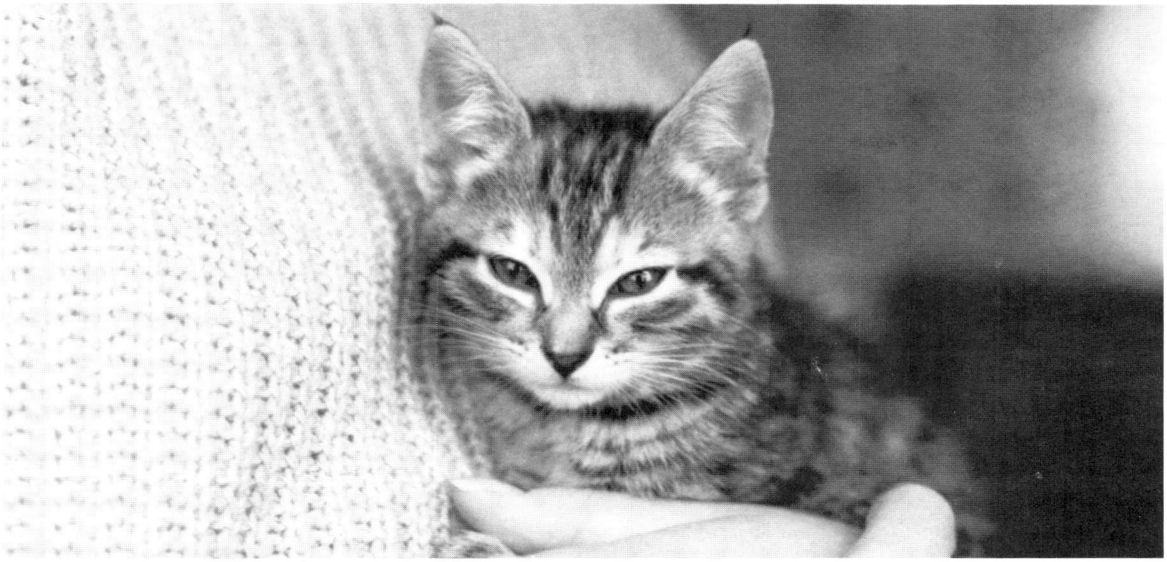

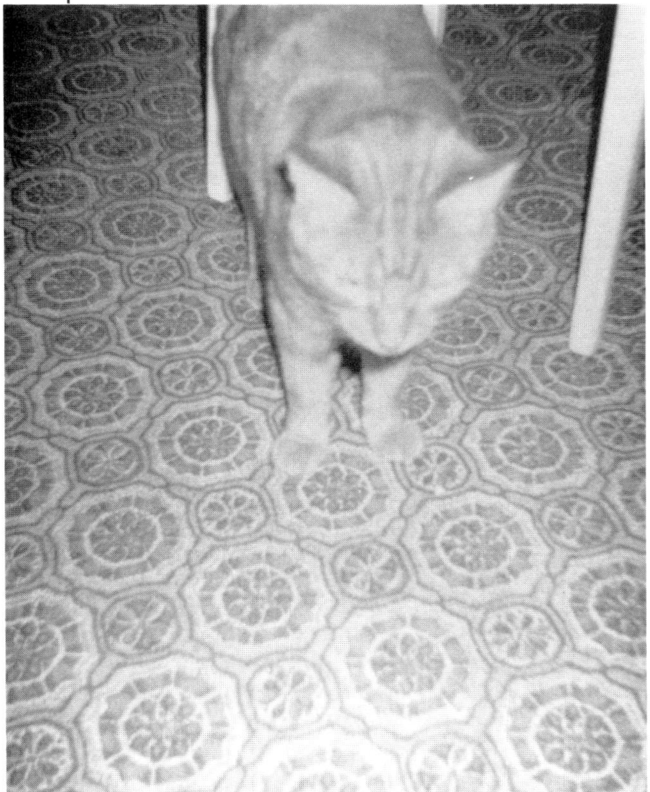

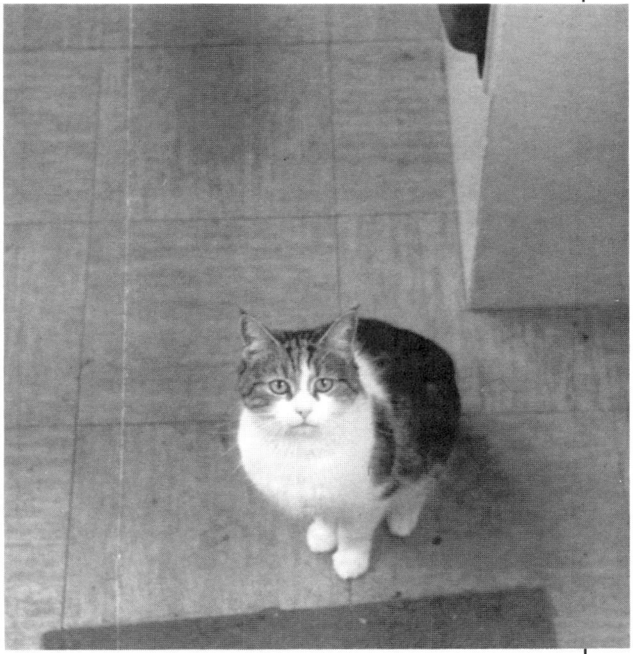

❧ The reason why we have so many pictures of the cat is not because I particularly like pet photographs but when you get to the end of the film there is always one shot left. That's when I take the cat.

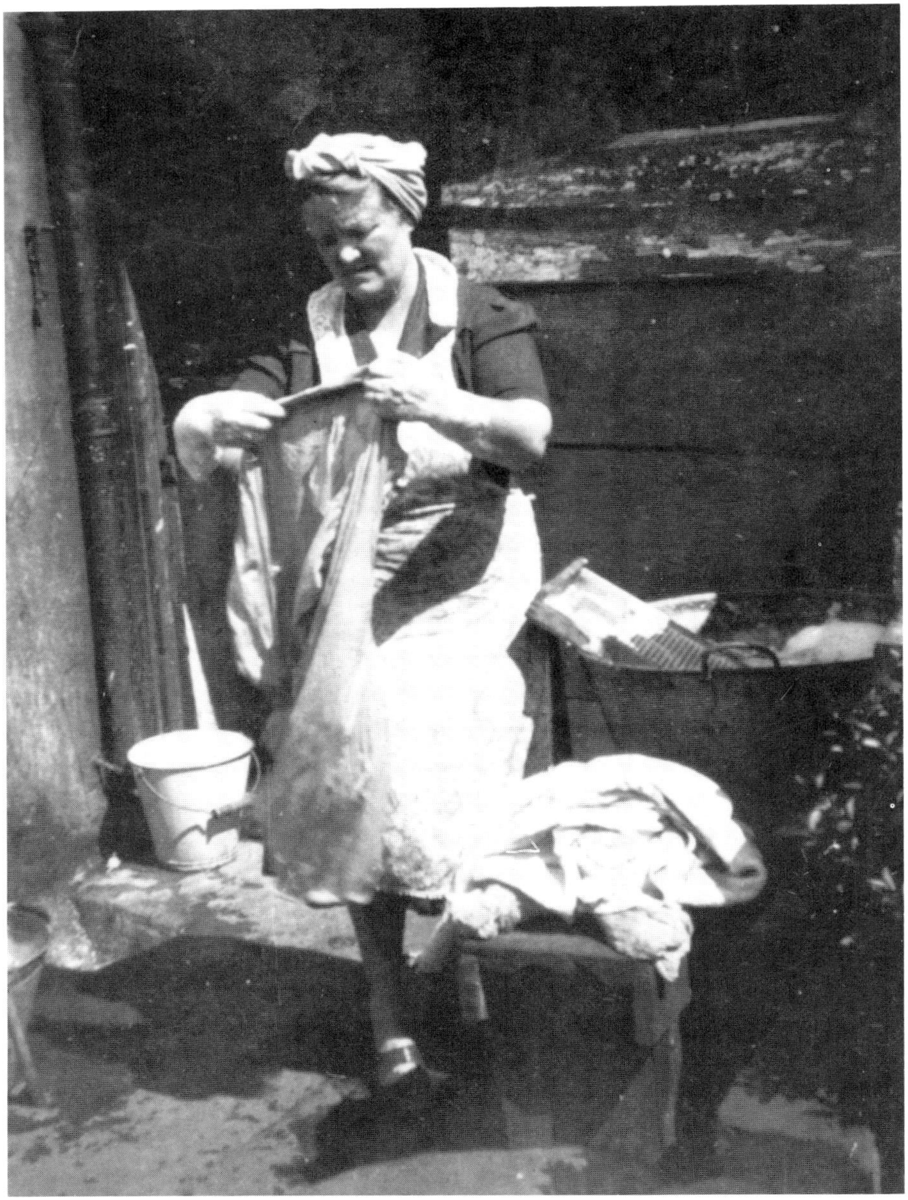

I'm much more interested
in what people don't take photos of.
Where are the pictures of us at work, or doing the housework,
or shopping, or on the loo?

CHAPTER FOUR

BRINGING HOME THE WORLD IN A PICTURE

Kodak advertisement 1935

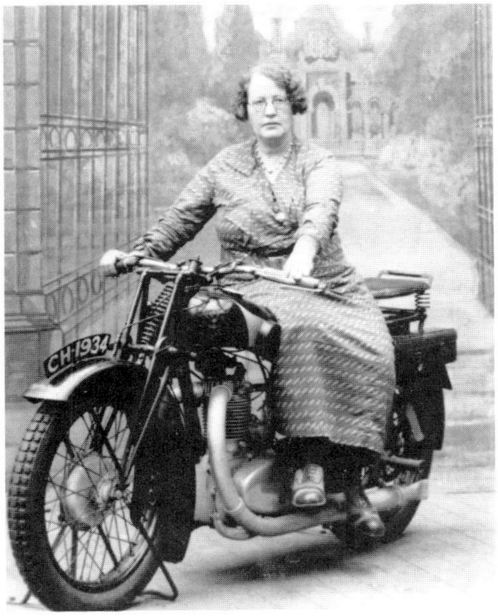

❧ My collection starts with the family snaps my mother took on special occasions; excursions, when visitors came, Sunday School anniversary days. There are not many, you didn't waste photographs on everyday things. Then there are those of my own wedding, our children growing up, various houses, gardens and holidays. Mostly these were taken by my husband. Me, in increasingly minute mini skirts in the sixties and an extraordinary maxi at a wedding in the early seventies. I did not have a camera of my own or take photographs much until I went to college as a mature student and did photography as part of my art course. Next come some bad copies of old photographs made by me with a borrowed close-up lens when I did not know if my ex-husband would share the family albums with me when we split up. He did though, so some are duplicated. The last batch are taken by me over the last nine years. A lot are of my daughter, who lived with me, as she grew from child to young woman, and some of my grown up sons when they visited or we did things together. The vast majority though are landscapes here and abroad that might be useful when I draw or paint. There are no people in them because I was usually on my own, but they record my pleasure in what I saw. Many resulted in pictures that I have since sold. Now that I write rather than draw I am not sure why I carry a camera. I am seriously thinking of leaving it behind when I go to Florence and Venice. You can, if you are not careful, spend more time composing a photograph than actually looking, hearing, smelling and feeling a place.

❧ A few years ago I joined a group who were doing a local history of Featherstone. The group already had a few old photographs of the town and its people and I became the custodian of the negatives. I had given up photography, or at least doing my own processing, and had sold all my darkroom tackle. I was so fascinated by these old snaps and postcards that I once again bought some processing gear and began to collect and copy them. This has become a great passion, not only to me but to lots of local people who eagerly await my annual calendar with its pictures of old Featherstone. I have been asking for old photos but I am still amazed to find people turning up with them. The thing I hate to hear most of all is, "My mother had hundreds of them but we threw them out when we cleared the house". When anyone starts to say it I close my ears. My collection has slowly built up until I have now got over 3,000 negatives. No one ever seems to save negatives! I hope one day the negs will go to someone who will appreciate them and maybe say, "Thank God he saved these."

❧ My grandad up and offed when my father was nine. There was an argument at the breakfast table over who was to pay for a pair of new boots my nan had bought. He said he had had enough so he got up and left. The next the family heard of him was when an Australian court wrote to inform my grandmother that she was no longer married on the grounds that she had deserted her husband.

The only photograph which survives of this shadowy family figure shows him standing with a group of men under a giant Canadian Redwood. He is very small, slightly blurred and marked with a cross. Poor though the image is it says it all. He has always been out of focus. Having got my grandmother pregnant and done the right thing he immediately left to seek his fortune by working his way

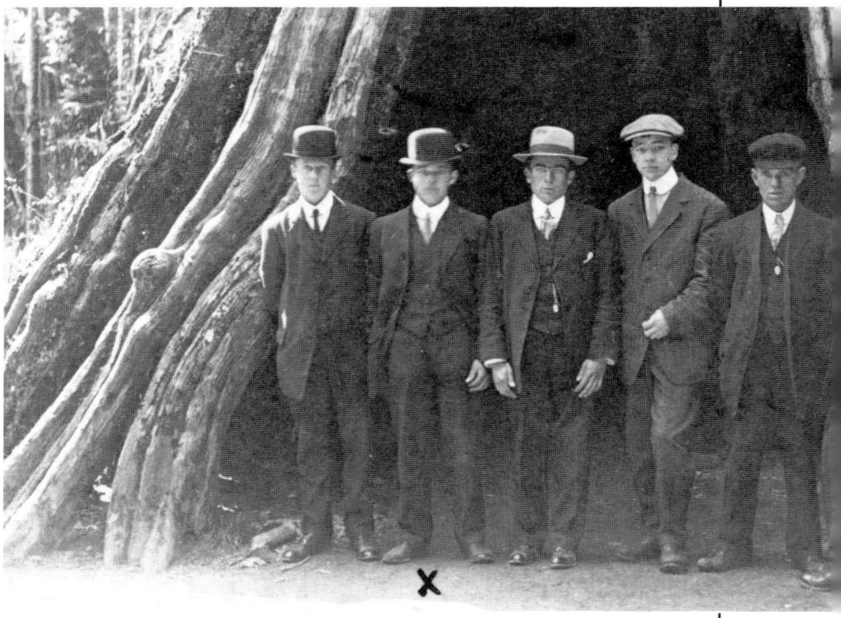

round the world as a stoker in the Merchant Navy. The First World War was a godsend; he enlisted and returned to grandmother but only for brief intervals. By this time she had become the manageress at a back street condom factory - all was under control - and he was driving mules. She was practical and fiery, he romantic and wandering. What better image to have of such a grandfather than one of a man in a bowler hat, marked with a cross standing with other men under the boughs of an exotic tree.

❧ In the early eighties most junk stalls had a few snaps stuffed in at the back of the topographical scenes and you could pick up the contents of some dead person's family file for a few shillings. I doubt if I could afford to now when most images go for a pound a time. A lot of the images were of weddings. You can learn a lot from a wedding photograph. Dress, standard of etiquette, class attitudes, fashion; it's all there so anyone who has gone out of their way and put together a collection of wedding pictures has something worth keeping and so neatly laid out as well. Most are taken to a formula, yet every one is unique.

The other type of picture I like is the friendship group: they too are real social history. Men often had cigarettes in their mouths when they posed and the sexes were usually grouped separately, that is except on the beach. What I particularly like is the mystery of it all. Who, I wonder, are these people? This is my particular favourite. I often wonder who they were.

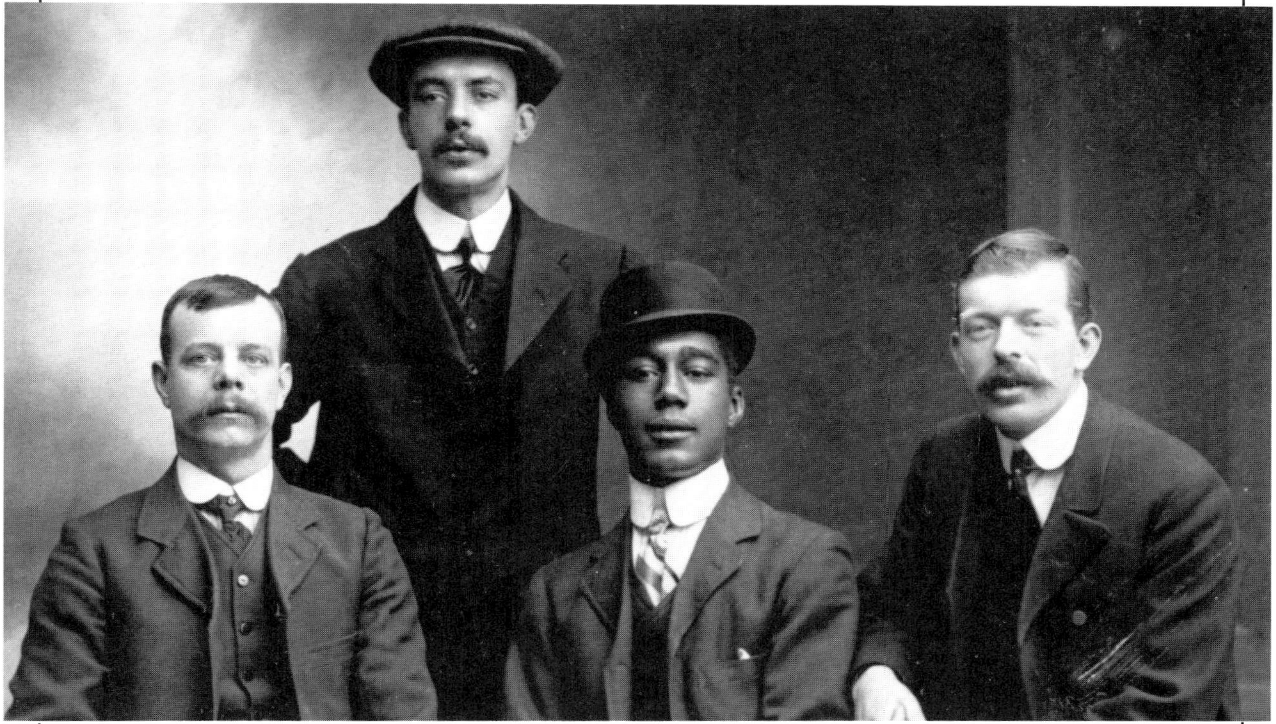

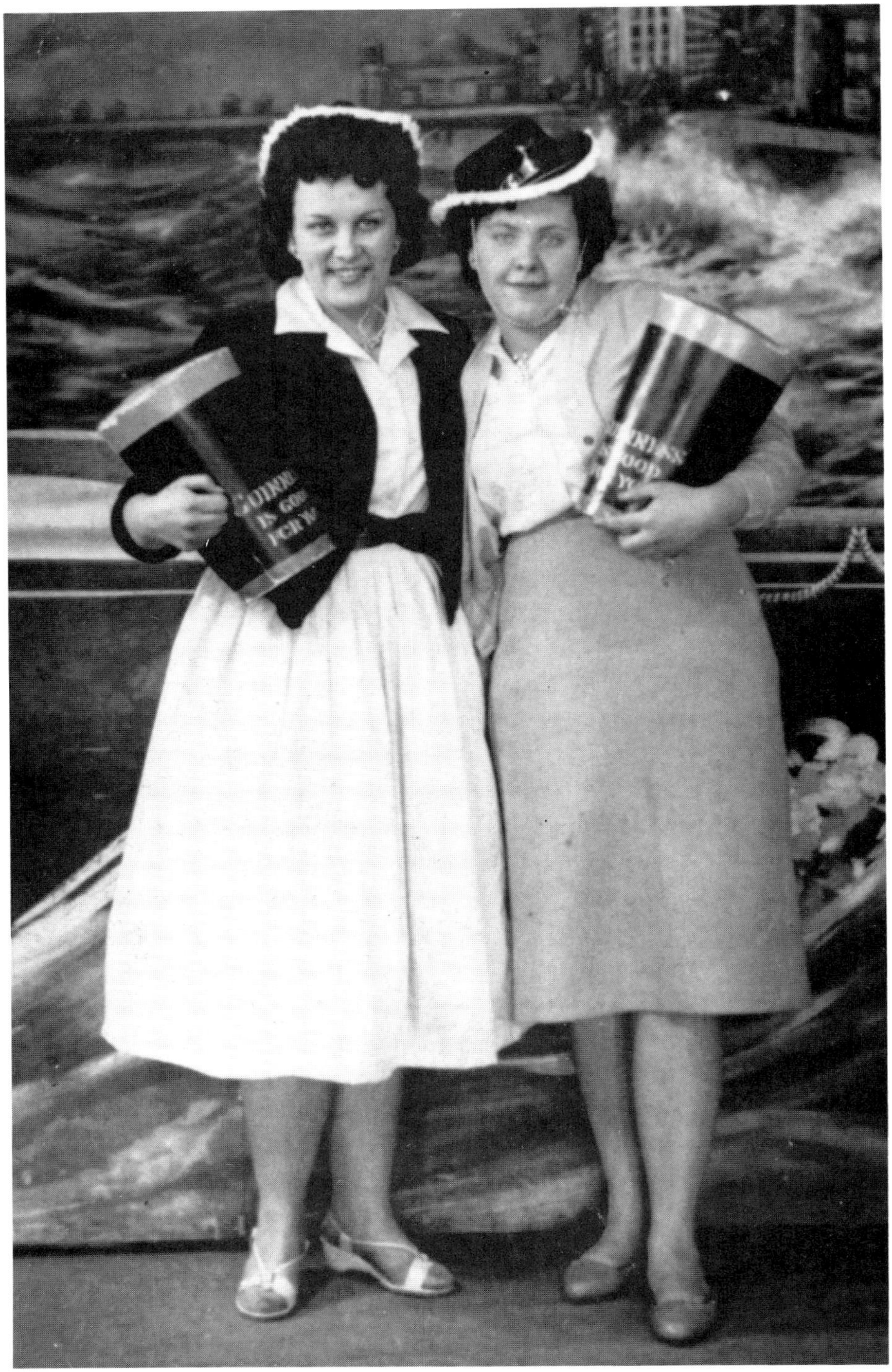

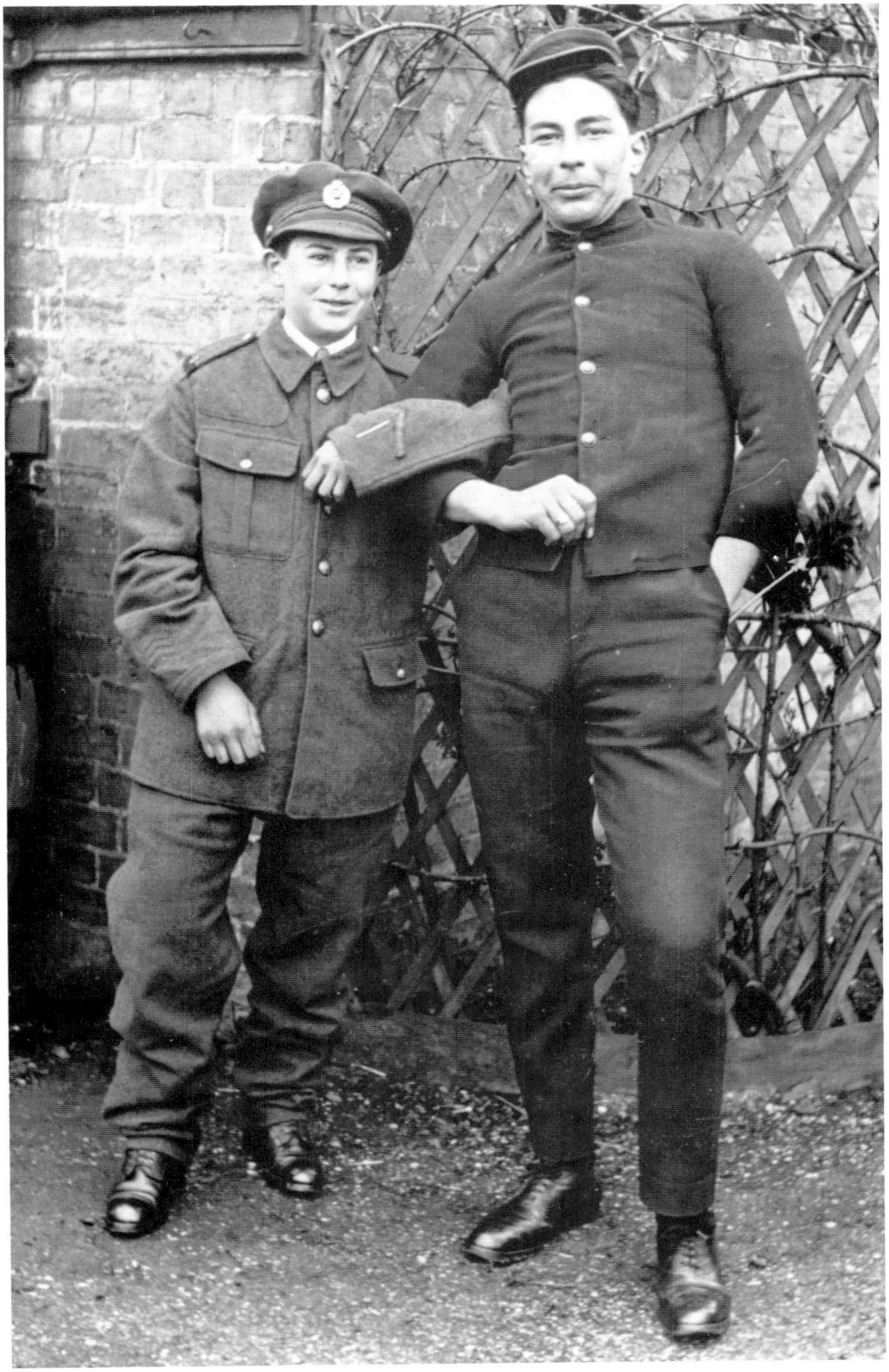

❧ I wonder if this is a true hypothesis. When work was looked on as a good thing, men, especially trained craftsmen, would have their photographs taken at their place of work surrounded by the machines they managed and the tools of their trades. When most work became repetitive and soul-destroying, they chose to be depicted at leisure. It is hard to imagine a group of workers choosing to be photographed standing beside the assembly line at Austin Rover or Rowntrees. The company might like such a photograph, but not the workers.

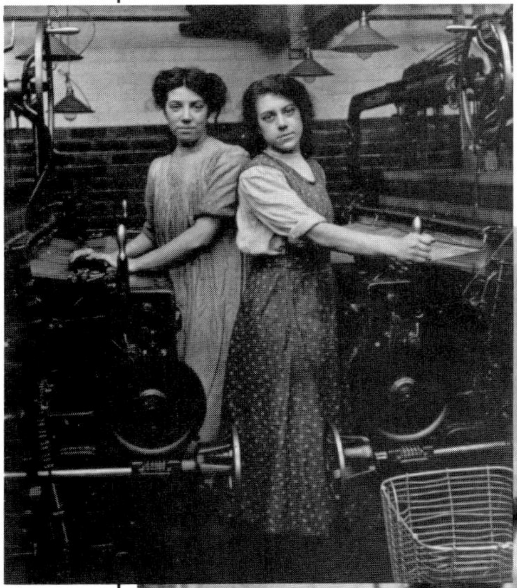

I find it difficult to cope with all those pictures you find of soldiers who fought in the war. I always wonder if they died or survived. We've only got two pictures of my Great Uncle Albert, killed during the Great War in 1916 at a village called Douchy-les-Ayettes. One shows him as an Anglican chorister, dressed in his surplice and the other in the khaki of his soldier's uniform. He was a Grenadier. All that was left of him that was recognisable, or so family tradition has it, was the palm of his hand. When they got the telegram to say that he had died, my great-grandad sat for two days in a chair, as if he was made of marble, and didn't move.

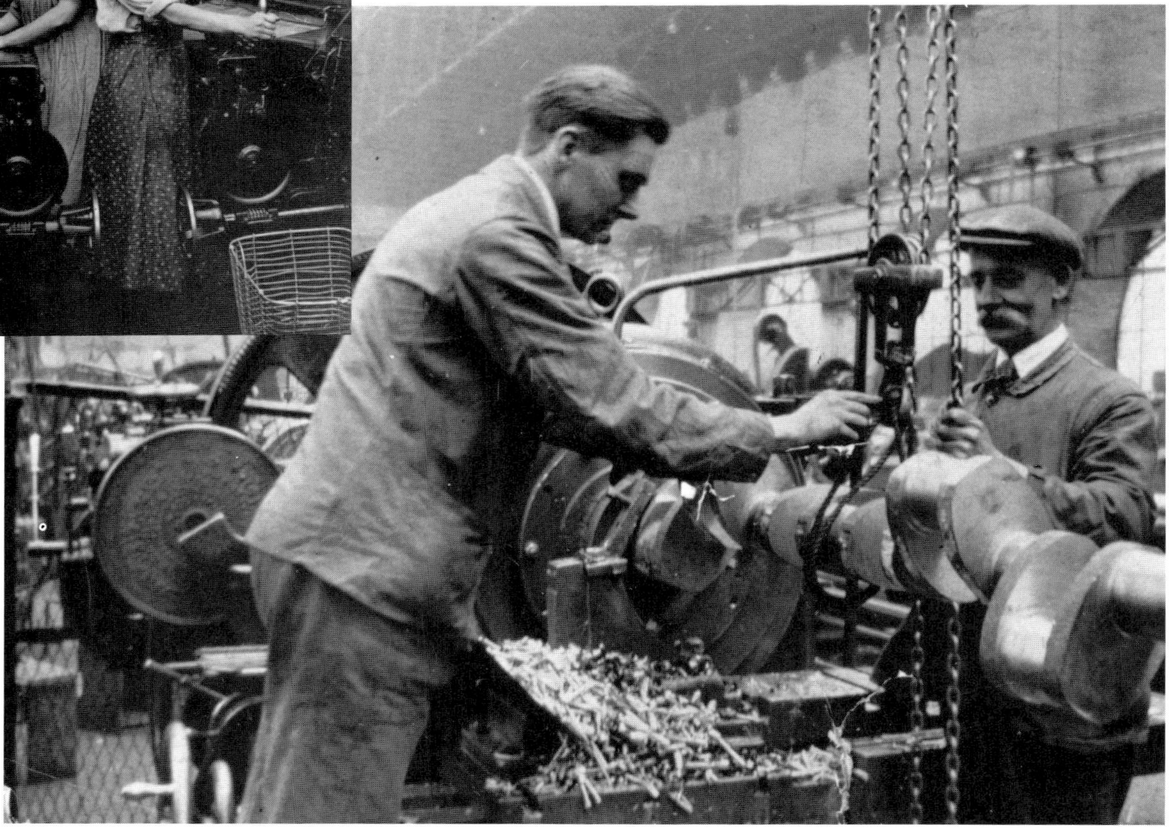

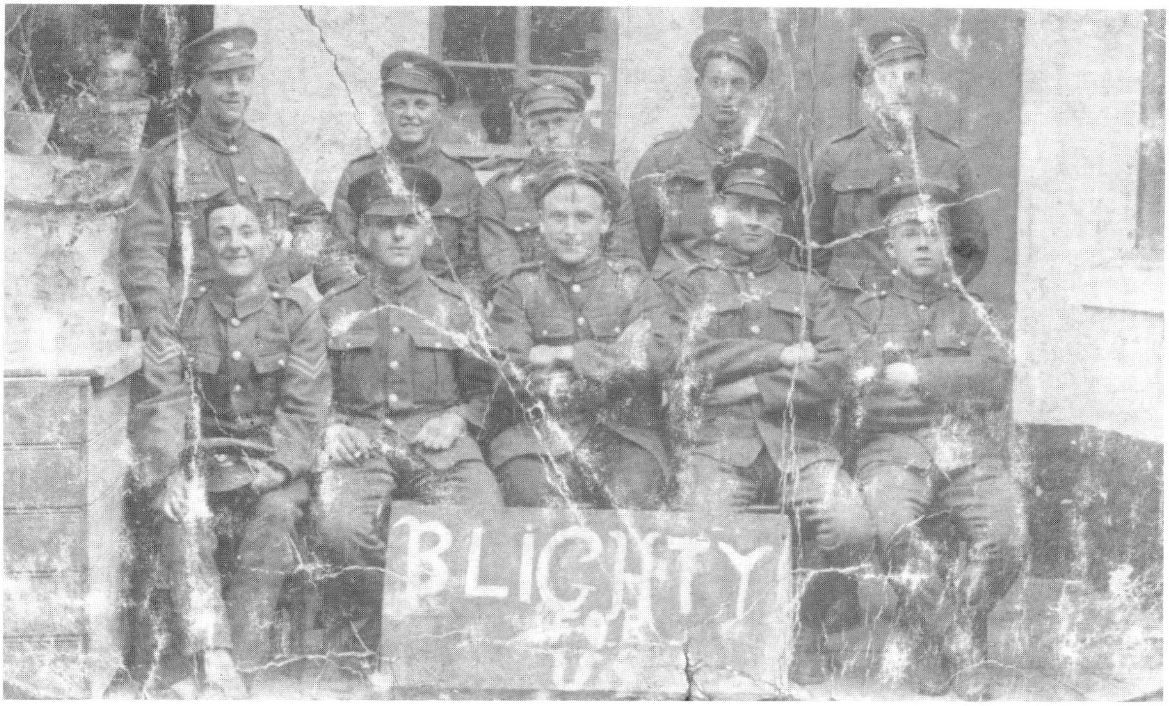
BLIGHTY

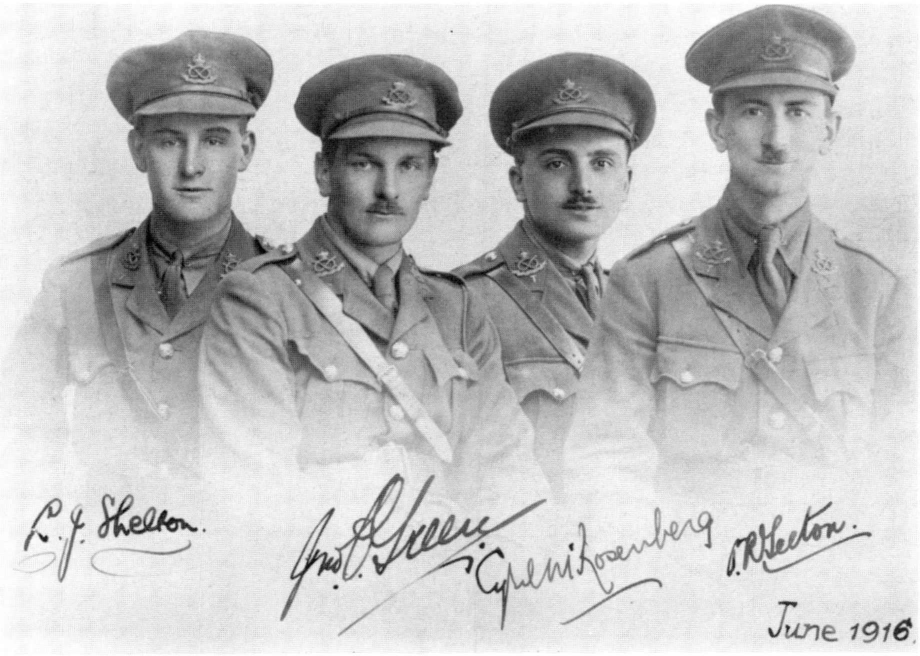
June 1916.

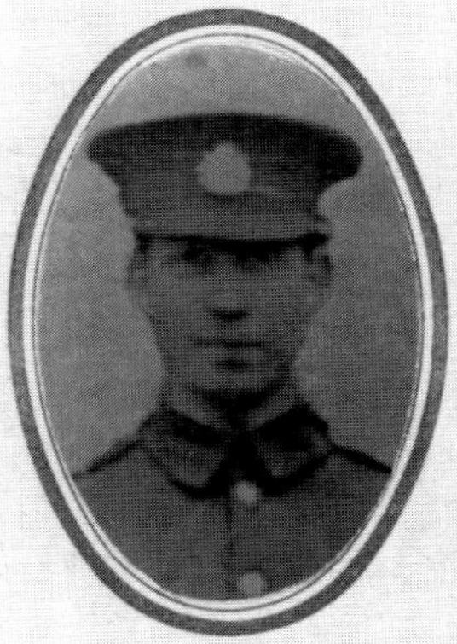

IN LOVING MEMORY OF

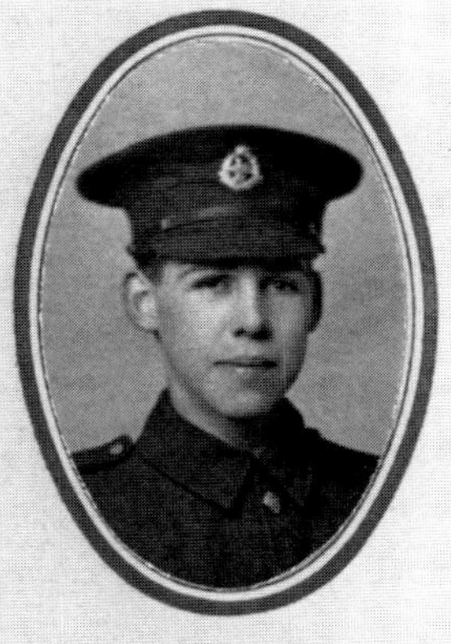

Frank Taylor Ormerod,

Aged 24 Years,

Private in the 1st Border Regiment,

Who lost his life in the Ægean Sea on the Transport "Royal Edward" on the 14th day of August, 1915.

Robert Taylor Ormerod,

Aged 18 Years,

Private in the 6th East Lancashire Regiment,

Who was killed in action on the Gallipoli Peninsula on the 9th day of August, 1915.

THEY GAVE THEIR LIVES FOR THEIR KING AND COUNTRY.

❧ My dad had an anecdote he told. At the age of five, on a wet, dull afternoon in 1915, he heard sounds of anguish coming through the terrace wall. Solidly built as it was, the Edwardian house was no barrier to the neighbour's cries. My dad remembered how his mother had tried to explain to him that the lady next door had got an official telegram which began, 'It is my painful duty to inform you ...' Even as children we had a slight shiver of understanding when we heard this story. Neighbours, after all, don't cry. But in the end, anecdotes are always about other people.

Then a couple of years past, Auntie May died. Her box of family photographs came to me. It was a treasure trove of relatives, a sudden inheritance of great aunts and great uncles. It was also a puzzle for amongst the photographs were two young men who nobody had ever mentioned. Exploring further, we found two letters. Both were to my great grandmother. One informed her of the death of her son, Robert, on 9 August 1915. Killed in action. The second advised her that her son, Frank, was missing, believed drowned, on the 14 August 1915.

Two proud photographs of lads in uniform. Two sons dead within the space of five days. A family grief so bitter no-one ever spoke of it. Suddenly, we understood the pain through the wall.

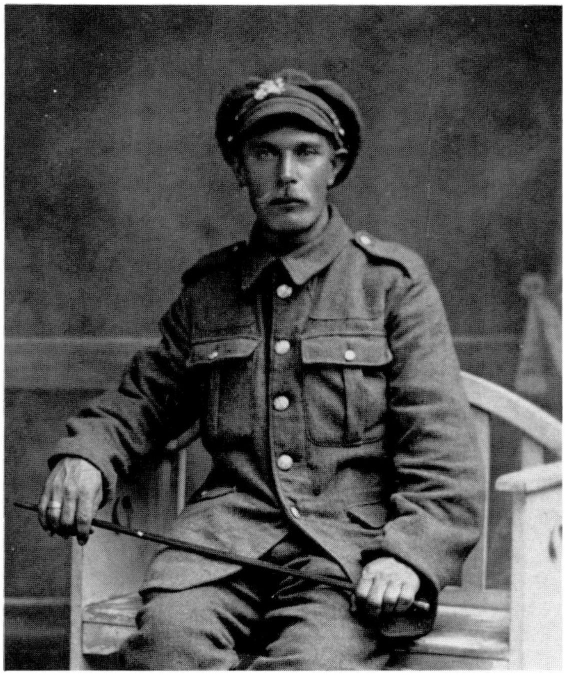
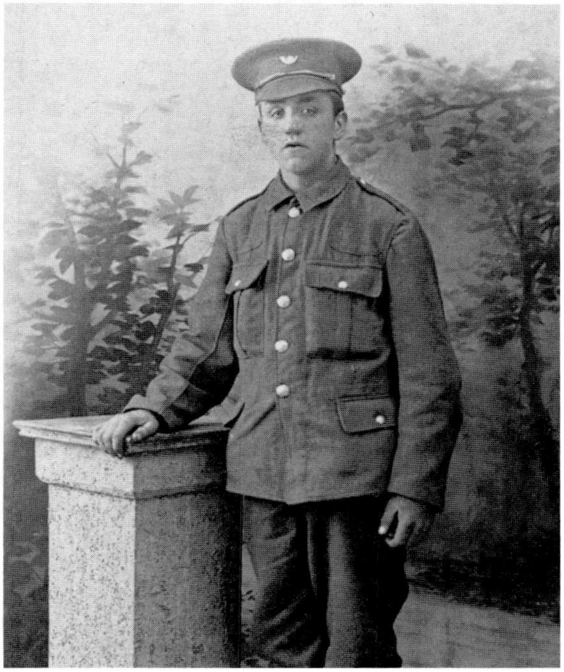
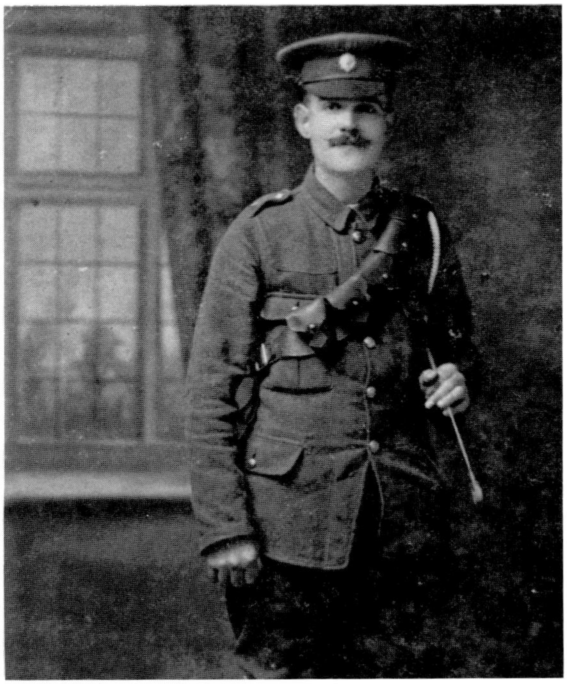
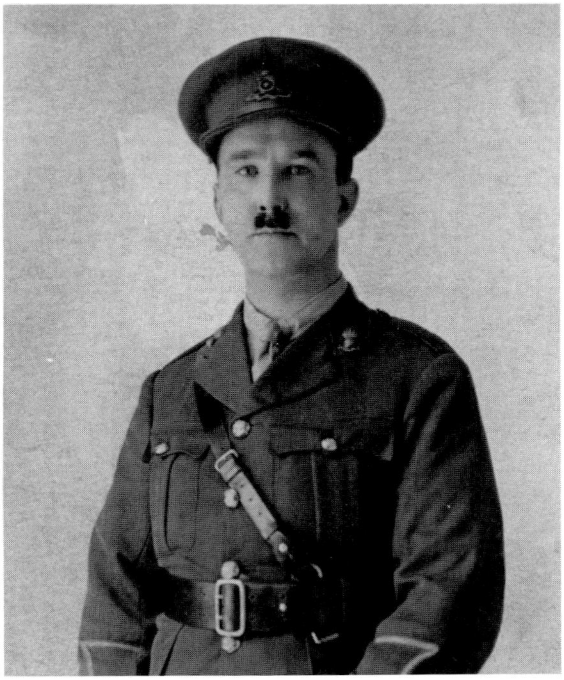

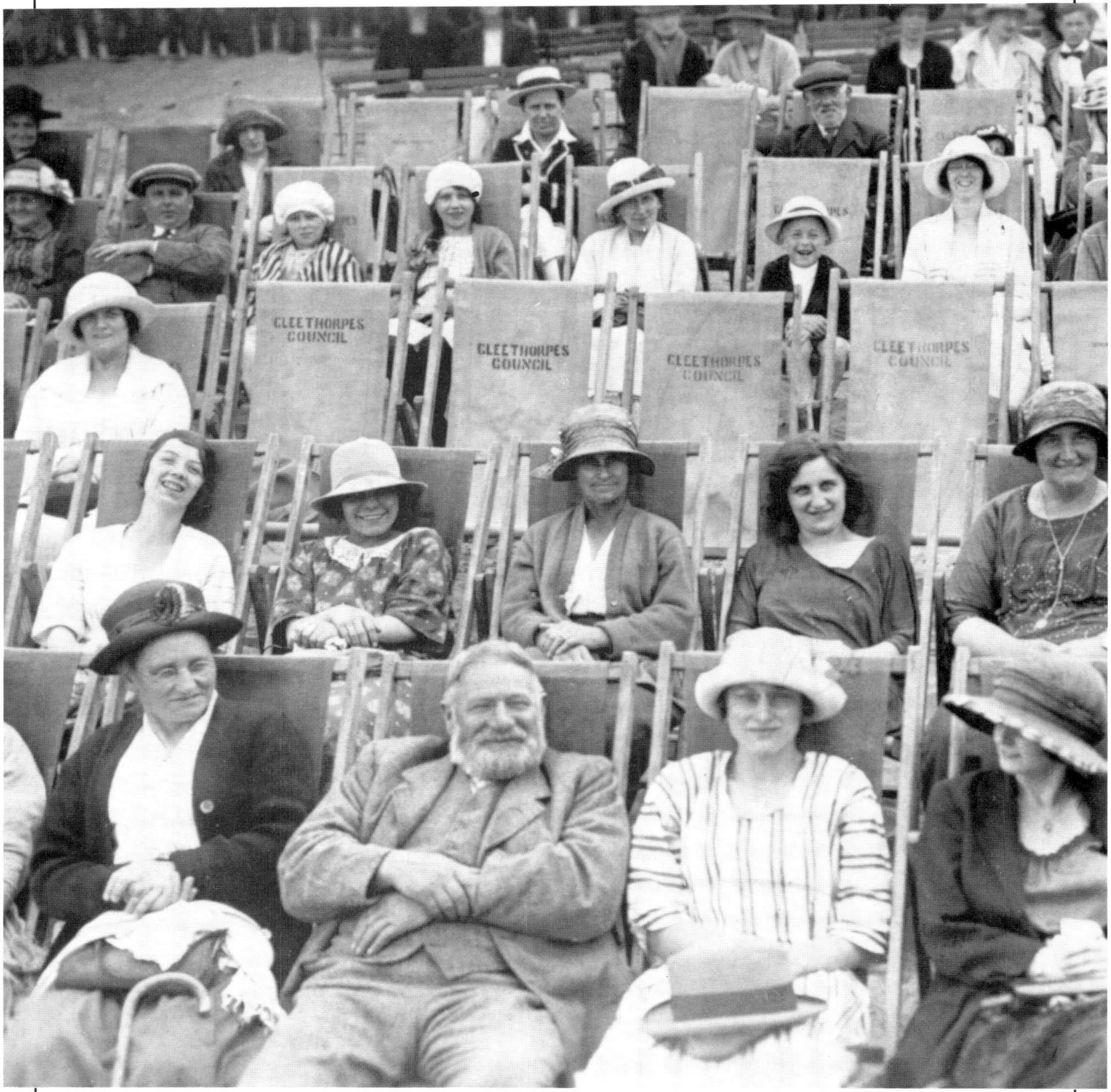
CLEETHORPES
COUNCIL
CLEETHORPES
COUNCIL
CLEETHORPES
COUNCIL
CLEETHORPES
COUNCIL

❧ Many years ago when I was little we went to Colwyn Bay on holiday. My mother spotted Lobby Lud and won the five pounds - a lot of money in those days. Someone from the paper went to take her picture but my mother thought he was a beach photographer touting for trade. This must have upset him, so he got his own back by taking a really horrible picture which appeared with a caption describing her as "middle aged". It completely spoiled my mum's pleasure in winning and indeed her whole holiday was ruined.

❧ Right from being babies my sister and I were photographed just before Christmas every year by Scrimshaw's Photographers in Leeds. This ritual carried on until I was in my early teens and Scrimshaw's either closed down or moved because of the massive redevelopment programme at the bottom of Woodhouse Lane.

It's very interesting looking back on these photos. My parents used to send them as Christmas cards to all our relatives. I guess they were very proud of us when we were growing up. In the latter years of this practice I used to dread the Scrimshaw day because I knew that the night before I would have to have my long hair set in rags so that I would have ringlets for the photos. I didn't mind the ringlets so much but when they were just full of rags they looked like sausages dangling around my head. I suppose if Mum had given them a good brushing out they'd have looked lovely and natural, but she never did. The Scrimshaw studios were over a shop and to reach them you had to climb a narrow staircase. The waiting room was very long and narrow. To keep us happy there were toys to play with. The one I remember best was a tin horse with casters under the hooves. The legs were so attached to the body that when we sat on it and jogged up and down it would move along the floor. We must have driven the waiting adults mad, endlessly going back and forth from one end of the corridor to the other.

In the studio itself all the props seemed old and very tatty yet, since photos were black and white, back-drops and props were unified and never looked drab on the prints. I remember they used to send a full set of proofs from which to choose. These were like photos but not fixed properly so they always faded beyond recognition after a few months.

DAYLIGHT STUDIOS.

The world's first photographic studio was opened in America in March 1840, less than a year after the announcement of the invention of photography. Britain's first studio was opened by Richard Beard, a former coal merchant, in March 1841, on the roof of the Polytechnic Institution in Regent Street, London. The rooftop location was to ensure as much natural light as possible. Illumination was provided by sunlight shining directly on to the subject's face. Exposures were long and having one's portrait taken was not a pleasant experience.

Improvements in processes meant that exposure times were shorter by the late 1840s. However, as much natural light as possible was still needed. A standard design for daylight studios evolved, with one wall and part of the roof being glazed. Studios usually pointed

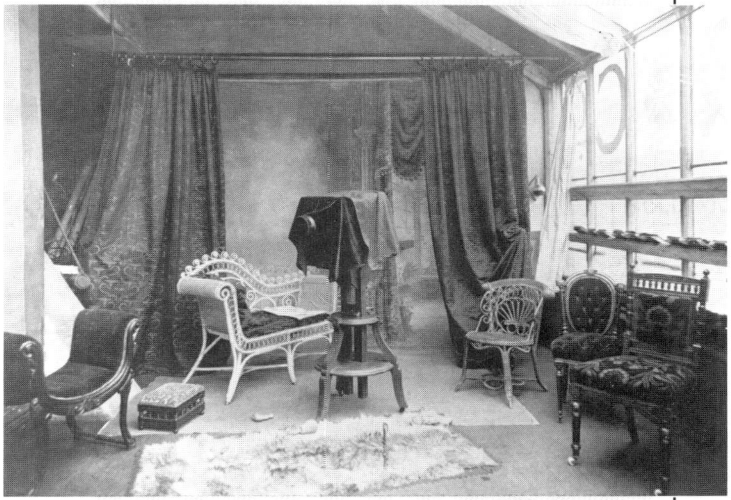

north so as to get the most satisfactory light. Daylight was controlled by using a series of blinds. This basic design remained unaltered throughout the Victorian period and well into our own century.

❧ I have a photo of when I was a young soldier in East Africa in 1945. Me and a mate are holding the head of a water buffalo that had been shot by our commanding officer. 'The Mad Major' as we called him, spotted the buffalo swimming in the bay. Eventually it was dragged ashore by the Major who had plunged into the sea, ignoring sharks which were attracted by the blood. We on shore had gathered quite a few natives who, on seeing all this meat on the hoof, didn't delay in hacking it to pieces with their porgies.

I managed to save the head and, as I am a butcher in civvy life, made some lovely tongue for the Major. He then took what remained and got the chippy to make him a shield to mount the magnificent pair of horns. Looking back on this photo brings to mind all kinds of memories of my early days as a young soldier in East Africa.

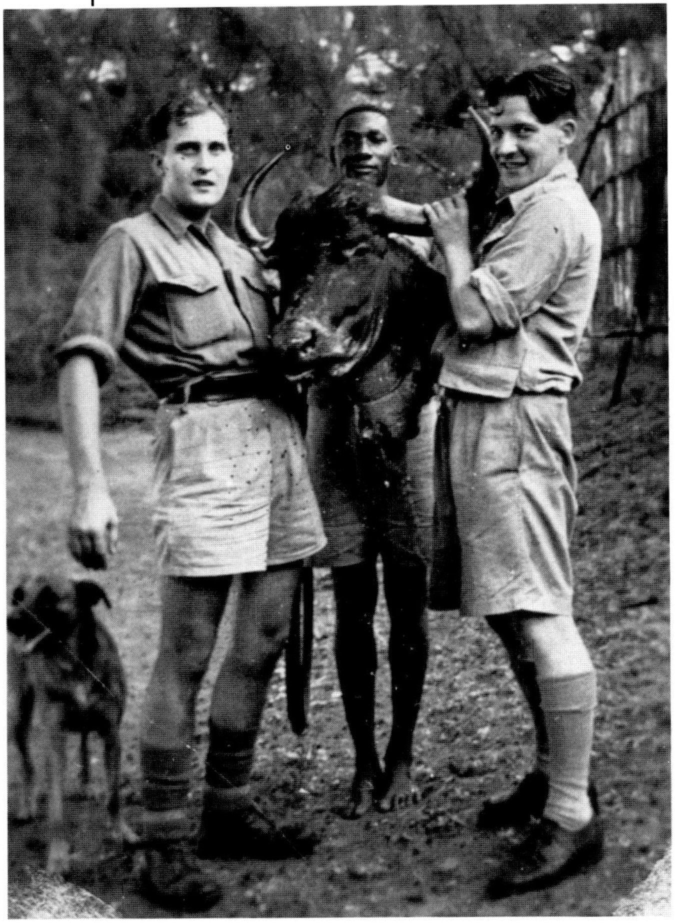

❧ Although a lot of friends and neighbours had come across, I was the first in the immediate family to travel to England. You have to remember that Trinidad had only a million people when I left in 1968. It is very small, you can easily drive across it in an afternoon.

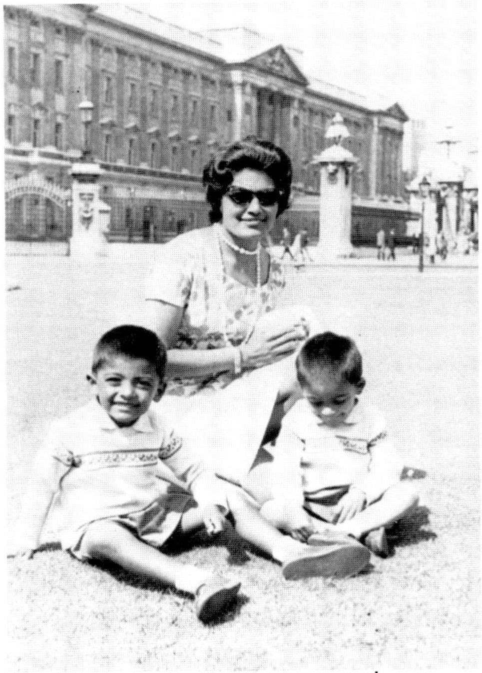

One of the first things you do when you get away is to have photographs taken in new surroundings to send back home. My mother says that my dad cried for a year after I came to England to train as a nurse. I was crying in Southampton, but you couldn't tell that from the photographs I sent back. My cousin went one step further; she took her two boys to Buckingham Palace and had her photograph taken there.

❧ One of Mum's most irritating and oft repeated maxims is that she has always treated my brother and myself alike. These two photographs are the best proof I have in how wrong she is in her assumptions. They show the first taste of school life for both of us. My brother was born before the war in Nottinghamshire where my Father worked for the Barber and Walker Mine Company. I was born after the war in Bentley, Yorkshire, where they had moved when a new mine was sunk shortly before nationalisation. My Mother, who had to give up teaching on marriage, was now persuaded to return to meet the post-war teacher shortage and I was dragged along with her. You can see from the photograph what a treat that was for me! There was a difference between Bentley Mixed Infants and Miss B's Prep school for young ladies, gentlemen - and terriers!

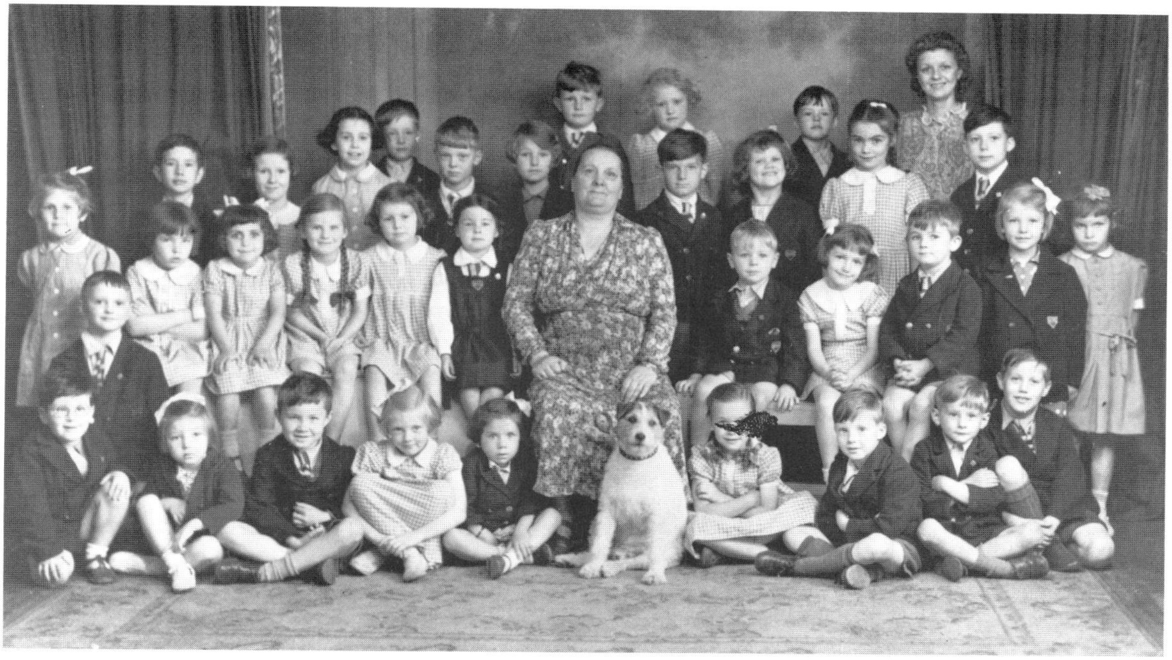

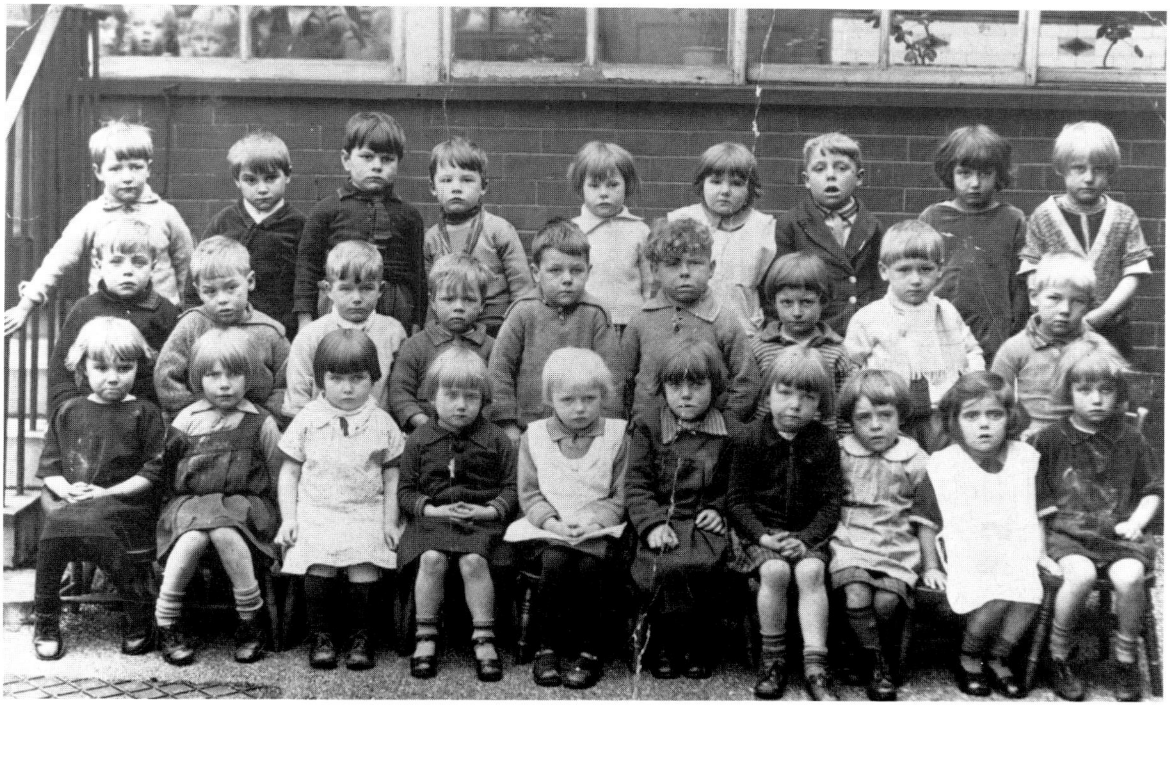

❧ In those days, in the early fifties, Meadow Dairy ran a competition. If your shop window was judged the best in the area, the head office sent down a photographer to take a picture of it. The shop girls and the manager, or in our case manageress, all lined up outside. I'm there with May Powell - she's the one in the button-up, rather than wrap-around overall - standing centre.

Moorends is hardly Doncaster, but seven of us worked in the Marshland's shop. My mother had heard that they wanted a junior and in 1952 got me the job there at 35 shillings a week. I was the general factotum. I scrubbed,

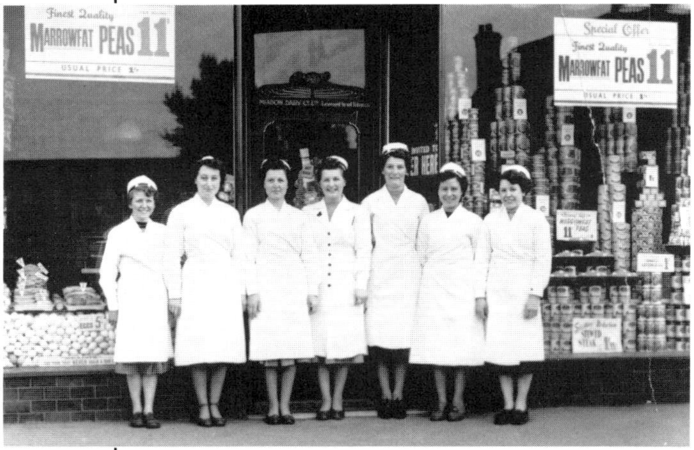

weighed the sugar into thick blue bags and cut portions of lard and butter. I also emptied the window. As a junior I was allowed to do this but filling it was a specialised task and so left to the manageress herself.

❧ Mother and Father met as students at Freiburg University.She was doing pharmacy, he was doing forestry. The wedding took place in Danzig in 1943. My father arrived from the area around Dunkirk and an uncle from the Russian Front. Just when the Nazis began to think they might lose, and as Britain was gearing up for total war; mobilising women in the Land Army and the Services, German soldiers were coming back from war zones for family celebrations.

Helmut was born a year later and my mother had to flee with her small baby from the advancing Soviet armies. By this time my father had been invalided out of the army having been shot up by the advancing Americans. He had no Nazi affiliations, spoke French, and Messkirch was in the French Occupation Zone.

His injuries meant that he had to abandon his planned career. So he became a Burgermeister instead.

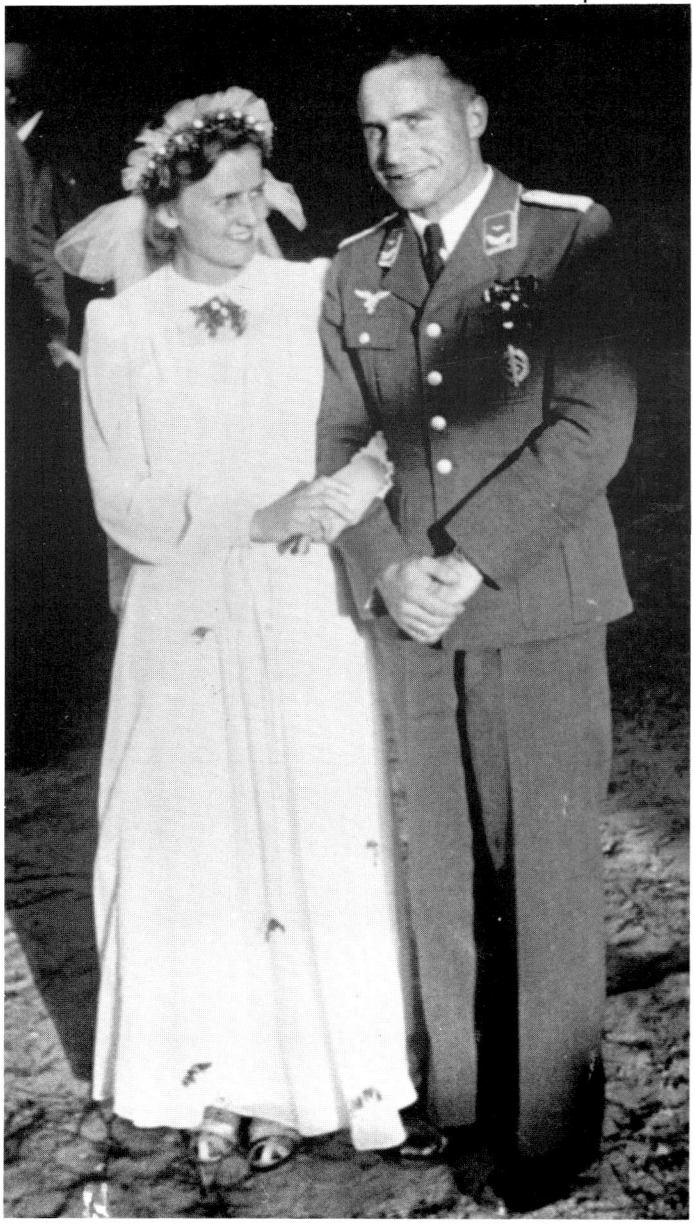

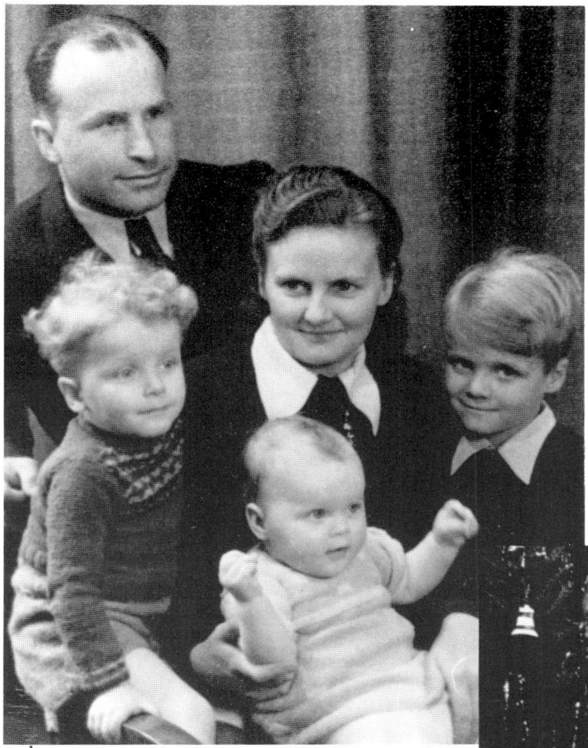

Eight years later, mother's family are in place; three boys and two girls, and we are going into the ritual of the annual family photograph in a determined way. Why our family had a professional in on Boxing Day I cannot say. Other German families didn't. Perhaps it was something to do with my father's social position. What you can see is evidence of the German Economic Miracle. The times when people scratched away for food had receded. We had already caught up with the living standards of the 1930s and were going ahead. .I didn't know at the time that mother was pregnant.Susanne was born prematurely that January and died after half an hour because there were no incubators at the local hospital. It was my first contact with death.She was a name on a little white cross on the family grave.

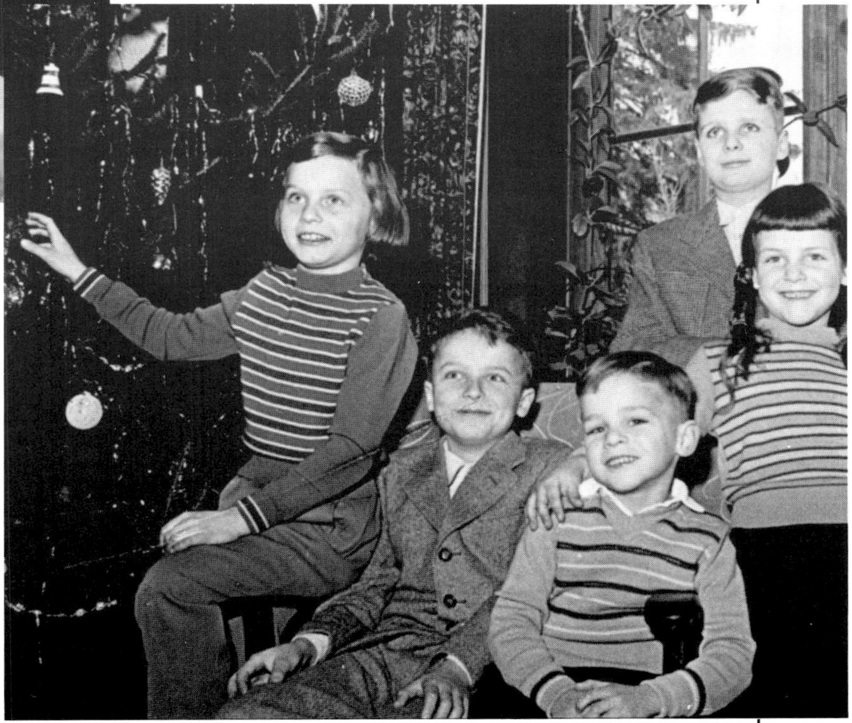

The first photograph shows him, my mother, their first three children. I am one year old. The picture was taken at the village photographic studio and it became a family tradition to have an annual formal picture. Originally studio photographs, eventually they were taken at Christmas at our house. When I was about twelve a local freelance photographer took over. His name was Franz King and he liked the American sound of his second name. When he lost his right hand in an accident he managed to continue his work.He was fitted with an artificial hand in a leather glove.It held a morbid fascination for us children.

It's the Christmas after I'd passed my A levels at the ripe old age of twenty. The norm was nineteen but I took a year out to live with a family in up-state New York. I returned with a good command of English and a very pronounced American accent.The dress I'm wearing has seen a significant alteration. I had it made for my Abitur graduation ceremony at a posh Catholic girls' school. In just six months the hemline has risen considerably. I was very much a citizen of the world. I bought my shoes in Paris and was moving more and more towards the political left while still retaining an affectionate attachment to fashion magazines and good hairstyles.

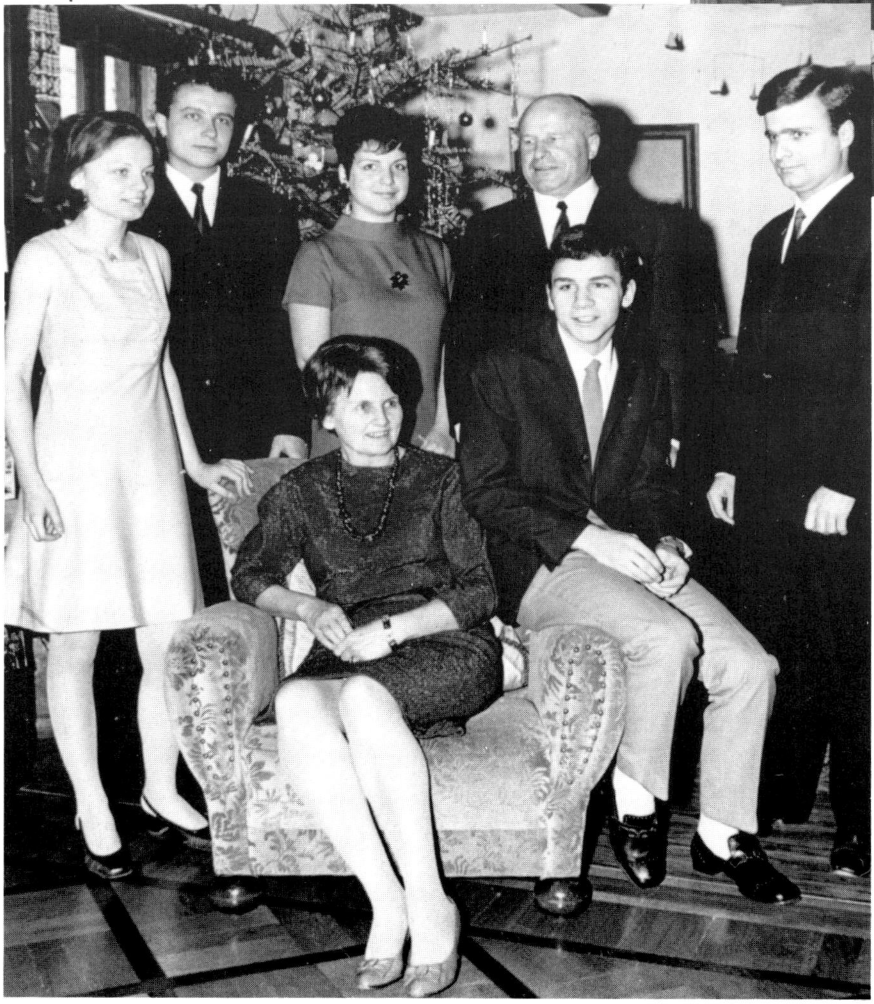

Two years later, on this picture, we are children of nature. The glorious revolutions of 1968 had broken out in my first year at Freiburg University, our hair had grown longer by

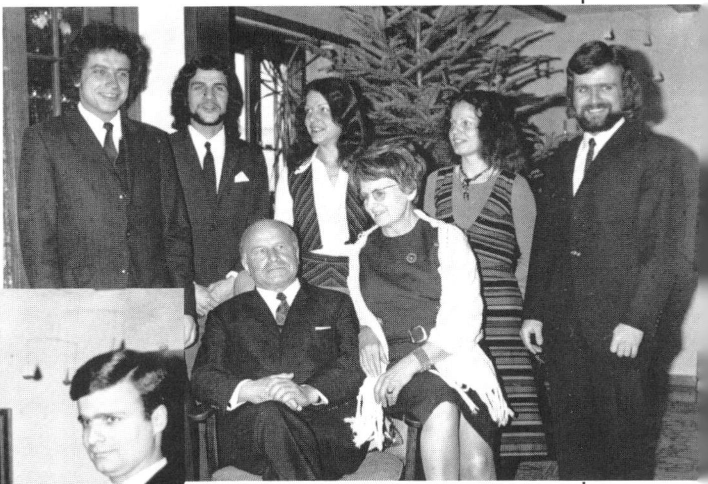

the day and the boys had sprouted beards to match their radicalism. My mother and father remain solidly conservative as they sit there in our living room; the children are not; rather they are peace people who read Germaine Greer and Kate Millett. I am getting ready to go to England.

My husband is English and we have three children who we bring up to say that they are European. All the family have become involved in the professions or the arts. On this photograph of mother's extended family there are teachers, dentists, a doctor and people involved in other aspects of the medical profession. What distinguishes the English from the others is the level of their pay. Mother remains politically indifferent; as a girl she saw where politics got you. Father is dead. The rest have doubts about reunification, think European and, having moved on from the Peace Movement, are deeply

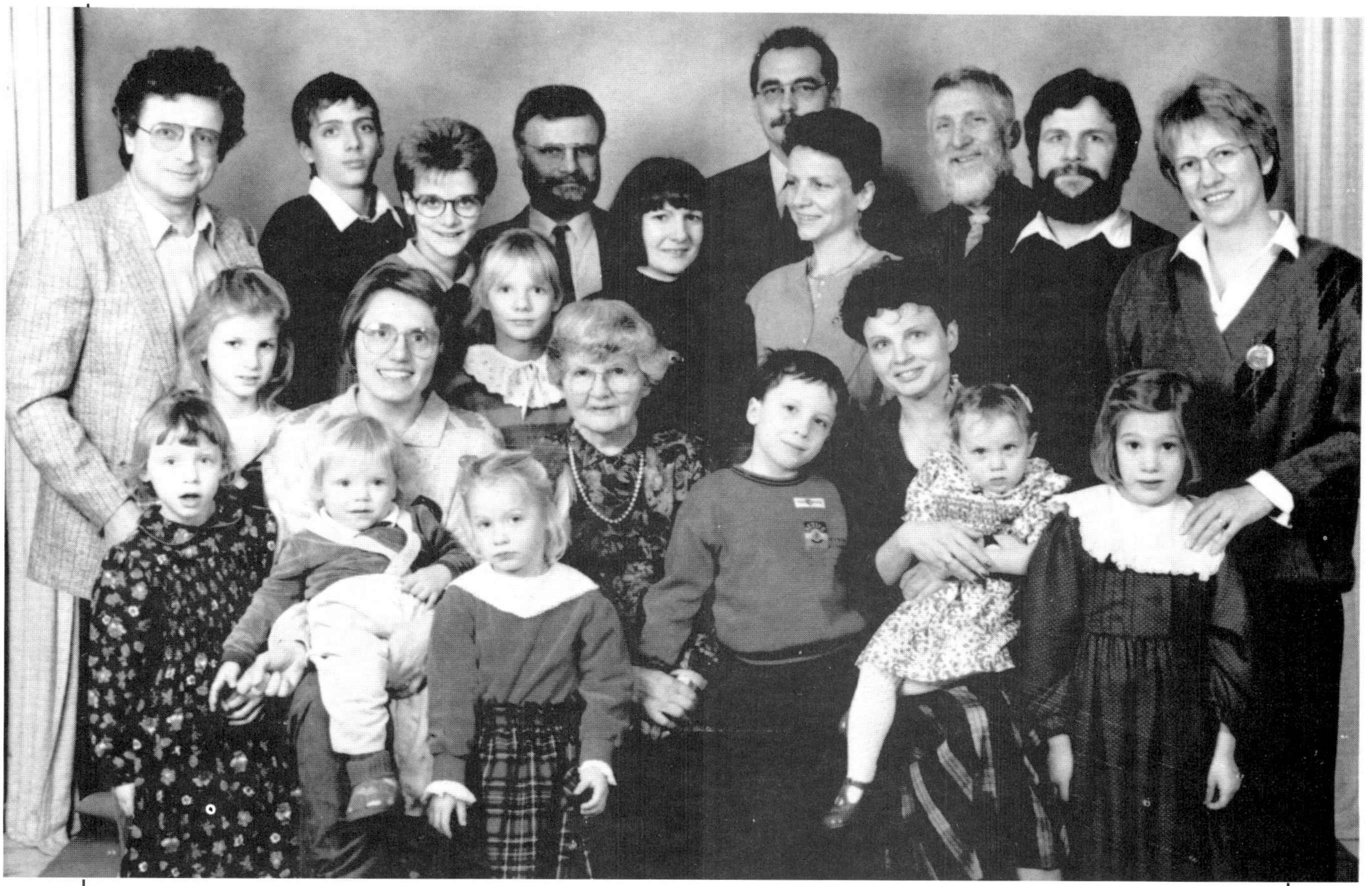

concerned about the environment. If you look carefully at these photographs, then you see the last forty years of European history emerge.

I hadn't looked at my more distant photos for quite some time.They took me on a slightly nostalgic journey and released many memories. Our children are fascinated by this proof that I too was once a child with a dirty face. Just as I was fascinated when I saw my father as a two year old in a lace dress such as was worn by little boys in the first decade of this century.

When Hannah was a baby I sat and watched her new-born, but ancient, little face transform. One minute I could see Great Aunt Hilda, the next my sister, Verena. Looking at my old family photos I can see glimpses of all of my children thirty odd years before they were born.

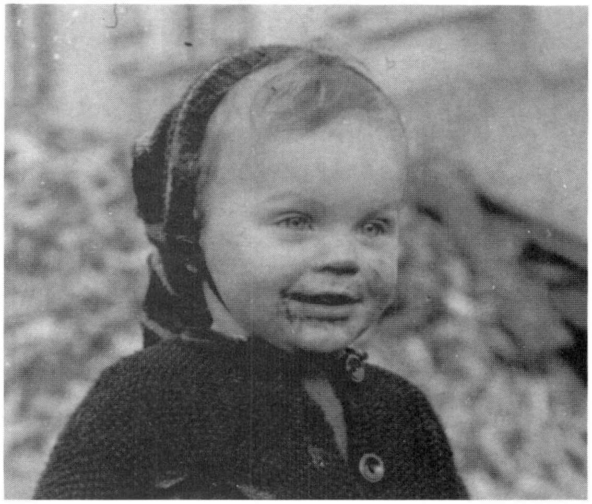

❧ When we were kids, Dad took us to Blackpool but he never took snaps. When we had moved off he did what everyone in our street was doing, booked a holiday on Glideaways and took himself off on a Six Capitals foreign holiday. It was to be the holiday of a lifetime and so that he could have a reminder of it be bought himself a camera. The snaps he brought back - and they were snaps - weren't particularly good. A lot were of people I would never meet, and he wouldn't meet again either, standing in groups around a courier on the steps of a one-night-stop watering place at the back of Brussels. Others showed him and Martin, an ex-German prisoner of war, who was there as a sort of unofficial translator, at great distances from the camera standing in front of Baroque buildings whose roofs were cut off.

The pictures themselves were small but that didn't matter because it was what he did with them that counted. Instead of sticking them into an album with a one line explanation he wrote an elaborate diary and pasted them into the text. In context the photographs gained something but I have to admit that beside the coloured postcards they looked a bit inadequate. He must have felt the same because as time passed he seems to have stopped taking his own pictures.

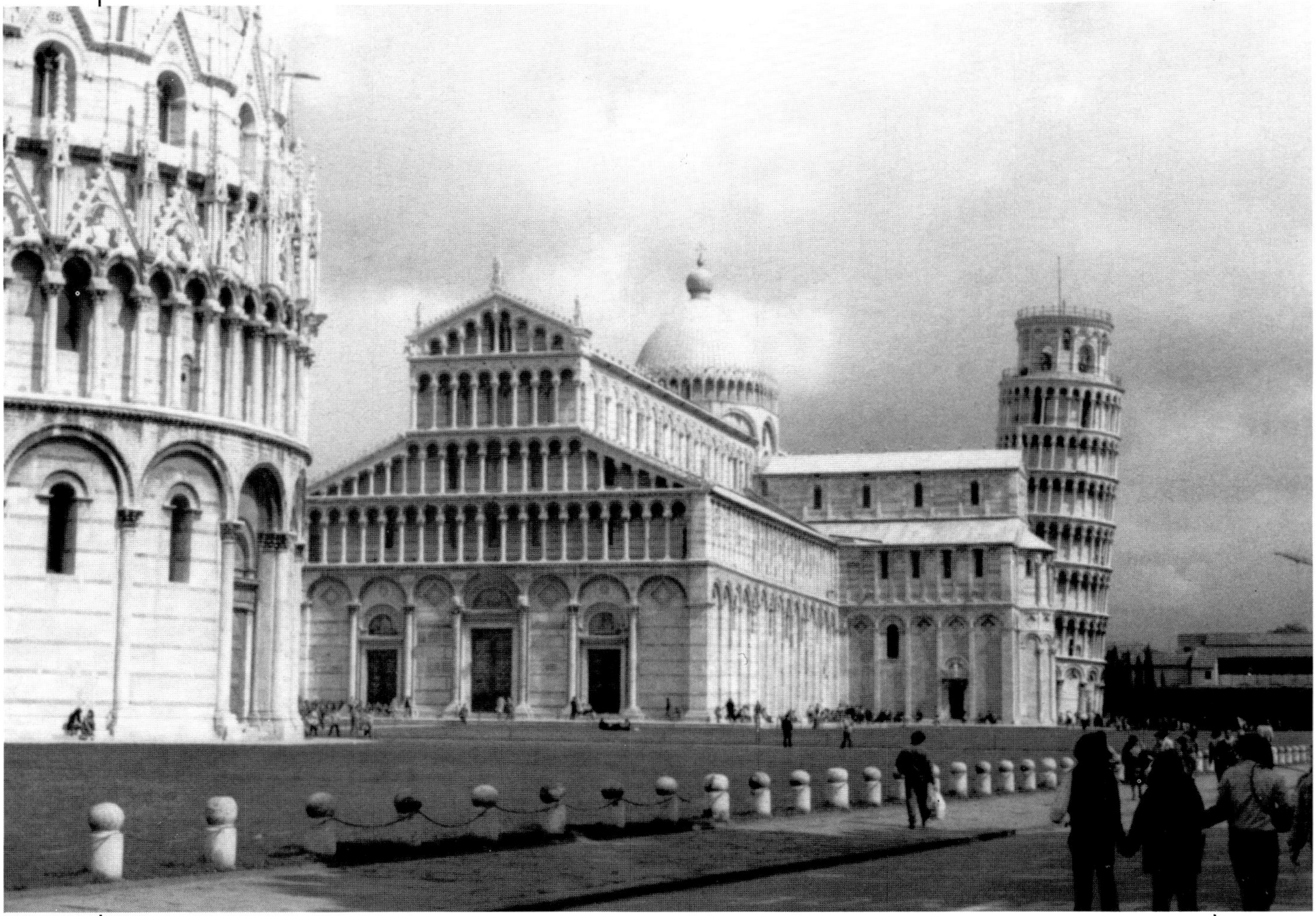

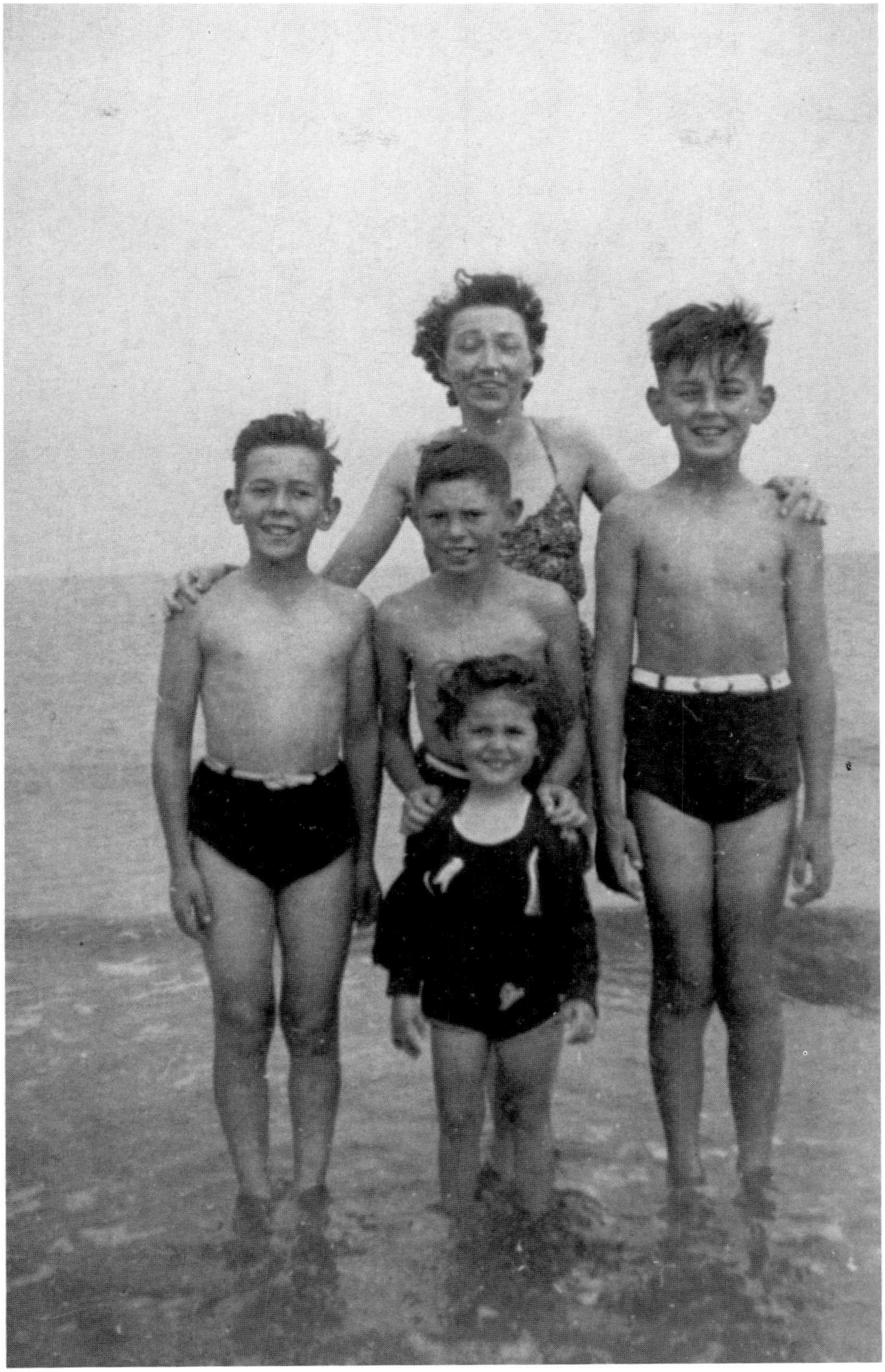

❧ We've got enough shots of places we do not remember to fill an album. When you are on holiday you waste so much film taking pictures of scenes which you think will be significant. When you get home you cannot even remember where they were taken. It's as if something wholly out of your control has taken over.

If they were pictures of monasteries or castles or even streets, it would be okay, but more often than not they are views out of the window of a hotel bedroom. If you look intently at this shot of an apartment in Tenerife, or it might have been Sicily - we went to both places that year - you can just see me smiling to camera.

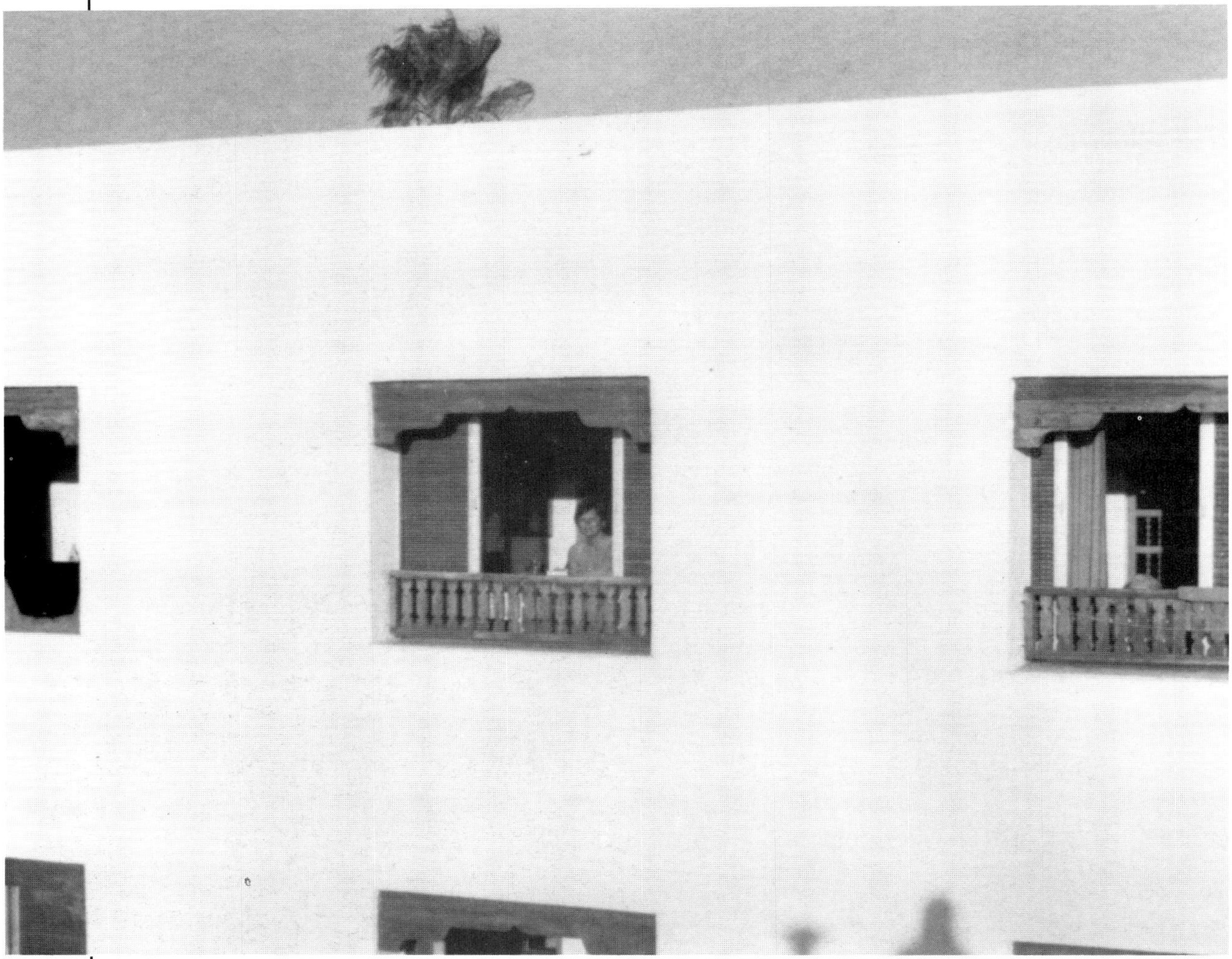

❧ I always wanted to take some shots of royalty. Last September the chance came; Princess Diana was to visit Shipley Resource Centre. She was due to arrive at ten thirty, so I got there at eight. Since I was the first there, I had plenty of time to check my Nikon FG20.

It promised rain and grey clouds trundled across the sky; not very good weather for a Royal visit.

Barriers had been erected to keep at bay the expected onlookers and those poor sods without a press pass. I got a good spec to the right of the wide entrance with a good view both of the road and of the forecourt of the resource centre. Gradually I was joined by others. By ten o'clock I was surrounded by hundreds of happy, eager sightseers and dozens of amateur and press photographers. Everyone was in good spirits; I could see happiness on hundreds of faces. One boy was doing a roaring trade selling tiny flags. Then the police arrived, some in civvies. You know what I mean; suits and sports jackets, personal radios grasped in strong hands. The uniformed officers lined the road and traffic was diverted.

That was when I lost my place. Plain clothes police officers insisted we were too close to the entrance, so we were all moved to behind the barriers. The idiots! There was no chance anyone was going to cause trouble, not today. Making it plain that we were unhappy at the intrusion, we moved to the other side of the entrance and pressmen took our places. Then I saw a perfect spot. It was on top of the stone wall which surrounded the resource centre. By this time the police were in a high state of alert. I clambered up followed by a dozen others who played copy cat.

A voice shouted, "She's here!" and up the road glided a Daimler. The police motorcycle outriders added an air of tension, so big and powerful. Everyone stood with mouths agape, as the cavalcade approached.

The roar from the crowd amazed me and, I have to admit, I had a lump in my throat. Professional photographers were hopping about all over the place. What a sight! Children shouted and their laughter rang out above the din. Applause broke out. The princess got out of her car and I stood firm on top of the wall. The bobbies had given up because all eyes were on the Princess. It's true what they say; she is very lovely. Her smile could melt the heart of the devil. Her eyes flashed, her cheeks were flushed, her stunning polka dot costume drew the admiration of all who had waited so patiently.

I shot half a roll of film in no time. Then she went inside for tea with the day patients in the centre. We waited and waited. We chatted away. We pushed the press off the wall; "This is our spot, mate. We got here first. Shove off!"

Suddenly she came out again, unveiled a plaque, met the mayor, shook hands, kissed children and even kissed an elderly man. I got that one. I also shot a frame of an Asian lady who was holding her child up high. It was a good shot. Then I spotted an old lady in a fawn coloured raincoat. Her face was lined with age and her hair like snow. She waved her little Union Jack flag from side to side. I snapped her just as she looked towards me.

ROYAL PHOTOGRAPHS.

The first 'official' photographs of members of the Royal Family were taken on the 17 May and 1 July, 1860. The photographer was John Mayall and the subjects Queen Victoria and her Consort, Prince Albert. Mayall's request for permission to sell copies of the portraits was granted and for the first time the real features of the Royal Family were brought before the general public. Approximately 100,000 copies of these photographs were eventually sold.

Mayall profited enormously from his royal coup as,indeed, he did from all his subsequent royal portrait sittings. In later life he became, for a short time, the Mayor of Brighton.

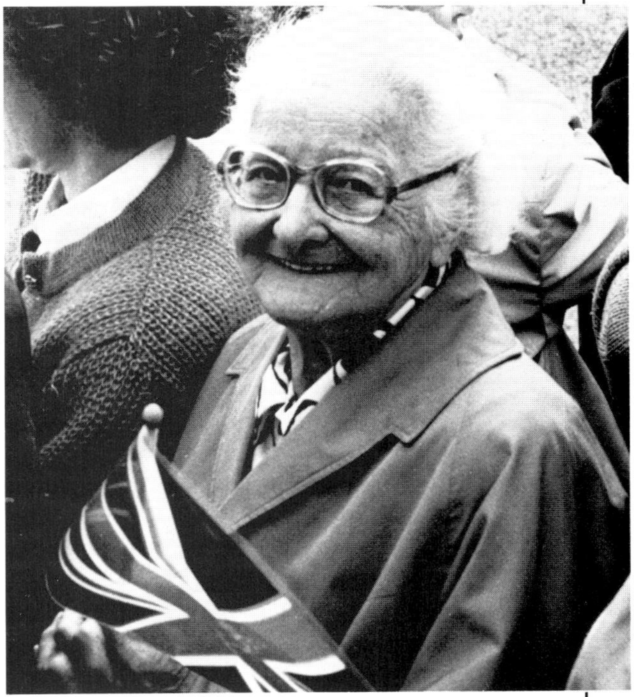

As long as I live I will never forget the atmosphere on that day. What the Princess does, she does well, and she knows it. She is a credit to our country, but then I'm a royalist.

❧ One morning I opened the curtains to discover that the British Union Party had graffiti-ed my windows. I found that detail out later in a scary telephone call in which they threatened to have a go at me and the children. We had been displaying Peace posters.

I cleaned if off but, a week later, received a return visit. Someone was watching me. I decided to go for the maximum publicity and called in the press. Somewhere in the newspaper archives there is a photo of me cleaning my windows. I also took a full frontal of the window, a reminder of the week in which our house became part of a political debate.

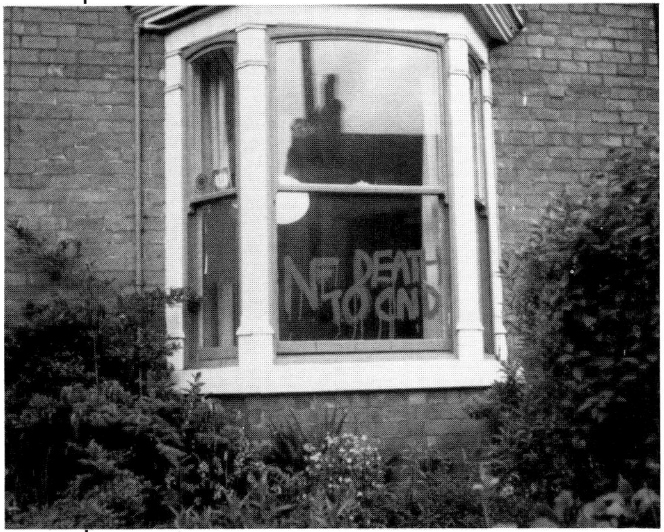

❧ I took my new German camera on CND and anti-apartheid marches in the early sixties. We seemed to have trudged over much of Tyneside in all weathers. I especially remember a cold, damp February march from North Shields to Newcastle through the working class districts along the Tyne. There was desultory singing of the new Ban the Bomb songs. *H-Bomb Thunder, We Don't Want Polaris* and *Family of Man*. The empty streets of Byker, Walker and Wallsend seemed pretty deaf to our straggly band of Quakers, older CP-ers and newly recruited youngsters who shouted, "Neither Washington nor Moscow, but International Socialism! "

I snapped away at the beginning of the march in a large and desolate park in North Shields where people were still chatty and cheerful, and again at the end on Newcastle Town Moor when they were footsore, exhausted and perhaps a wee bit disappointed.

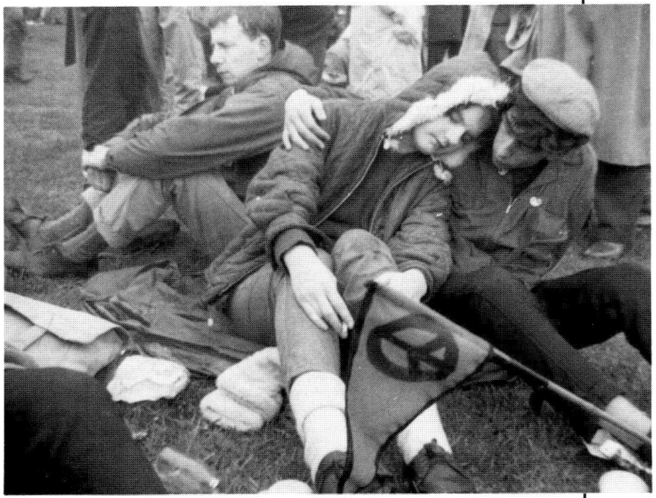

❧ If you are a guest inJapan you get overwhelmed by their generosity. The Japanese take a lot of photographs and pass them on to you, so when I returned my baggage was filled not with fans, rice bowls and chopsticks, but with wedges of photographic mementos of the visit. Me trying to go native and dressed by my host's wife in one of her best kimonos; me in the company of three managing directors - all in their twenties - looking at a trouser pressing machine; me in a boardroom waiting for something to happen. Me, me, me. I seem to be on every picture bar one. This is of a ruined stone building with a domed roof. It is set in parkland behind a modern fence and in the foreground someone I had not met is wandering off the picture.

This building stood immediately under the point at which they exploded the Hiroshima bomb. No-one would take me to see the museums dedicated to the people who died on that day in 1945 or who have died since that event. They said that those were there to remind the Japanese about the horrors of war, places to which they brought generations of fifteen-year-old school children. I was shown what remained of one of the victims, though. The flash from the nuclear device was so intense that his or her shadow was etched onto a bleached wall.

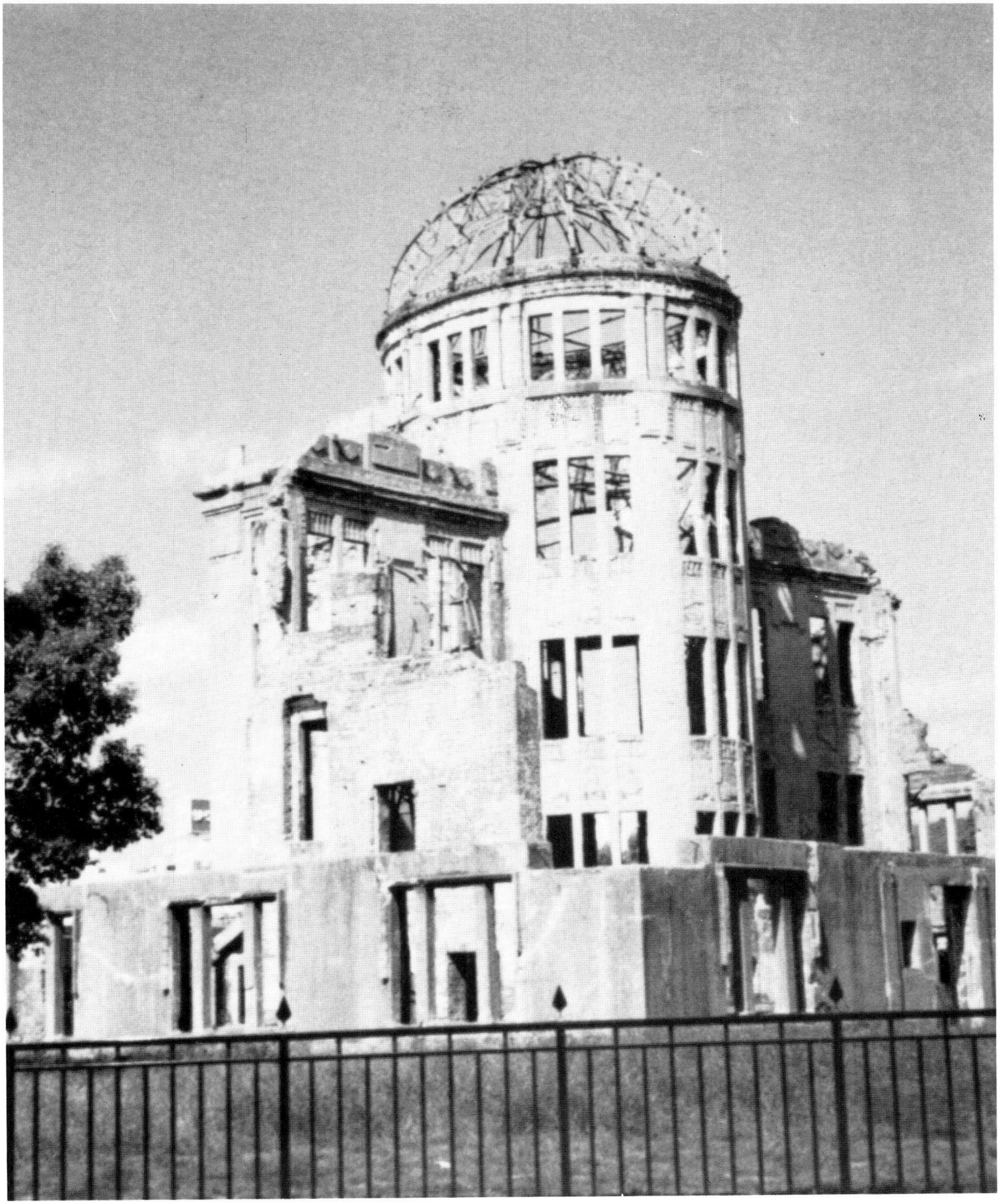

❧ I'll always remember Steve saying, "Bloody Hell!" as we came over the bridge into Fryston. I had never heard him swear before but then the last time he had seen the colliery village the canteen had been there and so had the workshops, pit head baths, offices and the winding gear; all the infrastructure of a working pit. Now, eighteen months later, all there was was a field of shale. But then the same was true of Glass Houghton, Whitwood, Wheldale; in fact all of the Castleford pits. When the strike was over these so called 'uneconomical pits' were flattened by British Coal.

There's something in the Bible about fertile fields being strewn with salt. That's how it was. Before they did it, though, they had to collapse the winding gear. This took on almost symbolic status. Men from all over came and took pictures of their pits coming down. At Fryston there was even a German television crew in attendance.

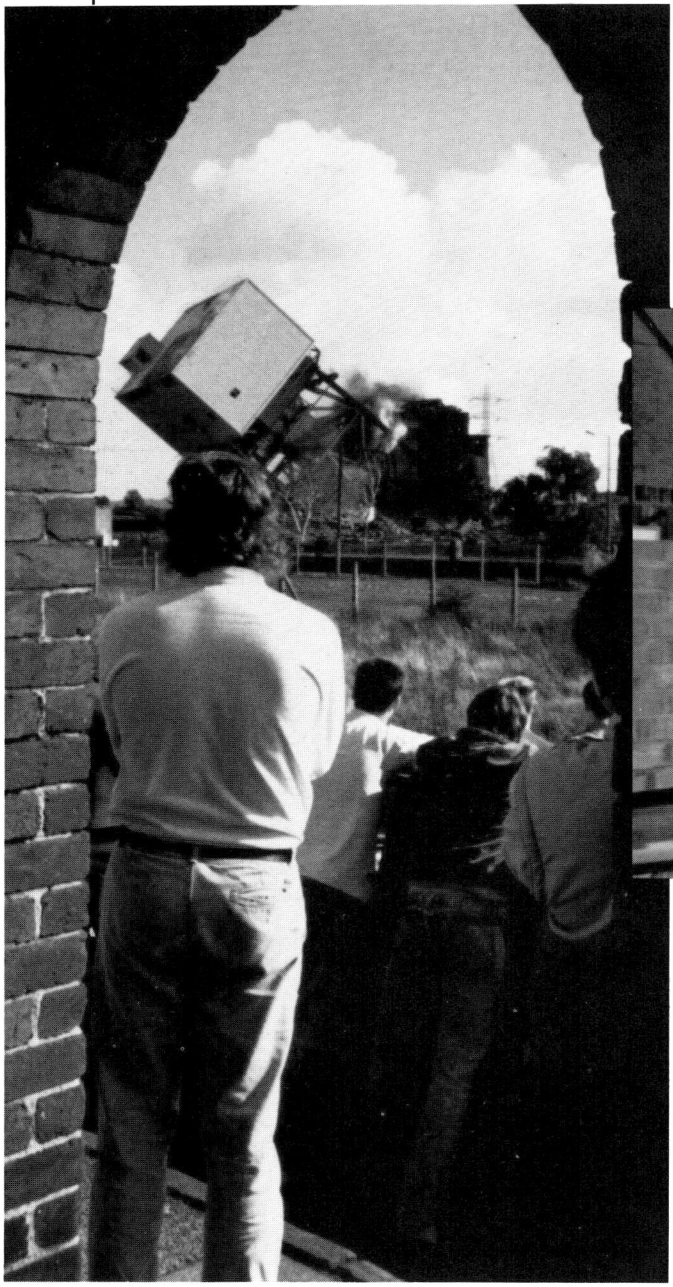

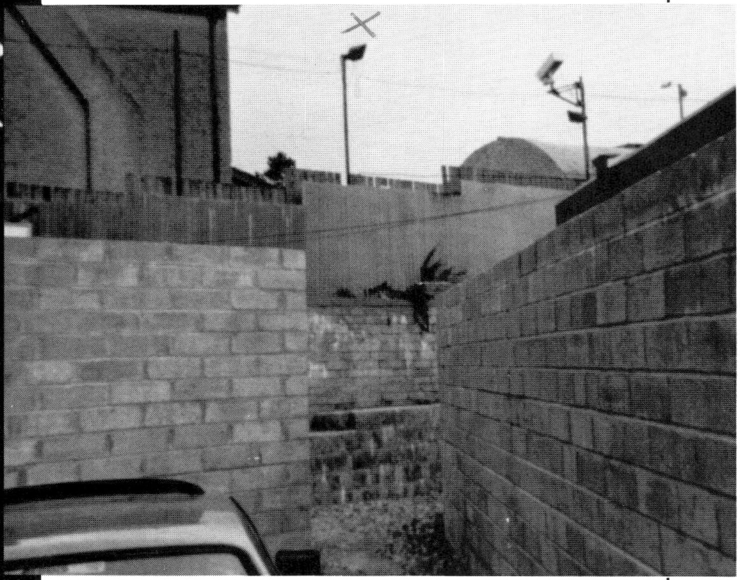

❧ Like all RUC stations in Northern Ireland, Castlederg is surrounded by a high security fence to stop sniper attacks. In front of this there is also barbed wire. This is to stop people leaving explosives near to the main perimeter. The gap between the barbed wire and the fence is covered by surveillance cameras. Below the light, at the place marked by a cross, is where the IRA left a holdall packed with plastic explosive and, just for good measure, ball bearings. The bomb was timed to go off at noon - At the time I was stood where I took this photo from. The bomb failed to go off - thank God! Otherwise up to thirty men, including myself, would be no more.

❧ Andropov was in control in Russia and things were relaxing when I went out as a student in 1983. I had bought my camera solely to record my days there and took a number of very interesting photographs. Some were even good. One, for instance, showed the queue at Lenin's tomb and captured both the size of the crowd and the coldness of the day. I am not sure just how many pictures I could have taken without some form of censorship.

I did not expect to be allowed to take pictures of government buildings or military installations but I was surprised when I was prevented from taking a picture of a woman in a market stall in Moscow selling fruit. There I was snapping away when suddenly I was aware of a man's hand approaching the lens. He told me that photography was forbidden.

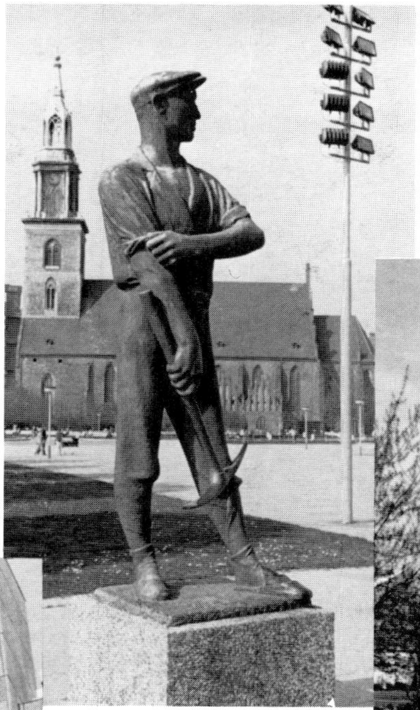

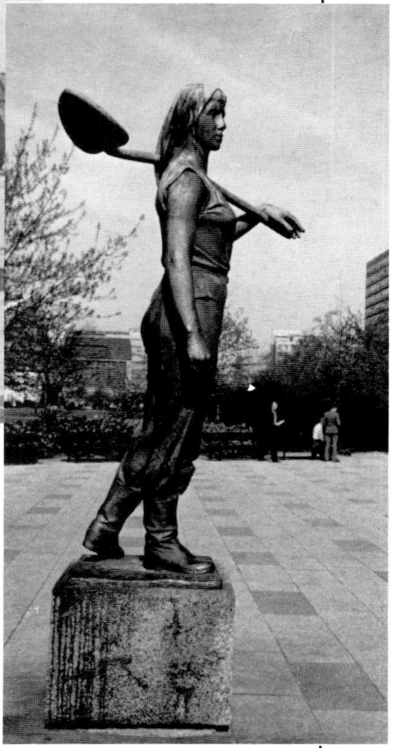

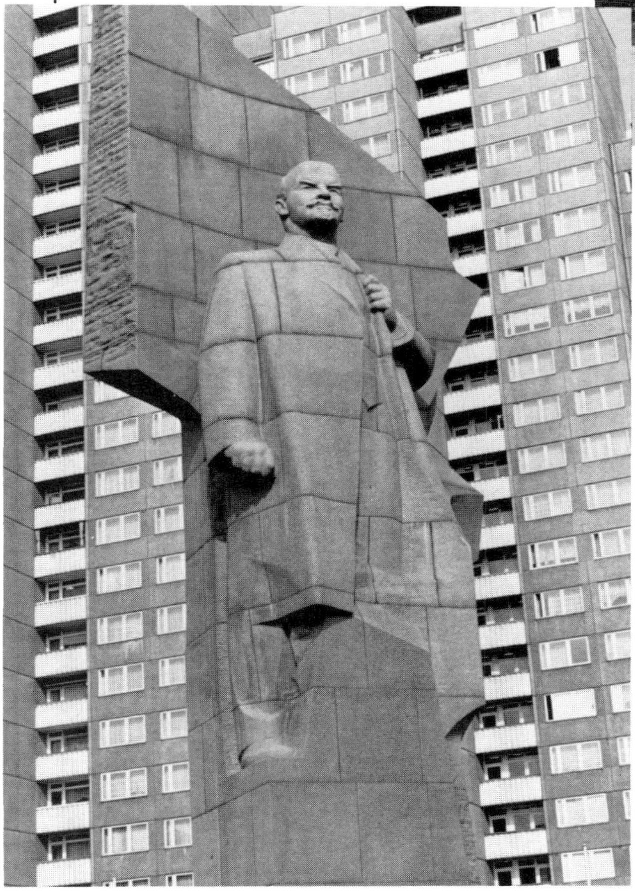

❧ Friedrichstrasse Station, East Berlin, about ten days before the fall of the old regime. It was chaos; huge crowds of East German pensioners with temporary exit permits, Polish traders going to sell goods for hard currency in the West, and the odd visiting Westerners like ourselves. The barriers which penned the crowd gradually narrowed to smaller and smaller spaces. There were no officials to control the crowd. My wife was getting more and more claustrophobic, and we were trapped behind an old gypsy woman with five big suitcases like her own personal Berlin Wall. The GDR's old regime had lost its grip, and German efficiency-cum-socialist organisation had failed.

When we finally reached the point where papers were inspected, I totally forgot the advice I'd been given 'Keep camera films above the level of the barriers where the X-ray metal detectors are'.
The result was that when I got home and got five films developed, only about three pictures out of the whole lot were visible, the rest were fogged.

Maybe that sums up how I feel about the GDR .

❧ In May 1989 my daughter and I spent a week in the old city of Dubrovnik, staying in the only hotel inside its traffic-free walls. We hardly left the city and walked every alleyway, saw all its treasures of architecture and art and felt, as far as visitors can, part of the city's life. We woke to the sound of the market stalls being set up below our window and watched the colourful carpets of fruit, vegetables and flowers spread along the trestles under the hands of black-swathed country women. Each evening, before dinner in our prettiest dresses, we joined the crowds on the broad marble streets. Later we sat by the harbour, twinkling with lights, drinking coffee and local liqueurs.

One afternoon we heard a jolly oompah-ing and round the next corner saw a small procession of dignitaries and children led by a local brass band. We never did find out what the ceremony was all about but I snapped those handsome young men with their bulging cheeks so intent on the music under their noses.

During the recent shelling of Dubrovnik I got out my photos and wondered . Which side were they on? Were they on opposite sides killing each other or lobbing shells into that beautiful city? Where are they all now?

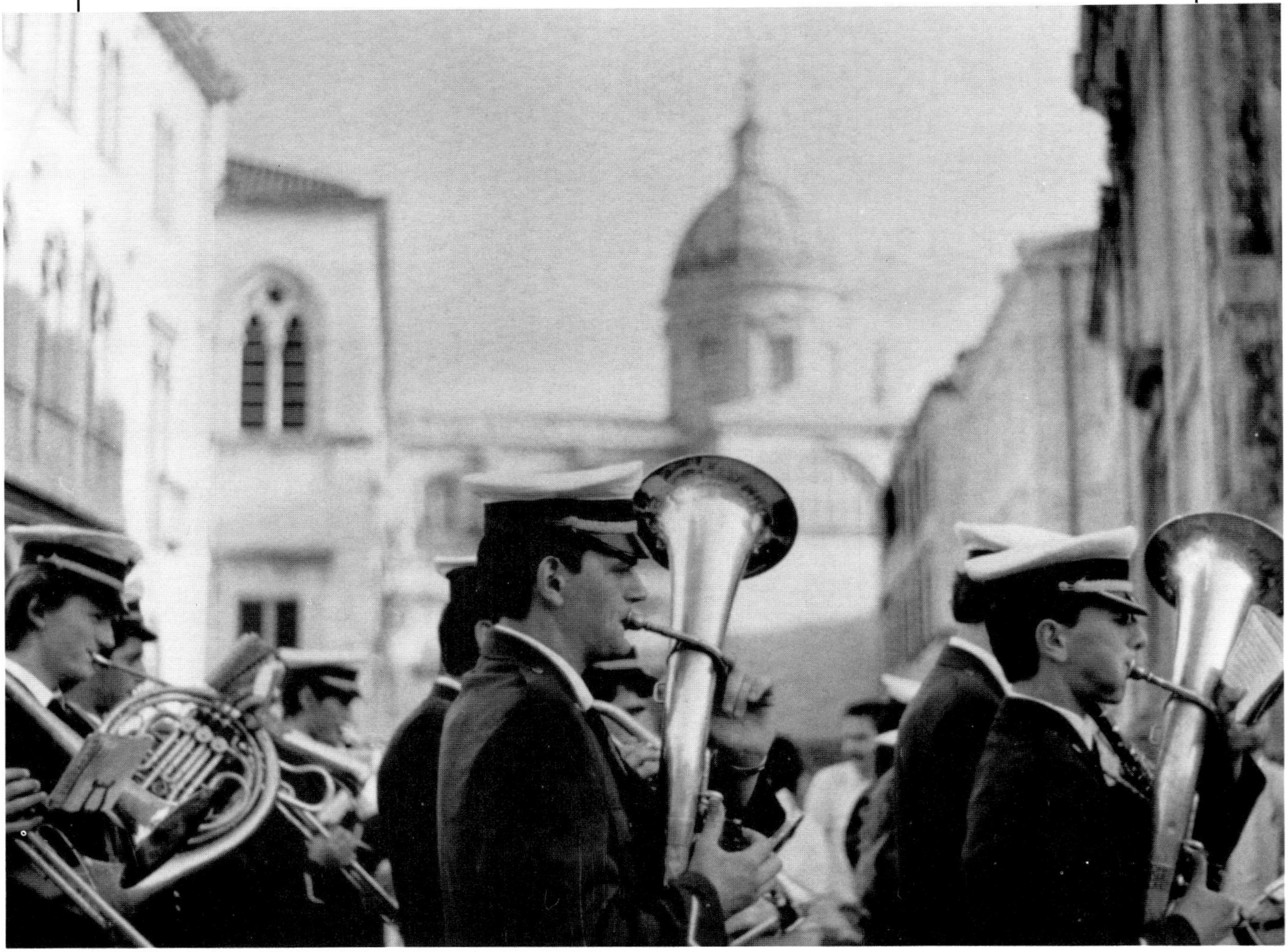

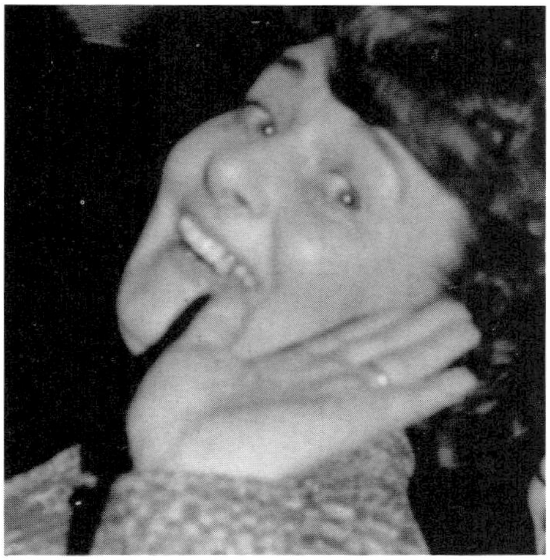